DATE DUE

Multinational Corporations and Developing Countries

by Joseph LaPalombara
Senior Research Fellow
and Stephen Blank
Senior Research Associate

A Research Report from The Conference Board

Contents

Tables

Exhibit 1.

Charts

About This Report

This report examines the relations of multinational corporations and developing countries. It focuses in particular on the perceptions and attitudes toward foreign direct investment of *strategic elites* in three key developing nations—Brazil, Malaysia and Nigeria. The report explores these responses in terms of the relations between multinational corporations and their home governments, the linkages between parent companies and their overseas subsidiaries, and the relationship of foreign subsidiaries and host-country governments.

Fieldwork for this study involved 359 systematic and open-ended interviews with four categories of respondents: (1) Brazilian, Malaysian and Nigerian leaders and decision makers drawn from the public and private sectors; (2) officials of the U.S. government in Washington D.C. and abroad; (3) headquarters, regional and local affiliate managers of 18 U.S.- and non-U.S.-based MNC's operating in these three countries; and (4) expatriate managers in the three host countries from other nonparticipating companies. The table below shows the distribution of respondents among these categories; a more detailed profile of the elite respondents is found in the Appendix to this report.

Participating companies were drawn from six industrial areas: chemicals; automotive and tractor; pharmaceuticals; household products; hydrocarbons; and electric and electronic products.

The study is divided into four parts. Part One introduced key issues and facts regarding the role of multinational corporations in the developing nations, provides a description of the general political and economic background in the three countries under investigation, and assesses their current and recent policies regarding foreign direct investment and foreign companies. Part Two deals with the overall impact of multinational corporations on patterns of national economic development, focusing in particular on national elite perceptions of the advantages and drawbacks for host-country development associated with the presence of foreign companies. This part of the report also reviews these countries' policies dealing with joint ventures and equity sharing and concludes by examining how local leaders perceive and evaluate their own nations' policies toward foreign investment.

Interviews Conducted in Study by Locus of Interview

With Local Elites in:	Individuals Interviewed	
Brazil...............................	50	
Malaysia............................	82	
Nigeria..............................	41	

With U.S. Government Officials in:		
Brazil...............................	5	
Malaysia............................	3	
Nigeria..............................	5	
Washington D.C.	2	

With managers of cooperating companies at corporate HQ............	54	

With managers of cooperating companies in:		(locals of country)
Brazil...............................	40	14
Malaysia (includes Singapore and Hong Kong).......................	27	6
Nigeria..............................	29	17

With other expatriate managers in Brazil, Malaysia and Nigeria....................	21	
Total	359	

Part Three looks at a range of issues and problems associated with the operational side of multinational corporate operations. These include international investment strategies, personnel policies, corporate organization and structure, labor and industrial relations, and social responsibility activities abroad.

Part Four summarizes the findings of the study and introduces the idea that Brazil might provide a model for future policies toward the multinational corporation in those developing nations that are able to achieve a relatively high degree of independent economic growth.

Acknowledgements

Most of those who made this study possible are anonymous. They are the eighteen multinational corporations that permitted extensive internal interviews with managers; officials of the United States government interviewed in Washington and abroad; and the industrial, political, professional, labor, public administrative, and other leaders interviewed in Brazil, Malaysia and Nigeria. We thank them collectively here.

In Brazil, valuable guidance was provided by James Gardner of the Ford Foundation in Rio de Janeiro. Geraldo Forbes shared his understanding of Brazil, of international finance and his friendship. Renato Boschi and Eli Dinez provided professional assistance of the highest quality; their interviews with Brazilian elites testify to the complexity of Brazilian politics and the skill of the social science researcher. Alfred Stepan, of Yale University, provided needed guidance and contacts that helped launch the Brazilian study.

In Malaysia, Dr. Stephen Chee, his associate, Dr. Khong, and staff at the University of Malaya provided extraordinary assistance to the project. Drs. Chee and Khong carried out many of the Malaysian interviews under severe time pressure. Professor Jean Herskovitz, of the State University of New York at Purchase, tried to keep us from misunderstanding Nigeria and generously shared contacts and Lagos telephone numbers. The help of several participating companies with arrangements on the ground in Nigeria, including housing and the use of operational telephones, was invaluable.

The elite interviews, on which several chapters of the report are based, were coded and the computer runs supervised by John DeMarco. Dr. Robert Black, then Conference Board Research Associate, staffed the study with tireless efficiency. Once again, Mrs. Heliena Kelly typed draft after draft. Dr. Lillian W. Kay, our editor, struggled to hold the report within manageable—and comprehensible—bounds.

J. LaPalombara
S. Blank

Foreword

JUDGED by the rhetoric of many international meetings, the situation of the multinational corporation everywhere in the Third World would appear precarious. A litany of misdeeds is endlessly recited by Third World representatives. Leaders of many MNC's react defensively to these allegations of corporate wrongdoings, insisting that the extension of enterprise abroad is not only benign but also an unquestionable boon to the host country lucky enough to attract foreign investment.

Verbal exchanges of this kind produce much heat but little light; they obscure exactly those aspects of foreign direct investment in the Third World that are in greatest need of clarification. Such charges and counterclaims may also divert attention from a central reality: In the Third World, foreign direct investment is needed as never before; but the conditions of venturing abroad will be much more complicated and challenging than ever in the past. This report was undertaken to throw some light on this murky, ideologically charged debate and thereby to gain a better understanding of the impact of the multinational corporations in developing countries.

Like its predecessor, *Multinational Corporations and National Elites* (Conference Board Report No. 702, 1976), the present report focuses on the political and social factors that affect the relationships between foreign firms and host countries. The most important data for this report derive from the perceptions and attitudes toward the MNC's of carefully selected host-country elites. These individuals often have strong views about the operating strategies and practices of the foreign firms in their midst. They are sensitive to the variety of ways in which corporate behavior will affect the multinational's relations with the host country. Above all, it is these persons who will influence both the content and the administration of public and regulatory policies pertaining to the foreign investor.

The countries included in this study—Brazil, Malaysia and Nigeria—are in no sense "average" Third World countries. They are leaders of the Third World and much more typical of the limited number of developing nations that are highly attractive to the foreign investor. Countries like Brazil, Malaysia and Nigeria have much-above-average chances of achieving self-sustained economic growth. They tend to be pacesetters in their geographic regions and internationally. Their responses to foreign investment are watched and emulated in the developing world.

A second source of data in this study is the responses of managers at headquarters and abroad of the eighteen U.S.- and non-U.S. based multinational corporations that cooperated in this study. The companies represent a broad spectrum of the interests of the multinational corporations in the developing world. Ten of the companies are American; two are British; two are Dutch. Canada, West Germany, Switzerland and Italy are each represented by one.

The Conference Board wishes to thank the State Department for providing partial funding for this project through the then Office of Private Cooperation in the Bureau of Educational and Cultural Affairs. We also acknowledge the contribution of the Luce Foundation to the funding of the Malaysian portion of this project.

This study was conducted autonomously by the Board. It is the fourth report on the Board's Multinational Corporate Conduct Program, which is under the general supervision of Walter Hamilton, Vice President, Public Affairs Research Division.

KENNETH A. RANDALL
President

Part One

Chapter 1
Multinational Corporations and Developing Countries

FEW THEMES have stimulated more rhetoric than the relations between multinational corporations and developing nations. Extensive debate about the role of the MNC in the developing world has not resulted in much agreement among defenders or opponents. For some (for example, former Secretary of State Henry Kissinger), the multinational corporation is seen as "one of the most effective engines of development"; for others, (such as Ronald Muller, co-author of Global Reach), the MNC is "one of the most powerful impediments to Third World development."[1] Does the multinational play a positive role in development as a key source of capital, technology and managerial skills? Or does it hinder development by creating patterns of dependence among the world's poorer nations?

The Debate Over Development

Neither the issues nor the objects of this debate are very clear. The term "developing nations" is a good example. Possibly the only trait they share is their poverty relative to the rest of the world. A U.S. Senate report of a few years ago set the world gross national product at approximately $3,000* billion, of which the developing nations, with the vast majority of the world's inhabitants, accounted for only about 12 percent. At the other

---

[1] Address by Henry R. Kissinger on "Global Consensus and Economic Development"; delivered by Daniel P. Moynihan, U.S. Representative to the United Nations, Seventh Special Session of the UN General Assembly, September 1, 1975. Ronald Muller, "The Multinational Corporation and the Exercise of Power: Latin America," in Abdul A. Said and Luiz R. Simmons, eds., *The New Sovereigns: Multinational Corporations as World Power.* Englewood Cliffs, N.J.: Prentice Hall, 1975, p. 55.

---

*Unless otherwise indicated the sign "$" refers to U.S. dollars throughout this report.

extreme, about one-fourth of the world's population has access to about 88 percent of world GNP.[2]

A starting point in this discussion is the realization that the developing nations as a group are extremely heterogeneous with respect to both level of current development and developmental potential. Brazil, which is dealt with in this study, has the tenth largest economy in the world; its major cities rival those of the developed West in many ways; the country itself is well on the way to becoming a major industrial power as well as a significant factor in international trade. Is it logical to lump countries like Brazil (or others like Mexico, South Korea, Malaysia or Argentina) with other states—many of them artificial and with little developmental promise?

Aggregate statistics often obscure as much as they reveal. Most analysts, for example, feel that economic growth rates in the developing nations are fairly high by world historical standards. One study estimates that real growth in the less-developed countries was 4.5 percent between 1960 and 1966, a growth rate higher than that enjoyed by countries like Britain and France in the second half of the 19th century, the period of their most rapid industrialization. This study suggests that the developing countries' growth rate in this period compares fairly well with the developed nations' 5.1 percent rate. The difference, the study observes, is heightened significantly by the much higher rate of population increase in the developing world. Per capita economic growth in the developing nations was thus only 2 percent, compared with 3.6 percent in the developed nations.[3]

According to other studies, however, over a longer period, per capita GNP in the developing nations grew almost as fast (or even faster) than in the developing world. One U.S. Department of State report notes that per capita GNP in the underdeveloped nations increased by 213 percent between 1950 and 1975, compared with an increase of 205 percent in the developed nations.[4] But overall per capita income in the developing nations reached only $437, while in the developed nations the per capita figure was $4,445. Even if the developing nations do have a higher growth rate (which is debated), it could well be hundreds of years before they catch up. If the amenities gap is ever to narrow, the developing nations would have to grow at a *much* higher rate than the industrialized countries. While the richer of

[2] Report to the Subcommittee on Multinational Corporations of the Committee on Foreign Relations of United States Senate, R.S. Newfarmer and W.F. Mueller, *Multinational Corporations in Brazil and Mexico: Structural Sources of Economic and Noneconomic Power,* 1975, p. 5.

[3] Newfarmer and Mueller, p. 5.

[4] The Department of State, Bureau of Public Affairs. *The Planetary Product in 1975,* Special Report No. 33, May, 1977. See also United Nations Economic and Social Council, *Transnational Corporations in World Development: A Re-Examination,* E/C.10/38, March 20, 1978, p. 205.

the developing nations maintained per capita growth rates of around 6 percent during the 1960's and into the 1970's, per capita income in the poorest nations did not increase at all.

[Overall, the gap between the richer and poorer nations continues to widen: In relative terms, the poorer nations are getting poorer and the richer nations richer, and this basic trend is likely to continue indefinitely.]

Development is another murky concept. What do the developing nations struggle to achieve? Greater wealth? To be sure. But, with rare exceptions, development also appears to bring about greater inequality within nations. Computations of per capita wealth often obscure the increases in relative well-being of particular groups that seem to accompany urbanization and industrialization everywhere. Moreover, because the psychological sense of relative deprivation finds articulate spokesmen in national and international spheres, the inequalities that accompany economic development are likely to be more politically destabilizing today and in the future than in the past.

If development means industrialization as it does for most of the developing world, the process will often result in new problems of unemployment and urbanization; generate unrealistic and excessive demands for infrastructure development; lead to the introduction of inappropriate technology as well as to the neglect of agriculture; and drain away capital as well as local entrepreneurial and managerial skills which might be better utilized elsewhere in the economy.

Economic development is widely viewed as a necessary condition for the assertion of national individuality and political independence. Yet, as nations develop economically, they seem to lose much of that individuality. Cities are more and more alike, laced with the same highways and choked by the same traffic congestion. Their populations aspire to live in the same urban high-rise apartments, to wear the same clothes, to eat the same food, and to watch the same television programs. The "preservation of national culture" is often relegated to a minor government department.

The relationship between development and autonomy is also uncertain. The least dependent society (dependent, that is, on other humans) must be the *least* developed, subsistence-based society. [The least developed societies are those in which members have the least control over their physical environment and live most at the whim of nature.] They are societies with a limited division of labor, limited social and physical mobility, limited capacity to visualize other roles and alternative economic and social arrangements.

As economic development accelerates, nations become more, not less, dependent. This holds not only for resource-poor nations but also for those that believe they are capable of industrializing entirely under their own power. In today's world, no nation that reaches for significant development can avoid becoming enmeshed in a seamless web of global economic, financial and political interdependence.

3

The myth of "developmental autonomy" deeply clouds the issue of the "model" to be followed in achieving growth. If industrialization is the exemplar of development, what model should be followed—that of the United States, Japan, the Soviet Union, China? Are the human costs of industrialization so high that a developing nation should deliberately seek to avoid it or slow it down? What are the alternatives to industrialization?

What about the relationship between political ideology and economic change? Does successful industrialization require private property, an open market and profitability, and the political arrangements that guarantee these conditions? Can industrialization be achieved without capital inputs from abroad, and the conditions that make such inputs likely? In this regard, it is essential that developing nations spell out in the clearest terms the role that foreign direct investment (FDI) can, and perhaps must, play in overall developmental strategies.

Whatever the particular indicators used to describe development may be, the process itself is manifestly destabilizing. Development implies new relationships between man and his environment—new modes of production, new institutions, new forms of consumption and recreation—even new values that come to characterize a nation and its people. In today's world, destabilization can become unnecessarily extreme when a nation's new elites or "modernizers" make the mistake of believing that development requires the wholesale destruction of traditional social organization, beliefs, values and behavior.

Less-developed countries, dependent historically on the exploitation of a single primary commodity will often have enclaves of modern production and consumption in the midst of extreme economic backwardness. Further economic development will frequently occur at the expense of the underdeveloped parts of the country, increasing the "dualism" of these societies, and intensifying inequalities. Creating the infrastructure essential for manufacturing and commerce may cause excessive bloating of cities and increased unemployment and underemployment. Public policies that insist on the encouragement of capital-rather than labor-intensive industrial development may actually benefit a small minority at the expense of most of a nation's citizens.

The multinational corporation is inevitably drawn into the storms created by development. MNC's at once represent the necessary conditions for economic and material betterment and provide scapegoats for the irrationalities and human costs that development itself brings about. They are the most visible instruments that weave the independent nation into the fabric of global interdependence.[5]

Foreign Direct Investment in the Developing Countries

Most of the activities of MNC's, however, are located in the developed,

[5]See Raymond Vernon, *Storm Over the Multinationals.* Cambridge: Harvard University Press, 1977.

4

not the developing world. This is so notwithstanding the proliferation of developing nations since World War II, and notwithstanding the location of natural resources and population growth in the Third World. In fact, the imbalance seems to be increasing. Table 1 depicts the global distribution of foreign direct investment of the developed market-economy nations. In 1975, more than 40 percent of all developed-nation foreign direct investment was located in four host nations: the United States, the United Kingdom, Canada and the Federal Republic of Germany.

The share of the global stock of foreign direct investment located in the developing nations fell from 31 percent in 1967 to 26 percent in 1975. Three percent of the investment going to the developing nations in 1975 was, in fact, directed to tax-haven countries such as Bermuda and the Netherlands Antilles, and was often enrouted back to the developed nations; 6 percent went to the OPEC nations—leaving only 17 percent of the global stock of foreign direct investment in all of the other developing nations.

Table 1: Stock of Direct Investment Abroad of Developed Market Economies, by Host Country, 1967-1975

Host Country and Country Group	1967	1971	1975
Total value of stock (billions of dollars)	$105	$156	$259
Distribution of stock (percentage)			
Developed market economies	69%[a]	72%[a]	74%
Canada...............................	18	17	15
United States........................	9	9	11
United Kingdom......................	8	9	9
Germany (Federal Republic)..............	3	5	6
Other................................	30	32	33
Developing countries	31	28	26
OPEC countries[1]	9	7	6
Tax havens[2]	2	3	3
Other................................	20	17	17
Total	100%	100%	100%

[1]Algeria, Ecuador, Gabon, Indonesia, Iran, Iraq, Kuwait, Libya, Arab Jamahiriya, Nigeria, Qatar, Saudi Arabia, United Arab Emirates, and Venezuela.

[2]Bahamas, Barbados, Bermuda, Cayman Islands, Netherland Antilles, and Panama.

[a]Details do not add to 100 percent because of rounding.

Source: United Nations Economic and Social Council, *Transnational Corporations in World Development: A Re-Examination,* E/C.10/38, March 20, 1978, p. 237.

Data gathered by the United Nations in 1972 indicate that in 1967 about three-quarters of the affiliates of MNC's headquartered in the developed nations operated in the developed world. The UN data show that between 65 and 75 percent of U.S.-based MNC affiliates were located in the developed market economies, as were 68 percent of the British, 82 percent of the German, and 60 percent of the French.[6] Japan is the exception to this rule in that more than half of its direct investment stock was in developing nations in 1975, although this proportion, like that of other developed nations, was lower than in 1967.[7]

Research carried out by the Harvard Comparative Multinational Enterprise Project confirms the United Nations' findings. The Harvard group found that 60 percent of the foreign manufacturing subsidiaries of large U.S. MNC's are sited in the developed nations and in the less-developed nations of Europe (which the UN counts as developed). For Britain, the share is 55 percent; for Germany, 62 percent; and for France, 57 percent.[8]

In 1957, 41 percent of the book value of U.S. direct investment overseas was in the developing nations; by 1973, the figure was only 24 percent (see Table 2). The British pattern is similar: 28 percent of British foreign direct investment was sited in the developing Commonwealth nations in 1962 and only 15 percent in 1974 (see Table 3).

Although the share of the world stock of foreign direct investment located in the developing nations declined over time, the absolute amount rose substantially—from $32.5 billion in 1967 to $67.3 billion in 1975. But 1976 may have marked a dramatic change in this pattern. Direct investment in the developing nations by multinationals headquartered in the United States fell by more than 50 percent against the previous year. Substantial increases in direct investment in developing countries by Japanese, Canadian, Belgian and Italian multinationals were not enough to offset the overall decline in the total direct investment flow to these developing countries.[9]

Whether 1976 marked the beginning of a new and considerably leaner era for direct investment in the developing nations—or whether the prevailing postwar pattern will reassert itself—the attitude of many MNC's toward the developing nations is well summarized by Peter Drucker. He observes that in a group of 45 major multinationals he studied ''75 to 85 percent of all growth, whether in sales or profits, in the last 25 years, occurred in the

[6]United Nations. *Multinational Corporations in World Development,* ST/ECA/190, 1973, p. 147.

[7]See *Transnational Corporations in World Development: A Re-Examination,* March 20, 1978, p. 40.

[8]Lawrence G. Franko, *The European Multinationals: A Renewed Challenge to American and British Big Business.* Stamford, Conn.: Greylock Publishers, 1976, p. 108.

[9]See *Transnational Corporations in World Development: A Re-Examination,* March 20, 1978, p. 249.

Table 2: U.S. Direct Investment Position Abroad at Year-end (Million U.S.$)

Country or Area	1957 Amount	1957 Percent	1962 Amount	1962 Percent	1967 Amount	1967 Percent	1970 Amount	1970 Percent	1973 Amount	1973 Percent
All Countries..............	$25,262	100%	$37,226	100%	$56,583	100%	$75,456	100%	$100,675	100%
Developed Countries	13,905	55	22,618	61	38,708	69	51,819	69	72,214	70
Developing Countries.......	10,316	41	12,960	35	14,928	26	19,168	25	25,266	24
Other	1,041	4	1,647	4	2,947	5	4,469	6	6,195	6

Sources: 1957, *U.S. Business Investment in Foreign Countries*, U.S. Department of Commerce, 1960
1962, *Survey of Current Business*, U.S. Department of Commerce, August 1964
1967-73, *Revised Data Series on U.S. Direct Investment, 1966-1974*, U.S. Department of Commerce, 1974.

7

Table 3: United Kingdom Overseas Direct Investment, Location and Growth, 1962-1974[a]

| Country or Area | Book Values (£ million) | | | | | | Average Annual Percent Increase | |
| | 1962 | | 1970 | | 1974 | | 1962-1969 | 1970-1974 |
	Amount	Percent	Amount	Percent	Amount	Percent		
Developed Commonwealth (including Canada)	£1,470	43%	£2,759	43%	£3,961	37%	12%	9%
Developing Commonwealth	936	28	1,300	20	1,633	15	4	7
United States	301	09	762	12	1,678	16	16	32
EEC (the six)	272	08	808	13	2,095	20	24	37
EFTA (the seven)	82	02	182	03	373	04	14	25
Other	344	10	593	09	883	08	10	11
Total	£3,405	100%	£6,404	100%	£10,623	100%	11%	15%

[a]Excludes oil, banking, insurance

Source: John M. Stopford, "Changing Perspectives on Investment by British Manufacturing Multinationals," *Journal of International Business Studies*, Fall-Winter, 1976, p. 15.

developed countries." He argues that "for the typical twentieth century multinational, that is a manufacturing, distributing or financial company, developing countries are important neither as markets nor as producers of profits."[10]

Latin America has by far the largest regional stock of foreign direct investment from the developed nations, although its share of the global stock of FDI dropped slightly between 1967 and 1972. Asia's share increased significantly during this period, while the African and Middle Eastern proportions both declined marginally. In 1972, Brazil and Nigeria received the greatest shares of developed-nation direct investment in Latin America and Africa, respectively. Malaysia's share in Asia was much less than either India's or Indonesia's, but was still substantial (see Chart 1).

Chart 1: Developing Countries—Concentration of Private Foreign Investment by the Developing Advisory Committee Countries (year-end 1967 and 1972)

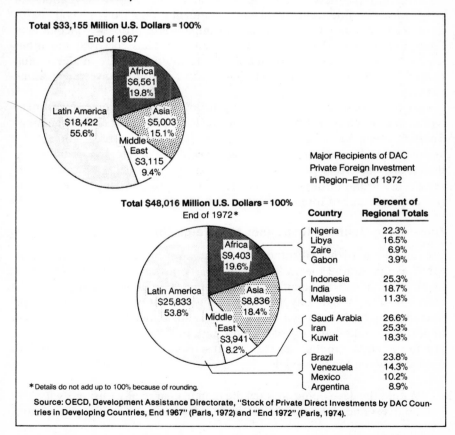

Total $33,155 Million U.S. Dollars = 100%
End of 1967

Africa $6,561 19.8%
Latin America $18,422 55.6%
Asia $5,003 15.1%
Middle East $3,115 9.4%

Major Recipients of DAC Private Foreign Investment in Region—End of 1972

Total $48,016 Million U.S. Dollars = 100%
End of 1972*

Africa $9,403 19.6%
Latin America $25,833 53.8%
Asia $8,836 18.4%
Middle East $3,941 8.2%

Country	Percent of Regional Totals
Nigeria	22.3%
Libya	16.5%
Zaire	6.9%
Gabon	3.9%
Indonesia	25.3%
India	18.7%
Malaysia	11.3%
Saudi Arabia	26.6%
Iran	25.3%
Kuwait	18.3%
Brazil	23.8%
Venezuela	14.3%
Mexico	10.2%
Argentina	8.9%

*Details do not add up to 100% because of rounding.

Source: OECD, Development Assistance Directorate, "Stock of Private Direct Investments by DAC Countries in Developing Countries, End 1967" (Paris, 1972) and "End 1972" (Paris, 1974).

[10] Peter F. Drucker, "Multinationals and Developing Countries: Myths and Realities." *Foreign Affairs,* October 1974, pp. 121-122.

Working with OECD data, an International Labor Organization (ILO) research team analyzed the distribution of foreign direct investment in the developing nations (including Southern Europe) by type and region of investment (see Table 4). Three basic types of investment are categorized: Type 1: exploitation of basic products; Type 2: penetration of protected markets; and Type 3: exploitation of cheap labor. Their findings, illustrated in Table 5, indicate that the overwhelming share of foreign private investment in the Middle East and the largest share in Africa was Type 1. Type 2, essentially import substitution, predominates in Latin America. The three types are almost evenly distributed in Asia, although the Asian share of Type 3 foreign investment is much greater than the share of any other region. The distribution of the types of foreign investment in the countries dealt with in this report—Brazil, Nigeria and Malaysia—appears to be reasonably representative of their regions.

Available data may underestimate the amount of foreign investment flowing into the developing countries, and into the OPEC nations in particular. For one thing, data on investment flows from several major developed nations—Germany, for example—are probably incomplete. Secondly, through the use of management contracts, licenses and other similar arrangements, the presence of the multinationals in developing countries undoubtedly is greater than figures on direct investment alone suggest.

Finally, these data also omit the rising flow of foreign direct investment within the developing world. Nations such as India, Mexico, Argentina, Taiwan, Hong Kong, and Singapore are growing sources of foreign investment, and multinationals headquartered in developing nations are increasingly active in their own regions and even globally.[11] Brazilian investors are found throughout Nigeria, for example, and Singapore remains the leading source of foreign investment in Malaysia.

Developing Country Responses to Foreign Direct Investment

Even where, by global standards, the amount of investment, the size of MNC affiliates, and the scale of their operations are small, foreign direct investment is still frequently a critical factor in a developing nation's economic life. What may be a small investment in a relatively minor operation by New York or London boardroom standards can be of crucial importance to the economy of the host nation. Peter Drucker, in the article previously cited, emphasizes that this discrepancy can be a key source of tension between MNC's and developing country governments:

"Within the developing country the man in charge of a business with 750 employees and eight million dollars in sales has to be an important man.

[11] See articles by Louis Wells and Carlos F. Dias-Alejandro in Agmon and Kindleberger, eds., *Multinationals from Small Countries*. Cambridge, Mass.: The M.I.T. Press, 1977.

Table 4: Developing Countries, 1970—Breakdown of Foreign Private Investment (by region and type)

Region	Type of Foreign Investment			Total	
	Exploitation of basic products (percent)	Penetration of protected markets (percent)	Exploitation of cheap labour (percent)	Million U.S. Dollars	Percent
Africa.........	60%	34%	6%	$ 7.9 m.	20.8%
Latin America...	33	62	5	20.8	54.6
Middle East......	91	9	—	3.6	9.4
Asia	30	36	34	5.8	15.2
Totals (in million U.S. dollars)......	$16.6	$18.0	$3.5	$38.1 m.	
Percent of overall total.........	44%	48%	9%		100%

Source: Computed from Y. Sabdo and R. Trajtenberg in collaboration with J.P. Sajhau, *The Impact of Transnational Enterprises on Employment in the Developing Countries.* Geneva, Switzerland: International Labour Organisation, 1976, p.2.

While his business is minute compared to the company's business in Germany, Great Britain, or the United States, it is every bit as difficult— indeed it is likely to be a good deal more difficult, risky and demanding. And he has to be treated as an equal with the government leaders, the bankers, and the business leaders of his country—people whom the district sales manager in Hamburg, Rotterdam, or Kansas City never even sees. Yet his sales and profits are less than those of the Hamburg, Rotterdam, or Kansas City district. And his growth potential is, in most cases, even lower." (pp. 123-124)

That foreign investment or the activities of foreign companies are often the subject of severe tensions between home- and host-country governments, or between host countries and foreign firms is no surprise. Nor are such tensions a recent phenomenon. Expropriation and nationalization, the seizure of assets and armed intervention to protect foreign-owned property, were not uncommon long before the era of the multinational corporation. But the rapid emergence of so many politically independent countries (in 1950, 37 developing countries were members of the United Nations; in 1977, there were 110); the growing concern in these nations with economic development and with the economic aspects of independence; and the expansion of the multinational corporation in the world economy have all focused attention on the role—positive and negative—of the MNC in national development and international economic relations.

As early as the 1950's, leaders in the independent developing nations recognized that economic modernization was tied to global economic and political factors. Some sought to encourage collective action to overcome obstacles to development, and, in particular, to stand aside from the international policies of the great powers by declaring that they were "nonaligned" in the Cold War.

In 1964, the "Group of 77" was formed at the United Nations Conference on Trade and Development (UNCTAD). The Group of 77 (soon to number more than 100 members) sought to represent the interests of the developing nations in a variety of international contexts.

In 1975, at Manila, the developing countries moved for the first time to adopt a series of common positions on major international economic development issues. This step had an immediate and direct impact on international negotiations under way within and outside of the United Nations system. The developing nations of the "South" now sought to engage the industrial nations of the "North" in an ongoing dialogue on matters relating to development and the global economic system. In particular, the developing nations stressed that they would seek "...to obtain greater equality of opportunity and to secure the right to sit as equals around the bargaining tables of the world."[12]

[12]Mahbub ul Haz, "Negotiating a New Bargain with the Rich Countries," in Guy F. Erb and Valeriana Kallab, eds., *Beyond Dependency: The Developing World Speaks Out.* Washington, D.C.: Overseas Development Council, 1975, p. 158.

A year earlier, the Group of 77 pushed resolutions through the UN General Assembly which called for the creation of a "New International Economic Order" (NIEO). Proponents of the NIEO argue that existing international economic institutions, including multinational corporations, inhibit development in Third World nations. To create a more equitable international economic system and to break the cycle of dependence, developing nations must achieve more influence over international economic policy. This would permit them: "(1) to initiate at the domestic level and ensure at the international level policies that will mobilize or increase their resources; and (2) to use these resources to strengthen their bargaining capacity to attain the measure of autonomy necessary to determine the type of welfare they wish to achieve."[13]

Tensions between multinational corporations and developing nations often reflect the deep feeling of ambivalence regarding industrialization in the developing nations. Almost all are committed to the goal of industrialization, even as they acknowledge the social and political cost of development. Leaders in these nations are unsure about the means of economic development. Does external assistance—through foreign aid or the participation of multinational corporations—lessen or increase social costs?

Differences of opinion such as these are a major source of tensions within developing nations. These tensions, in turn, frequently lead to ambivalent responses to the presence of foreign corporations. On the one hand, Charles Kindleberger observes, "...'uncompromising nationalism and economic populism' and the aim to 'terminate dependence on the United States' or the developed world seem...to characterize the environment in which the multinational corporation has had to operate vis-á-vis developing governments in the last decade or so."[14] On the other hand, governments of the developing nations (especially in the corridors of their own ministries) urge greater MNC participation and investment. MNC executives complain that leaders of developing countries take a different line on foreign investment for each audience, and policies toward the foreign investor become stakes in host-country policies.

Patterns of Developing Country Policy Toward Multinational Corporations

If leaders of developing nations are hesitant, even fearful, about industrialization, the momentum of the movement in that direction is too

---

[13]Felix Pena, "Multinational Enterprises and North-South Relations," in Erb and Kallab, 1975.

[14]Charles P. Kindleberger, "The Multinational Corporation in a World of Militant Developing Countries," in George W. Ball, ed., *Global Companies: The Political Economy of World Business*. Englewood Cliffs, N.J.: Prentice Hall, Inc., 1975, p. 71.

strong to halt. The pressures of population and poverty often impel governments to be less discriminating than they might be where there is an overwhelming need for capital, technology, managerial know-how, and access to foreign markets.

The capacity of these governments to negotiate with multinational corporations has increased sharply as the skills of their administrative cadres have improved and as competition among multinationals from different countries has increased. In addition, after a period of intense preoccupation with the multinationals, in the mid-1970's many leaders in developing countries saw that the multinational corporation was only one— and not the most important—dimension of the problems that confronted their nations. Critical problems of the global economy, of North-South relations, and of economic development were not caused by the multinationals and, while the MNC's remain a convenient symbol of these problems, hammering the multinationals does little to provide solutions.[15]

In all countries in which MNC's operate, the network of regulation and control has become more and more dense. National legislation relating to multinational corporations (reports a recent United Nations survey) focuses on four broad areas. The first is *foreign-investment decision making.* This includes procedures for the selection of foreign investment and the screening of foreign investment proposals, control of takeovers, establishment of sectors reserved for local firms or in which foreign participation is restricted, and incentive schemes designed to attract foreign investment interest, particularly in certain regions of the country or in certain sectors of the economy.

The second focus of national foreign investment legislation is *ownership, management and employment:* restrictions on foreign ownership involving either specific local participation requirements or a requirement for eventual divestment; requirements regarding local participation in management; and restrictions relating to employment creation and the use of expatriates. The third area is *taxation and financial transactions.* This includes the determination of taxable income (often in the form of bilateral double-taxation agreements) and the regulation of corporate financial transactions—particularly the repatriation of capital and profits and debt financing by foreign enterprises.

The fourth area of regulation deals with the *administration and supervision of national foreign-investment legislation.* The report suggests that, in the developing countries, such legislation is increasingly administered by interministerial investment boards or commissions, or by special agencies established for the purpose of coordinating all matters relating to foreign investment. This is one dimension of a tendency among the countries

---

[15]United Nations Centre on Transnational Corporations, *National Legislation and Regulations Relating to Transnational Corporations.* New York: 1978.

studied toward the coordination and integration of legislation relating to private investment in general—and foreign direct investment in particular.

The United Nations report surveys the foreign investment laws and regulations of 37 developing countries. It states that, in nearly all of these countries, major investment proposals are thoroughly scrutinized either at the time the foreign enterprise is established or in connection with an application for incentive benefits. It notes, however, that criteria for screening investment or incentive applications, although numerous, are often not precise enough to serve as a fixed standard for evaluation. Although there is a tendency in developing countries to encourage local equity participation in foreign enterprises, the proportion of those countries studied that require majority local ownership is still small (6 out of 37). The movement toward increased local equity participation is nevertheless apparent.

In most countries, foreign direct investment in certain sectors of the economy is prohibited or restricted. Such sectors include defense-related production, nuclear power, public utilities, inland transportation, telecommunications, radio, television and the press. Commercial banking and insurance are increasingly included among the closed sectors, and wholesale and retail trade are often reserved for local entrepreneurs.

Investment incentives constitute an important part of most developing nations' private investment policies. In a few cases, regulation may be limited to foreign firms receiving incentive benefits. Elsewhere, benefits may be designed to encourage local equity participation by being limited to joint ventures or to enterprises with a minority foreign participation. Investment laws tend to deal with the financial aspects of investment in general terms. When they are more specific, they frequently take the form of a limitation on the proportion of profits that can be repatriated. In most financial aspects of foreign investment and in the determination of taxable income, host-country regulations are vague and general.

Arrangements for supervision and control after the establishment of a foreign enterprise are frequently unsatisfactory, the UN report concludes. Disclosure requirements may vary among government departments, and coordination of ministerial or departmental regulations is normally poor. Problems also tend to arise in connection with registration or licensing, the expansion of an enterprise or its merger with another company. The settlement of disputes between host countries and foreign enterprises constitutes one of the most sensitive areas of the relationship. Virtually all western hemisphere developing nations (and some in Asia and North Africa) insist on local jurisdiction for investment disputes, membership in the International Centre for Settlement of Investment Disputes notwithstanding. Some regional agreements (such as the Andean Common Market, ANCOM) also cover the settlement of disputes.

The UN report suggests that while foreign investment legislation is too complex to permit generalizations beyond these, three general patterns of foreign direct investment regulation are discernible. One general pattern prevails in most African and certain Asian nations, as well as in the Central American Common Market (CACM), and is characterized by relatively few regulations and restrictions and a greater number of incentives. The pattern found in the Asian Middle East and North Africa is similar, except that most of these countries have established local participation quotas. The South American pattern is characterized for the most part by greater restriction and control. The three patterns are summarized in Exhibit 1.

Increasing Differences Among Developing Nations

The developing nations have struggled to maintain a common front in recent negotiations with the developed nations, although they have adopted more moderate positions on several key issues than in the past. Efforts by the developed nations to split off the non-oil producing developing nations from the OPEC countries have not been successful. Wealthier developing nations (such as Brazil) have taken a strong line, possibly to demonstrate their solidarity with the poorer members of the developing world. But despite heroic efforts by the Group of 77 to maintain a common front, and the concern of the richer developing nations to keep in step, the heterogeneity of the nations of the developing world and the variety of their interests and needs, are increasingly evident.

Much of this heterogeneity rests on basic "givens." Some of the developing nations are plentifully endowed with natural resources: petroleum, minerals and, of growing importance, soil and climate suitable for extensive agricultural production.

The history and experience of a developing nation constitutes another crucial "given." Because colonial powers drew borders between countries without reference to ethnic, tribal, religious or linguistic factors, every African nation today embodies an inherent source of instability as an element of its colonial heritage. The British predilection for "indirect rule" provides one legacy; the French approach to colonial rule another. The large number of university-educated Nigerians is an aspect of its colonial legacy—a condition for which the newly independent Nigeria is not responsible. Zaire, the former Belgian Congo, received quite a different legacy. Literally, no native was awarded a university degree during the era of colonial administration.

Asian cultures seem to have been more resilient than African in the face of European domination, while the Indian cultures of South America all but disappeared. Colonial systems could alter entire social structures. The British brought Chinese to work in the tin mines of what is now Malaysia and also carried the seeds for the rubber tree from Brazil to Malaysia. European and American slavers mined the West Coast of Africa for human cargoes (with the assistance of local rulers) and violently altered social, economic and political structures there.

The level of political and economic development at the time of independence constitutes another "given." Were there cadres of trained local administrators? Had there been some experience with local self-government? How well-developed was the economic infrastructure? Were there railroads, ports, communications? Had efforts been made to develop the entire local economy, or merely one sector—or none of it at all?

What did the country face to win its independence? A long and violent struggle or a more gradual process? Were patterns of trade with the former colonial nation maintained or sharply interrupted? Were long-term economic and assistance agreements laid down at independence, or was the newly independent nation determined (or forced) to fend for itself? Did the new nation plunge immediately into internal strife: rebellion, civil war, partition? What about external pressures? Rapacious neighbors? Did it become a stake in the Cold War?

The effect of these "givens" has been heightened by policy choices for development. The public-sector's role in the economy is substantial in all developing countries, given the demands of modernization and industrialization. But while some nations have opted for a high degree of centralization, administrative discretion, and a large segment of public ownership in the economy, others seek to lessen the role of government and to emphasize private-sector growth. While few nations have chosen a "Chinese model" of development—excluding foreign corporations—the degree of acceptance of foreign corporations varies considerably. All developing nations would like to have the technology, capital and managerial skills multinational corporations provide—but not all are willing to pay the cost involved in terms of providing stable investment regulations, provisions for rapid remittance of profits and capital, and so on. Developing countries are more or less capable of exploiting the growing competition among MNC's, particularly as they come increasingly from different home countries. They also differ in their capacity to negotiate favorable terms with foreign corporations.

Resources are a necessary, but not sufficient, element of success. Countries with substantial natural resources have failed to develop coherent national development policies and programs and have squandered their wealth. Others, with less natural endowment (for example, Singapore and the Ivory Coast), have devoted intense efforts to development and to the maintenance of a favorable investment and business climate.

Initial stages of economic development may, in fact, be easier to achieve than later stages that are closer to self-sustaining growth. As development proceeds, the easy decisions have all been taken and the early, high-return investments (basic communication systems or port development, for example) all made. Profit margins are narrower and the social costs of mistakes may be higher. Development targets can no longer be framed in terms of such general goals as miles of road completed or number of elementary schools constructed. Choices made at this stage with regard to policies which favor import substitution or the development of export

Exhibit 1: Patterns of Foreign Direct Investment Regulation in Selected Developing Countries

Parameter	Pattern 1 (mostly Asia—excluding India—Africa, CACM)	Pattern 11 (mostly Middle East, North Africa)	Pattern 111 (mostly South America)
1. Administration	Case-by-case screening largely restricted to award of *incentives* (non-discriminatory).	Case-by-case screening at establishment (degree of discrimination varies).	Separate administration for foreign investment. Screening at establishment.
11. Investment screening criteria	Emphasis on functional contributions of investment. Little indication of extensive cost/benefit analysis. Screening largely for award of incentives.	Emphasis on functional contributions and conditions of investment. Little indication of extensive cost/benefit analysis.	Criteria formulated for cost/benefit analysis, often extensive. Includes social cost criteria in some cases.
111. Ownership	Few requirements. Few sectors closed to foreign investment.	Joint ventures prevalent.	Strict regulations on owner-ship and investment (exc. Brazil). A large number of closed sectors.
1V. Finance	Few repatriation limitations.	Few repatriation limitations.	Repatriation ceilings in most areas (exc. Mexico). Screening of foreign loans. Special control of payments to parent company.

Exhibit 1: Patterns of Foreign Direct Investment Regulation in Selected Developing Countries (continued)

V.	Employment and training	Announced indigenization policies but little headway in practice.	Local quotas for work force. Few local quotas for management.	Specific across-the-board indigenization requirements.
V1.	Technology transfer	No controls.	No controls.	Screening and registration of all technology imported.
V11.	Investment incentives	Long-term tax incentives for establishment.	Establishment incentives limited to five years—in most cases non-renewable.	Incentives tied to specific contributions, but incentives may be curtailed for foreign-owned firms.
V111.	International dispute settlement	Adherence to international dispute regulation. Regional investment regulation: UDEAC, OCAM, EAC, OAMP.	Same as Pattern 1 Regional investment regulation: Arab Economic Union	Local adjudication and regional harmonization of investment regulation: ANCOM, CACM.

Source: U.N. Commission on Transnational Corporations, *National Legislation and Regulations Relating to Transnational Corporations.* (Report of the Secretariat) (NY: United Nations. 1976; E/C. 10/8–12.1.76), pp. 21-22.

capacities, which channel manpower development in one or another direction, or which put in place this or that technology will determine whether or not development aspirations are achieved.

Governments at this stage must also begin to confront some of the social costs of development. Development strategies must be reformulated to include policies to create a better distribution of income; to deal with imbalances in rural and urban development; to establish more effective social welfare protection for newly urbanized workers and their families; and to regulate local business practices. As certain nations approach the goal of self-sustaining growth, their economic policies may become more conservative. They are playing the game and beginning to win. They now have much more to lose by seeking to change the rules.

For some of the developing nations, the achievement of political and economic stability seems within reach. For others, even some with great natural resources, it is a goal that cannot be obtained. Nations of South America, which have been independent since the early 19th century, may experience continuing political turmoil, but their existence as nations is not in doubt. But many delegations now sitting at the United Nations represent countries without historic or cultural identities. Some of these new nations may never achieve adolescence, let alone maturity. Strife between ethnic groups in a developing nation, even open internal warfare, might create fissures in society so wide that they can never be bridged; or it might be the catalyst for national unification. Success in coping with these problems underlies further achievements; failure decreases confidence in existing institutions and political arrangements and leads contending groups to seek alternative solutions all the more vigorously. With resources available and successes under their belt, some of the developing nations have become more and more self-confident.

Policies instituted by developing nations to gain leverage in the developed world affect other poorer nations most seriously. The effect of OPEC price increases on developed nations was serious to be sure, but the impact on other developing nations—especially the poorest nations dependent on imported petroleum and petroleum-based products—was catastrophic. No developed nation is included on the list of "MSA's"—the international bureaucratic term for the countries "most seriously affected" by oil price increases. Most commodity arrangements will have the same effect: They will provide windfall profits to those (including developed nations) that own resources and they will injure those without, especially the poorest, for whom substitution or retooling is impossible.

In this environment, it becomes more and more difficult to think in terms of the unity of the developing world. Instead, we see a rapidly increasing fragmentation along a number of dimensions: richer and poorer; less and better endowed with natural resources; inside or outside of regional or producers' organizations; committed to altering the international economic system or prepared to play within the system's existing rules.

Chapter 2
National Settings: Brazil, Malaysia and Nigeria

BRAZIL, MALAYSIA and NIGERIA are developing nations, sharing many of the tensions and frustrations associated with modernization and industrialization. But these three countries cannot be considered as typical of the developing world. They were selected for this study because of their economic and political importance, both regionally and internationally, and because of their growing interest to foreign investors and multinational corporations. The three accounted for 21 percent of the total direct investment stock in developing nations in 1975, up from 16.7 percent in 1965.[1] Brazil and Nigeria are emerging powers in their respective regions, and Brazilian ambitions extend well beyond South America. Far smaller than neighboring Indonesia, Malaysia still plays a significant role in Southeast Asian politics and is an active participant in international economic forums.

All three have encouraged foreign direct investment in the past and will almost certainly continue to do so. Each is also concerned with increasing the benefits it receives from foreign investment and, through the use of incentives and restrictions, each seeks to encourage foreign corporations to direct greater resources to solving its critical national developmental problems. Leaders in these countries are increasingly aggressive (although not hostile to the foreign investor) and basically optimistic about their capacity to control their relations with foreign corporations. They feel that foreign companies can and should contribute more to their countries, and they do not shy away from playing firms from different home countries against one another to win a better deal for themselves.

Nigeria

Nigeria was a highly arbitrary creation, pieced together from disparate elements—none of which was the focus of consistent British colonial in-

[1]United Nations Economic and Social Council, *Transnational Corporations in World Development: A Re-Examination,* E/C.10/38, March 20, 1978, p. 254.

terest. European interest in Nigeria focused initially on the West African slave trade. The first direct British involvement was in 1852, when British soldiers forced the King of Lagos to abandon the slave trade. Lagos soon became a British colony.

In 1900, the British Colonial Office, which had been responsible for the Lagos Colony, took over control of the Niger Coast Protectorate from the Foreign Office. In 1906, the two were combined and, in 1914, this joint colony merged with the areas north of the Niger and Benue Rivers, the Protectorate of Northern Nigeria (which from 1886 to 1900 had been administered by the Royal Niger Company, a crown-chartered trading company), to form "The Colony and Protectorate of Nigeria."

Aspects of British colonial culture coexist with local cultures in Nigeria today. This dualism is evident in the daily life of many Nigerians—even of highly educated and urbanized Nigerians who frequently maintain close ties to their villages and traditional life-styles far from the major cities. English remains the official language of the country whose inhabitants speak hundreds of different local dialects.

Size and Population

Nigeria, less than one-ninth as large as Brazil, is about the size of Texas, but has the eighth or ninth largest population in the world. Estimates vary widely, but its population is at least 80 million and may be 100 million. One of every four black Africans is a Nigerian, and Nigeria contains the largest Muslim *and* the largest Christian populations in all of Africa. Nigeria is still largely a land of villages, but Nigerian cities are growing explosively: Lagos' population has increased from 300,000 to more than 3 million in the past 15 years, and the flood of Nigerians to the cities and towns poses a serious problem for government leaders and economic planners.

Birth and death rates are significantly higher in Nigeria than in the other two countries and life expectancy is lower. Infant mortality is very high.[2] Populations are increasing at similar rates in all three countries—by about 2.5 or 3 percent a year—high by developed country standards but scarcely comparable to the runaway population growth rates in some other developing countries. The population in each country has grown by about 14 percent in the past five years, which means that these are very youthful nations: The majority in each of the three countries is, or will soon be, under 15 years of age.

Ethnic, linguistic and religious differences are more menacing to social and political stability in Nigeria because there is no clearly dominant culture. The country contains at least 250 distinct ethnic groups that represent cultural backgrounds as different as those of Britain and France,

---

[2]Overseas Development Council, *The U.S. and World Development Agenda.* New York: Praeger Publishers, 1977, pp. 5, 7, 163.

or of Germany and Italy. The typical view that Nigeria is composed solely of three contending ethnic groups—Yoruba in the West, Ibo in the East, and Hausa-Fulani in the North—is misleading. Together these groups do not constitute a majority of Nigeria's people; the "minority" ethnic groups, in fact, make up the majority of the nation.

Since Independence

At independence, Nigeria was a federation of three regions, each controlled by a political party supported by the region's dominant ethnic group. Regional politics were characterized by efforts on the part of these parties to minimize opposition, and national politics focused on increasingly intense competition among the regions for control of the federation's resources. Political competition heightened ethnic, communal and regional identification, and greatly augmented the force of "tribalism" in Nigerian politics. These centrifugal forces strained still further the federal bureaucracy and military—the two national institutions not dominated by regional or communal loyalties that had in large measure held the federation together since independence.[3] In January, 1966, a group of army officers overthrew the federal government; a second military coup followed in July. Efforts to reorganize the federation led to the outbreak of civil war in 1967 between the federal government and a secessionist Biafrian regime in Eastern Nigeria.

The lack of an historic national identity, the deeply rooted centrifugal forces in Nigerian society, and the bitterness of the civil war led most observers to conclude that the divisions in the nation could never be surmounted. Since the conclusion of the war, however, successive Nigerian governments have made reconstruction and national reconciliation a cornerstone of national policy. Most observers now acknowledge that impressive achievements have been made in neutralizing these deep cleavages, although traditional regional and ethnic identities remain a crucial factor in Nigeria today.

Natural Resources

Through the mid-1960's, Nigeria was one of the poorer nations of Africa. Until independence in 1960, its economy was dominated by great European and British trading companies. As late as 1949, it has been estimated, the three largest expatriate trading companies accounted for 49 percent of all traded items in Nigeria.[4] The colonial government of Nigeria did little to

---

[3] Robin Luckharn, *The Nigerian Military: A Sociological Analysis of Authority and Revolt 1960-67*. Cambridge: Cambridge University Press, 1971.

[4] Peter Kilby, *Industrialisation in an Open Society: Nigeria 1945-1966*. Cambridge: Cambridge University Press, 1969, p. 62, as cited in Andre Hilton, "Foreign Investment in Nigeria," unpublished dissertation, University of Pennsylvania, 1975.

control the marketing of export crops before World War II, although it did much to promote and facilitate their production. Its primary interest was to maximize trade in exports and imports. Everything else was left to free enterprise, which was dominated by Europeans. Although it has been suggested that European economic involvement in Nigeria stimulated African entrepreneurial initiative, Nigerians were specifically discouraged from direct competition with expatriates.[5]

The concentration of economic power in the hands of expatriate firms provided a major source of Nigerian resentment. The insensitivity of the expatriates and colonial officers in business and government to local aspirations provided fuel for nationalist movements.

Nigerian economic growth accelerated after World War II. Gross Domestic Product (GDP) increased by 4.1 percent per annum between 1950 and 1957, and 4.5 percent between 1957 and 1962. Growth rested on the development of agriculture—particularly cocoa, groundnuts (peanuts), cotton and palm oil. External examinations (for example, by Sir Arthur Lewis for the OECD in 1966) pointed out that Nigeria's favorable prospects for future growth rested primarily on the expansion of agricultural exports.[6] But the outbreak of war in 1967 halted economic expansion.

The search for oil in Nigeria began in 1908, but oil was not discovered in commercial quantities until 1956. By 1965, oil production reached 300,000 barrels a day, and production continued to expand during the civil war. In 1970, Nigeria's oil boom began. Production peaked in 1974 at 2.25 million barrels a day, fell in 1975, and stabilized at about 2 million until the oil glut of 1977 drove production down to about 1.6 million barrels a day. Nigeria is the sixth or seventh largest producer of crude oil and the third largest crude-oil exporter. It ranks behind Saudi Arabia as a supplier of crude to the United States.

Since 1970, oil has increasingly dominated Nigeria's economy. In 1963, oil earnings accounted for only 3 percent of government revenue, and for only 17 percent as late as 1967. By 1976, however, oil earnings reached $8 billion, some 90 percent of total government revenue.

Oil revenues have made Nigeria the "gold rush country of Africa."[7] Dependence on oil revenue makes Nigeria's boom extremely vulnerable, however. The recent international glut of oil, together with the weakening of the American dollar (in which Nigerian oil is priced), led to a sharp reduction of crude oil production in 1977, and to a serious shortfall in

[5]James S. Coleman, *Nigeria: Background to Nationalism.* Berkeley: University of California Press, 1968.

[6]Sir W. Arthur Lewis, *Reflections on Nigeria's Economic Growth.* Paris: Development Centre of the OECD, 1967.

[7]John Darton, *The New York Times,* October 30, 1976, and James Flanigan, "Nigeria: Where the Real Action Is." *Fortune,* December 1, 1976.

anticipated revenue in the face of rising world prices. By early 1978, some Nigerian leaders estimated that the loss of expected revenues for the year might run as high as 20 to 40 percent, although soaring oil prices in 1979 have reversed this trend. In any case, oil is a diminishing asset: Based on current estimated reserves and the current rate of production, Nigeria's oil reserves will be exhausted by 2001. The challenge facing Nigeria's leaders today is to ensure that the revenues derived from oil production contribute to overall national development so that dependence on this single resource can be reduced as quickly as possible.

Malaysia

Spices rather than slaves brought European traders to the ports of the Malay peninsula. Early in the 16th century, the Portuguese occupied Malacca (on the west coast of the peninsula) and, later in the century, the British East India Company appeared at Penang, to the north. European interests focused on trade rather than colonies, and not until 1867 did Britain bring together a group of these trading ports—Penang, Malacca and Singapore—into a crown colony: the Straits Settlements. Only with the initiation of modern tin exploitation in the mid-1870's did the British begin to take an active interest in the hinterland of the Straits Settlements.

The Union of Malaya was formed in 1946, after the Japanese surrender, by uniting Penang and Malacca with the nine states of the Malay Peninsula. Singapore, together with Sabah and Sarawak on the island of Borneo, became crown colonies at this time. Malaya was declared to be independent in 1957. In 1962-63, an agreement between Malaya and Britain led to the formation of a new Federation of Malaysia, which included Malaya, Singapore, Sabah and Sarawak. In 1965, Singapore seceded from the Federation and established itself as an independent state.

Size and Population

Malaysia is a small country, about a third the size of Nigeria, with a population of 12.5 million. Eighty-five percent of the Malaysians live in West or Peninsular Malaysia. The remaining 15 percent live in East Malaysia, in the states of Sabah and Sarawak on the island of Borneo, 400 miles to the east across the South China Sea. This is a country of villages and small towns: Almost three-quarters of the population is rural and the largest city, Kuala Lumpur, has a population of only about 500,000. The Malaysian government has attempted—with considerable success—to inhibit massive internal migration, especially toward urban centers.

While it has been replaced by Bahasa Malaysia as the official language, English is still widely spoken in business and in government offices, and British customs and institutions are widespread. Existing federal structures in government grow largely out of Britain's preference for "indirect rule" of its colonies, and the influence of British legal and educational systems remains pervasive.

Cleavages in Malaysian society are less complex than in Nigeria but constitute an equally—if not greater—destabilizing political force. Half of the population in Peninsular Malaysia is Malay, 37 percent Chinese, 11 percent Indian, and 2 percent a mixed group of other nationalities. (In Sabah and Sarawak, the majority of the population is made up of indigenous Bornean groups, and about a quarter of the population is Chinese.) Chinese first came to Malaysia hundreds of years ago to work in the tin mines, but most were brought to Malaysia by the British at the end of the 19th century to expand tin production and to work on rubber plantations. Indian laborers and their families were also brought to Malaysia by the British to build a railway system throught the Peninsula.

Malaysian Chinese culture has been resistant to external influences, but ruling Malay groups assimilated British colonial life-styles. More recently, however, there has been growing pressure from the Malay cultural heartland, the small rural villages, to reject external (and non—Islamic) cultural influences.

The Chinese community has traditionally dominated Malaysian commerce and the nation's economic life, but the British relied on the Malays to run the colony's administration. At independence, the Malay community provided most of the new nation's political leadership. Thus, unlike Nigeria, where dominant ethnic groups in each region competed for the control of the federation's resources, ethnic cleavages in Malaysia have been identified with particular roles in society—the Malays with political power and the Chinese with economic power and with the ownership of assets (see Table 5).

This arrangement was relatively stable during the first decade of independence. The Chinese cooperated with and participated in governments led by the United Malay Nationalist Organization (UMNO, the leading Malay political party). The disparity between the political predominance of the Malays and the economic predominance of the Chinese was not seen as a destabilizing force in Malaysian politics. In 1969, however, Malaysia was shaken by a wave of communal rioting and violence. The riots forced the Malaysian leadership to reexamine national policies, particularly with regard to the economy and development, as they affected relations among the racial communities.

Natural Resources

From the perspective of the balance of its resources, Malaysia may be the most favorably endowed of the three nations in this study. It is the world's leading exporter of natural rubber and the world's leading producer of tin. It accounts for more than 30 percent of the total world production of tin— twice as much as Bolivia, the second largest producer. It supplies more than

Table 5: Asset Ownership by Race, Peninsular Malaysia, 1970 (in percents)

	Shared capital in limited companies	Planted acreage in modern agriculture		Fixed assets in industry	
		Corporate sector	Noncorporate sector	Corporate sector	Noncorporate sector
Total................	(M $5,289 million)	(1.8 million acres)	(0.7 million acres)	(M $1,307 million)	(M $171.3 million)
Malaysians...........	39.3%	29.2%	94.1%	42.8%	97.6%
Malay	1.9	0.3	47.1	0.9	2.3
Chinese..............	22.5	25.9	32.8	26.2	92.2
Indian	1.0	0.3	10.1	0.1	2.3
Other................	13.0	2.7	1.8	14.3	0.8
Government	0.9	—	2.3	1.3	—
Non-Malaysians.......	60.7	70.8	5.9	57.2	2.4
Total................	100.0%	100.0%	100.0%	100.0%	100.0%

Source: C.C. Robless, "The Feasibility and International Consistency of the New Economic Policy," in Stephen Chee and Khov Siew Min, eds., *Malaysian Economic Development and Policies*. Kuala Lumpur: *Malaysian Economic Association*, 1975, p. 43.

50 percent of the world's palm oil. Malaysia is also the world's leading exporter of tropical hardwoods and of pepper. In addition, it now produces about 200,000 barrels of crude oil a day.

Malaysia is blessed with plentiful natural resources in a balanced array. As the international market price of one commodity has fallen, the price of another has risen. Moreover, Malaysia has been extremely good at product and market development. World leadership in rubber, palm oil, and timber was achieved by successful planning and management.

Brazil

Brazil was a Portuguese colony for 300 years. In 1822, Dom Pedro, the son of King John VI of Portugal, declared Brazil independent of Portugal and proclaimed himself emperor. Thus Brazil has been an independent nation for almost as long as the United States—although the Brazilian monarchy was overthrown and a republic established only in 1889.

Brazil's people and culture (which includes European, African and Indian elements) are more diverse than Nigeria's or Malaysia's, but there has been a sense of national consciousness in Brazil for a much longer period. Brazil shared in the nationalism which swept Latin America in the early 19th century. Although colonial influences remain, most have been assimilated into a unique national amalgam in the course of Brazil's long history.

Size and Population

Brazil is the fifth largest nation in the world in area and seventh in population. Its land area takes up half of South America, and is larger than the continental United States. Its population is at least 110 million, possibly pushing upward to 115 million.

Almost 60 percent of Brazil's people live in urban areas. Several Brazilian cities are huge, even by world standards. At least six have more than a million inhabitants; Rio has more than five million and São Paulo, with ten million, is the largest industrial center in the southern hemisphere. Much of the country, however, is relatively empty. The North (Amazon) and Center-West (Mato Grosso), which together make up almost two-thirds of Brazil's area, contain only about 10 percent of its population. The densely populated southeast, however, with only 11 percent of the national territory, contributes more than 85 percent of the country's industrial production; employs 70 percent of the industrial work force; provides half of the voters in national elections; contributes over 80 percent of the national revenue; has 50 percent of the large banks and 80 percent of the bank deposits.[8]

---

[8]Thomas E. Weil and others, *Area Handbook for Brazil,* (DA Pam 550-20). Washington, D.C.: Government Printing Office, 1975, p. 12.

Brazil's population is highly diverse in racial and national origin. Estimates of the compositon of the population in the mid-1970's suggest that while less than 1 percent can be classified as Indian, about a third have some Indian ancestry. Brazil has the heaviest concentration of blacks and their descendants outside of Africa: At least a third, and perhaps half, of the population would be considered black by the U.S. definition of race. More than half of the population consider themselves white descendants of European stock—Portuguese, Germans and Italians in particular. Racial differences are critical elements in Brazilian society. Brazil has long considered itself to be a multiracial society with few racial tensions. But students of Brazil, as well as Brazilians themselves, underline continuing racial prejudice.

Natural Resources and Early Economic Development

Brazil possesses extensive mineral resources and is the sixth largest producer of iron in the world; its reserves are estimated to constitute a quarter of the world total. It is one of the world's major producers and exporters of agricultural products. Agriculture employs more than 40 percent of Brazil's labor force, and provided until very recently over 50 percent of the country's export earnings. Brazil is the largest coffee growing and exporting nation; a major producer and exporter of sugar and cotton; and derives much of its current export earnings from soybeans.

From the founding of the Republic in 1889 until World War I, its economic growth rates exceeded those of the United States. World market conditions for coffee and other agricultural products, and earnings from duties on imports, made it possible for Brazil to maintain a favorable trade position for many decades. The Brazilian government, aided by British investments in railroads, involved itself directly in financing infrastructure development, and in other capital investments associated with the country's early industrial development.

Well into the present century, however, Brazil's economy was heavily dependent on the export of coffee and a few other primary products. These exports paid for manufactured goods and, later, for the intermediate products that went into Brazil's industrialization.

Despite its vast mineral and agricultural resources, Brazil is deficient in energy, particularly fossil fuels. Oil is a critical problem. Brazil has never produced more than 20 percent of its requirements, and the rate of growth of new domestic sources barely enables it to maintain that proportion. Although Brazil is speedily increasing its hydroelectric capacity, it is forced to rely heavily on imported petroleum. The rapid inflation of world oil prices after 1973 has imposed an extreme burden on the Brazilian economy.

Chapter 3
Government, the Economy, and Politics

BRAZIL, MALAYSIA and NIGERIA share certain characteristics that are highly relevant to foreign investors. For example, the role of national government in all three economies is very significant and growing in importance. The growth of public sector not only impinges on economic development; it also directly affects the quality of national politics. All three countries also manifest marked and growing economic inequality—a fact that is potentially destabilizing.

Let us look at some of these factors more closely.

Political Systems

The political systems of these three countries have a number of features in common. Despite certain outward trappings, they have few similarities with the pluralistic and participant political systems of the Anglo-American world. Although all three countries are federal in structure, the requirements of development and of maintaining political and economic coherence in rapidly changing societies have led to a high degree of centralization. By Western standards, all three governments are authoritarian. Although there are official oppositions in Brazil and Malaysia, their role is considerably hedged about; in Nigeria, where political parties were outlawed until recently, open opposition was still more limited. The Malaysian government's policy regarding civil rights is less arbitrary than Brazil's or Nigeria's, but the continuing danger of Communist insurgency provides a rationale for restrictions on individual freedom where the government feels they are required.

Military Governments in Brazil and Nigeria

Brazil and Nigeria have military governments. In January, 1966, a group of senior Nigerian military officers overthrew the civilian government that had ruled over an environment that had become progressively more turbulent since independence. They were ousted by another group of officers in a second coup six months later, which proved to be the prelude to the civil war that broke out in May, 1967. The military has remained in control—although there was a successful coup in 1975 and an unsuccessful attempt in 1976. The government has pledged to restore civilian rule in 1979, and steps in this direction are being taken as planned. However, presidential elections in the Summer of 1979 suggest that the centrifugal nature of Nigeria's civilian politics remains in evidence.

The overthrow of the civilian government led to several basic alterations in Nigeria's political system. The four original regions of the country were divided into twelve and later nineteen states in order to reduce the power of the major regional-ethnic groups in national politics. Leaders of minority groups gained influence in the government and the military—although northerners retained a preponderant role in the country's leadership. Party leaders were replaced by the military as general policymakers, but permanent secretaries and other top public administrators significantly increased their role in the policymaking process.

The formal transfer of political authority has been much smoother in Brazil since the Brazilian military overthrew the government of Joao Goulart in 1964. Brazil's experiment with open, democratic policies seemed to many to have brought the country to the brink of economic and political chaos, and there was widespread agreement that some sort of highly centralized—even authoritarian—regime was needed to restore order and confidence. General Castello Branco was installed as president, and the regime he constructed was in many ways a return to a more traditional authoritarian political system. Presidential terms of office are now set at five years, however, and the succession of presidents, carefully orchestrated by the military and rubber-stamped by tightly controlled political parties, has progressed smoothly—at least to the outside observer.

The military is the most influential political group in Brazil. It has selected the presidents-elect from the ranks of top military staff, and has ensured that transfers of national power were peaceful. The military is not monolithic, and officers have quite different views on critical national issues. Moderates and hardliners clash on many issues regarding political participation, democratization and the restoration of civilian rule—all of which spill over into the determination of the presidential succession. The military, like the civilian leaders with whom they are associated, also differ regarding the degree of inequality economic development requires, or can be politically tolerated or managed. The military is highly "modernized," both technologically and politically. Its officers reflect the same "technocratic" training and values found in the upper levels of the state administration. The military leaders have, for the most part, agreed to turn over the operations of the state administration to highly trained civilian technocrats with a strong commitment to government intervention and management. Brazil's military leaders and technocrats are extremely nationalistic in the sense that they view Brazil as a natural global leader of the 21st century and seek to ensure that present policies aim clearly at this goal.

In both Nigeria and Brazil, the military regimes describe themselves as "corrective" and have pledged to restore civilian government. Brazilian military leaders argue about the degree of "decompression" that can safely be permitted in Brazilian society, but there is no sign that the government will soon honor its commitment to bring about a return to civilian rule.

In Nigeria, however, the government has adhered to a strict schedule for the restoration of civilian government. A new constitution, based on the American model, has been adopted; local elections have been held as a first step toward the re-creation of civilian political institutions; and elections for state houses of assembly, the national Senate and House of Representatives and President, were held in the Summer of 1979. The evolution of political institutions and patterns of political behavior is at an earlier stage in Nigeria than in Brazil, however, and centrifugal forces are considerably more powerful there—so that, even while acknowledging the determination of the Federal Military Government to turn over the government to civilians, questions remain about the feasibility of civilian rule.

Malaysia

Despite continuing external and internal pressures (caused by the dual threats of communism and communalism), the Malaysian government has been impressively stable. The Federation of Malaya came into existence in the midst of a Communist-led insurrection against the British that began in June, 1948. Because of continuing guerrilla warfare, independence was delayed until 1957, and the state of emergency was not ended until 1960. Communist insurgency remains a worrisome but not, it appears, a dangerous problem. Many foreign investors feared that the fall of Vietnam would lead to heightened guerrilla activity in Thailand and Malaysia, but this has not been the case. The antiterrorist campaign waged jointly by the Malaysians and Thais seems to have effectively neutralized the insurgency threat. Although influenced by the rise of Islamic militancy, Malaysia's political system has not been destabilized by this phenomenon.

Malaysian stability was also threatened when Singapore left the newly formed federation in 1965 and, more severely, with the outbreak of communal rioting in 1969. Communalism—the struggle among Malaysia's racial communities—is the most serious problem now facing Malaysia (and the foreign investor in Malaysia as well), but most observers agree that the political system instituted at independence has functioned reasonably well in coping with this, as with other, problems.

Malaysia is a constitutional monarchy with a king, elected by the royal rulers (sultans) of the Malaysian states from among their own ranks, who serves a four-year term. The monarch has no official power, and government is carried on by the prime minister and cabinet with the consent of the two houses of parliament. Malaysia was ruled after independence by the Alliance, a coalition of three communal parties: the United Malay National Organization (UMNO), the Malayan Chinese Association and the Malayan Indian Congress. The Alliance came into existence after unsuccessful efforts to create noncommunal political organizations led to the recognition of "the existence of diverse and conflicting communal interests and the need for an instrument to manage and mediate them."[1] The leadership of the Alliance, representing the leadership of the ethnic communities, sought to reconcile the interests of the communities and ensure their electoral and political support for the government.

The Alliance rested on a series of understandings among the communities. The Malays were politically dominant, and the electoral system ensured a Malay majority in the federal parliament, as well as in the state governments, even where non-Malays were a majority of the population. The chief ministers of the states and the members of the federal cabinet would be largely Malay. Non-Malays received full and equal citizenship if born in Malaya and more liberal naturalization rights than existed during the colonial period. They also received full political participation, religious freedom, liberal use of communal languages, and the opportunity for economic activity.

Until 1969, the system appeared to be working remarkably well. Since 1969, tensions within the original coalition, defections from it, and opposition outside of it have all heightened substantially. After 1969, a wider coalition—the National Front—replaced the old Alliance. Almost all communal groups, however, still seem to acknowledge the basic effectiveness and legitimacy of the leadership coalition and of the Malaysian government.

Economic Development

Economically, there are striking differences among these three countries. Brazil is the superstar, with the tenth largest economy in the world. Considered for so long to be the "country of the future," many people—Brazilians and non-Brazilians—doubted that Brazil would ever fulfill its promise. From the late 1960's to the petroleum crisis of the early 1970's, Brazil experienced an "economic miracle" with growth rates among the highest in the world.

Because of the oil boom, Nigeria's GNP has also grown rapidly. It reached $21 billion in 1974 and should touch $30 billion by the end of the decade, thus overtaking South Africa as the continent's largest economy.

[1]Milton J. Esman, *Administration and Development in Malaysia.* Ithaca, N.Y.: Cornell University Press, 1972, p. 24.

The Malaysian GNP of $8 billion is much smaller, although on a per capita basis it is about 75 percent of Brazil's. World Bank data show Brazil with a per capita income in 1974 of $920 and Malaysia with $680. Despite its great oil income, per capita GNP in Nigeria remains much lower—$280 in 1974.[2]

Calculations of GNP vary considerably, especially for Brazil and Nigeria, and data on economic growth rates are even more unreliable. Brazilian GNP grew rapidly from 1968 to 1974—the years of the "economic miracle"—probably at a rate exceeding 10 percent a year. But Brazilian growth throughout the entire period since World War II has been remarkable, with an average annual growth rate of about 7 percent. Nigerian GNP also grew by as much as 10 percent a year between 1960 and 1974, although growth here was focused on a far narrower segment of the economy than in the other countries. Malaysian GNP in the 1960's expanded at an annual average rate of between 6 and 7 percent; average annual increases in the 1970's are probably slightly higher—although growth has been less smooth than in the previous decade. World Bank data indicate that *per capita* GNP increased substantially between 1960 and 1974 in all three countries (see Chart 2).

The composition of its economy reflects the unbalanced development Nigeria is experiencing. Petroleum accounted for more than 45 percent of gross domestic product (GDP) in 1974 (up from 33 percent in 1970) and may be more significant today. The contribution of manufacturing to GDP

Chart 2: Per Capita GNP: Annual Rates of Growth

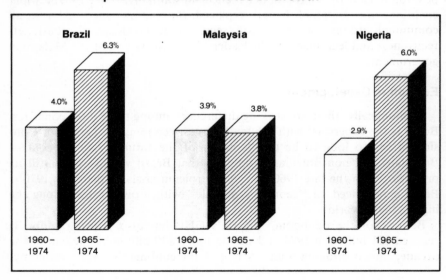

Brazil		Malaysia		Nigeria	
1960–1974	1965–1974	1960–1974	1965–1974	1960–1974	1965–1974
4.0%	6.3%	3.9%	3.8%	2.9%	6.0%

[2]World Bank, *Atlas*. Washington, D.C., 1976, p. 5.

declined marginally in Nigeria between 1970 and 1974 (from 5 to 4 percent)—because of the dramatic growth of oil production—and the contribution of agriculture to GDP has declined to about 25 percent. The makeup of the Brazilian and Malaysian economies has changed more gradually. The contribution of agriculture to GDP in Brazil declined from 23 percent in 1960 to about 15 percent in 1970, reflecting the growth of the industrial sector. Agriculture, including the production of rubber, has remained at about 30 percent of GDP in Malaysia, a level that reflects the increasing importance of palm oil and timber (as well as rubber) in the Malaysian economy. During 1971-1975 (the life of the Second Malaysian Plan), manufacturing output rose sharply—by almost 11 percent a year—but the contribution of manufacturing to GDP rose more slowly, increasing from 12 to 15 percent. Current economic development plans, however, emphasize growth in this sector, with a 1990 target of 26 percent of GDP.

Brazil pursued a policy of import-substitution industrialization from the end of World War II until 1967, and has subsequently emphasized exports, especially of manufactured goods, as the key to its future growth. As a result of both strategies, as well as Brazil's highly sophisticated and centralized economic management system, Brazil has achieved a substantially higher level of industrialization than almost any other developing nation.[3]

International Aspirations

All three countries aspire to international economic and political leadership. Brazilian and Nigerian leaders have again and again expressed their determination to take leading roles on the regional, continental and even the international stage. Both have strenuously sought to diversify trading relationships and to assert their independence from traditional "special relationships." (In this respect, the remarkable growth of Brazilian-Nigerian ties in recent years should be underscored.) Malaysia, too—although quite lacking Brazil's sense of *grandeza*—has emphasized its leadership role in Southeast Asia, within ASEAN, (the Association of South East Asian Nations) and among the world's commodity producers.

International Trade

All three countries are leaders of the developing world in international trade. Table 6 ranks developing nations by the dollar value of their exports in 1974, the latest year for which such complete data are available. Nigeria is in the second level of petroleum exporters, and Brazil has the largest non-oil exports of any developing nation. Brazil's 1974 import figures reflect the

[3]Werner Baer, "The Brazilian Growth and Development Experience: 1964-1975," in Riordan Roett, ed., *Brazil in the Seventies.* Washington, D.C.: American Enterprise Institute for Public Policy Research, 1976, p. 52.

Table 6: Rankings of Developing Countries by Dollar Values of Exports and Imports (in millions of U.S. $, with ranks in parentheses)

Country	Exports 1974		Exports 1963	Imports 1974
Saudi Arabia	$35,657 (1)		$2,026 (2)	$ 1,865 (18)
Iran	24,002 (2)		1,881 (3)	5,672 (7)
Kuwait	10,957 (3)		1,437 (8)	1,552 (20)
Venezuela	10,732 (4)		2,506 (1)	4,200 (10)
Nigeria	9,567 (5)		591 (18)	2,737 (16)
Libya	8,259 (6)		1,863 (5)	2,763 (15)
Iraq	8,177 (7)		1,039 (13)	2,273 (17)
Brazil	7,951 (8)	1 [a]	1,881 (4)	14,162 (1)
Indonesia	7,426 (9)		731 (17)	5,672 (8)
United Arab Emirates	7,371 (10)		340 (20)	1,605 (19)
Hong Kong	5,959 (11)	2	1,744 (7)	6,768 (5)
Singapore	5,811 (12)	3	1,271 (11)	8,380 (2)
Taiwan	5,533 (13)	4	789 (16)	6,964 (3)
Korea	4,461 (14)	5	455 (19)	6,844 (4)
Algeria	4,336 (15)		830 (15)	4,058 (12)
Malaysia	4,233 (16)	6	1,347 (10)	4,155 (11)
Argentina	3,932 (17)	7	1,368 (9)	3,570 (13)
India	3,927 (18)	8	1,761 (6)	5,043 (9)
Mexico	3,540 (19)	9	1,254 (12)	6,504 (6)
Philippines	2,671 (20)	10	857 (14)	3,436 (14)

[a]Largest non-OPEC exporters

Source: Adapted from Riordan Roett, ed., *Brazil in the Seventies.* Washington, D.C.: American Enterprise Institute for Public Policy Research, 1976, p. 79.

enormous drain on its resources caused by rocketing oil prices after 1973. What observers consider to be heroic efforts to increase exports (aided by rising commodity prices) and limit imports have substantially reduced Brazil's trade deficit since 1974, however.[4] Nigeria's imports have soared since 1974, increasing in value by more than 40 percent between 1976 and 1977. Early in 1978, the Nigerian government negotiated a billion-dollar international loan to help finance development projects, and the 1978 federal budget demanded austerity and "sacrifices for all," and imposed drastic restrictions on imports.

Malaysian exports rank only marginally behind Hong Kong and Singapore, and the two major Asian export-platform nations, South Korea and Taiwan. Because of the recovery in world demand for primary products

---

[4]"The Brazilian Gamble," *Business Week,* December 5, 1977. Also "International Economic Survey," *The New York Times,* February 5, 1978.

in 1976 and 1977 and the hardening of product prices, Malaysian exports, primarily of raw materials, rose sharply in this period, exceeding the targets of the Third Malaysian Plan by a wide margin.

Brazilian exports, especially of agricultural goods and iron ore, increased dramatically after 1968. By 1977, Brazil seemed likely to become the world's second greatest exporter of agricultural products—just behind the United States—but the export of Brazilian manufactured goods has also increased sharply, increasing by 1975 to 28 percent of total exports. By 1979, manufactured goods for the first time in Brazil's history became the leading export category.

Rubber, tin and palm oil constituted 47 percent of Malaysian exports in 1976, down from 58 percent in 1970. In this period, exports of manufactured goods increased from 11 to 22 percent, although —as noted above— the share of manufactured goods in Malaysia's exports has declined in the past two years. Nigerian exports, of course, are totally dominated by oil. Crude oil accounted for 94 percent of its exports in 1976. Nigeria was a major exporter of agricultural products in the 1950's, but is now a substantial net agricultural importer—even of foodstuffs and of products formerly exported.

Malaysia's international trade is evenly distributed among several major partners. Japan accounts for about a quarter of Malaysia's imports and about a fifth of its exports; the United States for about 16 percent of its exports and 13 percent of its imports; the EEC for a fifth of both exports and imports; the ASEAN area for slightly less than a quarter of Malaysia's exports and about 16 percent of its imports.

The United States is Brazil's major trading partner, although its share of Brazilian trade has diminished somewhat in recent years. In 1962, the United States took 40 percent of Brazil's exports and provided 26 percent of its imports; in 1972, it accounted for only 31 percent of Brazilian exports—although it provided 28 percent of Brazil's imports. The Federal Republic of Germany is Brazil's second largest trading partner, and accounts for about 10 percent of Brazil's exports and 15 percent of its imports. Argentina and Italy are also important trading partners, and Japan has become a major source of imports for Brazil.

The United States is the principal customer for Nigerian oil, purchasing more than half of the total output. It should be noted that this accounts for about two-thirds of all U.S. imports from Sub-Saharan Africa. The United Kingdom, the Netherlands, and France are Nigeria's next largest purchasers, each accounting for about 10 percent of its crude oil; the rest of Europe accounts for another 10 percent of Nigeria's oil sales. The major sources of Nigeria's imports are the United Kingdom, West Germany, the United States, and Japan.

Data on imports (Table 7) reveal important patterns. They show, for example, Brazil's efforts over the five-year period, 1969 to 1974, to increase its trade with the EEC, as well as growing U.S. trade with Malaysia. Most importantly, the data clearly indicate the dramatic expansion of Japanese trade with Brazil and Nigeria. Indeed, between 1969 and 1974, Japanese exports to Nigeria and Brazil expanded about three times more rapidly than U.S. exports to these nations.

Table 7: Sources of Imports for Brazil, Malaysia and Nigeria

Country	Imports from:	(1974, f.o.b., U.S. $ Million)	5-year increase (percent)
Brazil	United States	$3,348	391%
	EEC	3,431	435
	Japan	1,350	1,177
Malaysia	United States	397	438
	EEC	873	231
	Japan	915	391
Nigeria.	United States	314	283
	EEC	1,508	255
	Japan	313	1,085

Source: Business International Corp., *IL&T—Latin America*, June 1976, p. 19; *IL&T, Asia*, June 1976, p. 4; *IL&T—Africa, Middle East*, June 1976, p. 6.

The Role of the State

The state is a major force in all three economies. It plays a critical role in infrastructure development—communication systems, transportation and education, for example—and is a primary source of investment capital. Increasingly, the state acts as an entrepreneur as well, initiating new investments either on its own or as a joint-venture partner with local or foreign investors.

Brazil

Because foreign investors remained relatively uninterested in Brazil until quite recently, the government took a major role in that nation's early industrialization. Public-sector ownership of industry went hand in hand with Brazil's economic development. That process accelerated after World War II. On some occasions, such as the creation of Petrobrás in the early 1950's, heated debates accompanied the state's entrepreneurial expansion. But the general process of public-sector leadership has been furthered under the "revolutionary" military regime that has ruled Brazil since 1964.

Today, the Brazilian state owns and directs the public utilities, petroleum, iron ore, atomic fuels, steel and inland transport industries. Ten years ago, state enterprises in manufacturing (excluding petroleum) owned 8 percent of total assets; the figure now exceeds 20 percent. If petroleum industries are included, the state's share of assets has increased from 17 to over 30 percent in this period. Nineteen of the twenty largest Brazilian corporations are state owned; almost half of the hundred largest firms operating there fall into the same category. Petrobrás is one of the largest corporations in the world.

Nigeria

In Nigeria, under colonial rule, the government was the main source of capital for infrastructure development and was involved in almost every aspect of the economy. But the economic policy of the colonial government and the Nigerian government after independence both stressed the free market and private initiative wherever practical. Since the end of the civil war, however, the government has emphasized that national independence must rest on the foundation of a strong and independent national economy, and it has assumed the leading role in guiding and stimulating economic development.

The public sector has increased enormously, financed by oil revenues. The capital expenditure budget of the federal government alone (and the state governments are also highly active) was about $3 billion in 1974-1975 and is projected at $13.4 billion for 1978-1979 (even after cuts made in the Spring, 1978 budget). While the first and second national plans (1962-1968 and 1970-1975) involved capital expenditures of about $4 billion and $6 billion respectively, the Third National Development Plan (1975-1980) called for some $60 billion in capital expenditures, $40 billion of which was to come from the federal government—and these figures have been revised upwards.

The Nigerian government has reserved basic sectors of the economy for public ownership (such as railroads, telephone service, and electricity) and has identified certain key sectors in which there should be direct public-sector control and a minimum of 55 percent public-sector ownership. These include iron and steel, petrochemicals, fertilizer production, and the local distribution of petroleum products.

The federal government has also acquired a 60 percent interest in two major foreign-owned commercial banks, and has taken a joint interest in various other industrial projects. More importantly, the Nigerian National Petroleum Company (NNPC) now owns a majority share in the subsidiaries of all oil-producing companies operating in Nigeria, and owns a 60 percent share in the distribution activities of the major foreign oil companies there.

Malaysia

The role of the public sector has also increased dramatically in Malaysia. State ownership was traditionally restricted to certain basic infrastructure facilities (airlines, railroads, public utilities). In addition, the state at times participated in industrial ventures deemed in the national interest. The government's response to the communal rioting in 1969 was the adoption of the New Economic Plan (NEP), designed to eradicate poverty in all racial communities and restructure the economy to eliminate racial imbalances.

The crucial goal of the NEP is that, by 1990, the Malay community will own 30 percent of all commercial and industrial activities in Malaysia; non-Malay Malaysians (mainly Chinese), 40 percent; and foreigners, 30 percent. It quickly became clear, however, that with the low levels of income and savings of the Malay community it would be impossible for them to reach the 30 percent target by 1990 on their own. Thus, since 1970, the government has taken a greatly expanded role in the economy, and particularly in the industrial sector, through a wide-ranging system of state corporations and public enterprises—permitting it to acquire industrial and commercial assets that are to be held "in trust" for the Malay community. The most important of these agencies is Pernas (the "national corporation"), a holding company established in 1969, and now involved in many commercial and industrial activities, including distribution, insurance, construction, real estate, mining and manufacturing.

Through this and similar organizations, the state role in the Malaysian economy has increased sharply. By 1990, it is predicted, some 22.6 percent of the corporate sector of the economy will be owned, directly or indirectly, by the government. Only 7.4 percent will be owned by individual Malays. The long-term goal of the NEP, of course, is that all of this should find its way into individual Malay hands—that assets "held in trust" should be released as quickly as feasible. But many people inside and outside of the Malaysian government—some Malays themselves—feel that the growing state apparatus will prove reluctant to redistribute these shares of the economy into individual hands. Some speak fearfully of the growth of "state capitalism" as the primary result of the NEP.

The Role of the State Bureaucracy

While the states' role in the economy is growing rapidly in each of these countries and administrators in the bureaucracy play an increasingly prominent role in the nations' economic life, there are important differences among them. In Brazil, cadres of highly trained, nationalistic technocrats are sheltered by the umbrella of the military regime and largely isolated from key political issues, such as the return to civilian rule and the implications of increasing inequality in Brazilian society. The situation in Nigeria is similar. The nature of the military regime and the ban on political activity, together with the overwhelming role of the state as a source of capital, provide a clear field for top bureaucrats to set key economic policies. Unlike Brazil, however, there has been much greater penetration of private-sector interests into the Nigerian administration. Despite government concern, administrators at all levels have frequently become deeply involved in private business ventures. Thus, while the state has expanded into the private sector as in Brazil, in a certain sense the booming private sector in Nigeria has expanded subtly (and not so subtly) into the state.

The problem in Malaysia is somewhat different. Civilian political leaders have maintained a high degree of control over the expanding state administration, but state administrators have become more and more *politicized* as a result of heightened communal tension and of the various steps taken to improve the position of the Malays in Malaysian society. Political leaders now struggle to hold younger Malay administrators in check, and to control the tendency to utilize the state administration as an arm of the Malay community in the competition among the racial communities. The "overzealousness" of Malay government officials is a frequent explanation for the excesses of certain policies and a cause of great concern within the non-Malay communities and among leading Malay politicians as well.

Societies and the Growth of Inequality

It is difficult to compare levels of economic and social development in a very meaningful fashion. Per capita GNP provides merely one indicator of relative developmental levels. Other indicators enlarge the picture. Malaysia, for example, has about the same number of passenger cars per 1,000 of its population as Brazil; 32 in Malaysia, 33 in Brazil. Nigeria has only two per thousand. With a population almost ten times as great, Brazil has about ten times more telephones than Malaysia. But Nigeria, with a population pushing close to that of Brazil, has only half as many telephones as Malaysia.

Perhaps the most useful indicator of overall development is energy consumption. Brazil reaches only 4.7 percent of the average U.S. per capita energy consumption; Malaysia 4.1 percent. Nigeria consumes only .6 percent. By any of these indicators, Nigeria is obviously far less developed than Brazil or Malaysia. But it would be hard to judge which of the two latter countries was more developed.

Brazil is the far more complex society. By virtue of its size, degree of urbanization, and the extent of industrialization, the scale and complexity of its society is similar to that of many developed nations. The size of government agencies and both local and foreign corporations in Brazil, for example, requires an enormous and sophisticated infrastructure of communication systems, of recruitment and training facilities, and of personnel and financial administration. While these factors, too, are indicative of development, a society can be complex without being fully developed. Complexity is not identical with development, nor with efficiency. On a scale of social efficiency (as opposed to complexity) Malaysia probably would rank higher than Brazil. Here Malaysia's size and, more important, the highly favorable balance between population and resources weighs greatly in Malaysia's favor in future development prospects.

Economic growth has been associated in all three countries with a tendency for inequality to increase throughout these societies. Growth is associated in the first place with uneven development and growing imbalances among regions. This is perhaps most notable in Brazil, where regional disparities constitute a major political issue and a continuing source of tension for multinational corporations.

While the civil war in Nigeria grew out of the competition among major regional groups for control of the resources of the federation—a reflection of perceived and actual regional disparities in growth and opportunity—differential growth rates of urban and rural areas may constitute a more serious problem today in Nigeria than traditional regional differences. Urban incomes in Nigeria are estimated to be about three times the average per capita income, while many rural incomes are far below the national average. One key reason for Nigeria's abysmal agricultural performance is that no one wants to stay on the land when the cities beckon so brightly.

Regional imbalances and inequalities are only one dimension of the problem. More serious may be patterns of widening social and income inequality within these nations. This issue has been most prominent in Brazil since the publication of the 1970 demographic census revealed a dramatic increase in the concentration of income distribution. Brazilian government officials underscore the fact that economic development depends on capital accumulation, and that accumulation requires sacrifice. They also emphasize that unrestrained price and wage increases were the key sources of the economic and political chaos that led to the "revolution" of 1964. They are proud of their ability to bring these factors under control, and to harness the country to their goals of economic growth.

Nevertheless, income inequality is growing in Brazil. The real wages of industrial workers have been deteriorating. To some extent, the explosive effects of this are dampened by the undeniable fact that, in absolute terms, industrial workers today are better off than they were ten years ago. But restiveness is there—and growing—as indicated by strikes among metal workers in the Summer of 1978, despite legal prohibition. It intensifies when Brazil's "economic miracle" sours. Restiveness is fueled by the claim that Brazil's fiscal system places an inordinate burden on the poor and is full of escape clauses and special privileges for the wealthy and near wealthy.

Inequalities in income distribution in Malaysia have been of particular political importance because they have coincided with racial divisions in Malaysian society. Communal rioting in 1969 led to a massive internal examination of income, wealth and property ownership. The government concluded that the economic imbalance between the Chinese and Malay communities was a source of Malay frustration and anger which would have dangerously divisive political implications for the nation unless the balance was quickly redressed.

Communal imbalances have been the critical political dimension of inequality in Malaysia to this point. But inequalities of income *within* the racial communities are substantial, increasing and of growing political significance. Intracommunity income inequalities are almost surely increasing, particularly within the Malay community. While a middle class emerges gradually within the Malay community, a small number of individual Malays have struck it rich, exploiting their own skills as well as the umbrella of protection offered by government legislation, and frequently living in an ostentatious style that raises charges of nepotism and patronage within the expanding public sector.[5]

In Nigeria, although statistics are not available to confirm or deny the contention, the extremes of wealth and poverty are probably greater than in either of the other countries. Overriding the urban-rural disparities described above is a pattern of social inequality in the distribution of income in which oil revenues have made a few Nigerians enormously wealthy. Thus far, oil revenues have provided Nigeria with a great deal of foreign exchange, but with much less human and economic development. The income earned from oil production provides the infrastructure needed for oil production but, beyond this narrow area, Nigeria still suffers severely from structural underdevelopment.

A very substantial portion of Nigeria's oil income has been devoted to consumption, particularly of foreign-made goods, and thus has flowed out of the country almost as quickly as it has come in. A small number of Nigerians—often middlemen, who bridge the gap between the Nigerian government and foreign companies—have enjoyed a disproportionate share of this new wealth. Observers contend that for many Nigerians (some would say for most) the net impact of oil revenues has been a cost—in the form of high inflation rates—rather than a benefit in the form of better job opportunities, better housing, or improved educational and health services.

The excesses of this situation in both Malaysia and Nigeria may be exaggerated. Both governments are concerned about the long-term effects of the growth of inequality, and both seek to take steps to remedy this. But leaders in both countries acknowledge the same dilemma: How much inequality is required to produce an indigenous (or, in the case of Malaysia, a Malay) business class—or, put the other way round, how widely can wealth be distributed before it undercuts the development of a local entrepreneurial class? One Nigerian manager in a foreign firm observes that a key national goal is to gain greater influence over foreign companies in Nigeria. To do this requires the existence of a cadre of Nigerian

---

[5]"Outgrowing their proverbs—the Bumis can do it," *Far Eastern Economic Review,* September 2, 1977, pp. 57-61.

businessmen—"a Nigerian business elite." "Spreading the wealth among 50 million people is not going to affect this country. There is time in the future, when the country is wealthier, for greater distribution—for the socialization of wealth. What is important now is to develop a group of Nigerian businessmen who can actually exert influence within the foreign corporations."

Chapter 4
Foreign Direct Investment: Profiles and Policies

THE THREE COUNTRIES in this study are prime objects of foreign investor interest. Brazil has led the developing world in foreign investment for many years, and investor interest in Malaysia and Nigeria has increased rapidly during the past 10 years. In 1975, Nigeria had the fifth largest stock of foreign direct investment (FDI) in the developing world, and Malaysia the seventh. Indeed, of all the developing nations, only Mexico and Indonesia have increased their stock of FDI during the past decade at a rate comparable to that of these three nations (see Table 8).

Brazil's stock of FDI—$9.1 billion in 1975—can be compared with levels of foreign investment in major developed nations. In U.S. dollars, UN data for the same year show Canada, $38.8 billion of FDI; the United States with $28.5 billion (although this amount has increased rapidly in the past few years); the U.K. with $23.3 billion; and the Federal Republic of Germany with $15.5 billion. In 1975, foreign direct investment in all of the OPEC nations together came to $15.5 billion.[1]

The Brazilian stock of foreign investment is much larger than the Nigerian or Malaysian, but other indicators provide different perspectives on the relative importance of foreign investment in the three economies. For example, Nigeria (assuming a 1975 population of 90 million) has $32.22 of FDI per capita and Brazil $82.72. But there was $184 of FDI for each Malaysian.

As a percentage of GNP, Brazilian foreign investment ranks lowest of the three countries: FDI there in 1975 was about 9 percent of GNP; it was 14 percent in Nigeria; and 29 percent in Malaysia. These figures reflect the enormous importance of foreign investment in Malaysia's economy, as well as the relatively high level of indigenous economic development in Brazil.

---

[1]United Nations Economic and Social Council, *Transnational Corporations in World Development: A Re-Examination.* E/C.10/38, March 20, 1978, p. 237.

Table 8: Less Developed Countries with Largest Stock of FDI: Ranking by Share of Total LDC Stock

Country	1967 U.S. dollars (billion)	1967 Percent of total FDI in LDC's	1971 U.S. dollars (billion)	1971 Percent of total FDI in LDC's	1975 U.S. dollars (billion)	1975 Percent of total FDI in LDC's
Argentina.	$ 1.8	5.5%	$ 2.2	5.1%	$ 2.0	2.9%
BRAZIL.	3.7	11.3	5.1	11.8	9.1	13.3
Hong Kong.	0.3	0.9	0.6	1.4	1.3	1.9
India.	1.3	4.0	1.6	3.7	2.4	3.5
Indonesia.	0.2	0.6	1.0	2.3	3.5	5.1
Iran.	0.7	2.1	0.9	2.1	1.2	1.8
MALAYSIA.	0.7	2.1	0.9	2.1	2.3	3.4
Mexico.	1.8	5.5	2.4	5.5	4.8	7.0
NIGERIA.	1.1	3.3	1.7	3.9	2.9	4.3
Peru.	0.8	2.4	0.9	2.1	1.7	2.5
Philippines.	0.7	2.1	0.9	2.1	1.2	1.8
Singapore.	0.2	0.6	0.4	0.9	1.7	2.5
Trinidad and Tobago.	0.7	2.1	1.0	2.3	1.2	1.8
Venezuela.	3.5	10.6	3.7	8.5	4.0	5.9
All others.	15.3	46.9	20.3	46.2	28.9	42.3
Total stock.	$32.8	100.0%	$43.6	100.0%	$68.2	100.0%

Source: Adapted from United Nations Economic and Social Council, *Transnational Corporations in World Development: A Re-Examination*, E/C.10/38, March 20, 1978, p. 254.

Foreign Investment Profiles

Since 1969, the balance of ownership in the Malaysian economy has been a key issue in domestic politics. Concern focuses not so much on the *amount* of ownership or control as on the *balance* of Malay and non-Malay interests. The New Economic Policy establishes ownership targets for the whole economy. The NEP emphasized, however, that these goals are *not* to be achieved by a redistribution of wealth among the communities. Restructuring the economy will be paid for by economic expansion. Continued and even heightened involvement of foreign investment in Malaysia is thus regarded as a vital necessity if the nation is to grow rapidly enough to permit it to achieve the NEP goals of racial balance.

The foreign investment community is nonetheless disquieted by those policies: The very effort to restructure the economy creates uncertainty for the private foreign investor. Many fear that, when the chips are down, the government will demand that substantial blocks of equity in individual foreign-owned companies be distributed to the Malay community, either directly or through government-run agencies.

Foreign investors are concerned that Malaysians may have an inaccurate impression of the weight of foreign ownership in the economy (see Table 9).

Table 9: Percentage Ownership of Share Capital in Limited Companies in Malaysia, 1970-1975

Source	Year			
	1971	1973	1975	1990 (goal)
Foreign....................	60.7%	58.1%	54.9%	30.0%
Malay	1.9	5.3	7.8	30.0
Chinese	22.5	27.8	27.9 ⎫	
Indian....................	1.0	1.2	1.2 ⎬	40.0
Other....................	13.9	7.6	8.2 ⎭	
Total...................	100.0%	100.0%	100.0%	100.0%

Source: Computed from Table in "Tinkering with the interest rates," *Far Eastern Economic Review,* September 2, 1977, p. 48.

The Malaysian International Chamber of Commerce and Industry argues, for example, that foreign ownership in 1975 accounted for only 55 percent of the share capital in limited (incorporated) companies and *not* 60 percent of the *entire* economy, as is sometimes claimed.

The Chamber also argues that foreign ownership in the economy as a whole is less than 20 percent; that in the total private sector it is probably less than 25 percent; and that in the "modern sector" of the economy it is substantially less than 60 percent—and possibly as low as 40 percent. It notes that while foreign interests in limited companies increased by about 50 percent between 1971 and 1975, Malay interests increased by about 67 percent.

It is difficult to calculate the exact scope of foreign ownership in Malaysia because of the heavy involvement of investors from Singapore and, to a lesser extent, Hong Kong. Some portion of this investment is recycled Malaysian (mainly Chinese) capital. On the other hand, several major British-owned enterprises—particularly in plantation industries and trade—have recently relocated in Malaysia and, presumably, are now considered local.

Table 10 shows the distribution of foreign investment in Malaysia by country of origin for 1971, 1974, and 1975.[2] The rapid increase of Japanese involvement in the Malaysian economy in the 1970's is apparent, as is Malaysia's impressive ability to maintain a balanced distribution of investment (as well as trade) among its major economic partners.

Table 10: Percentage Distribution of Foreign Investment in Malaysia, by Country of Origin, 1971-1976[a]

| | Year | | |
Country	1971	1974	1976
Japan	11.9%	13.2%	22.7%
Singapore	29.3	30.6	22.1
United States	24.3[b]	14.0	15.4
United Kingdom	20.9	17.4	12.5
Hong Kong	9.4	9.7	12.4
Other	4.2	15.1	14.9
Total	100.0%	100.0%	100.0%

[a]Foreign investment—about 50 percent of all foreign direct investment—given "pioneer" status.

[b]U.S.A. figure for 1971 includes Canada, Bahamas and Puerto Rico; these are included in "Other" for 1974 and 1976.

Sources: 1971 data from Richard D. Robinson, *National Control of Foreign Business Entry: A Survey of 15 Countries.* New York: Praeger Publishers, 1976, p. 35; 1974 and 1976 data compiled by U.S. Embassy, Kuala Lumpur, Malaysia.

[2]Table 10 includes only the investment given "Pioneer Status," about 50 percent of all foreign direct investment in Malaysia. The Malaysian government says that the distribution among countries of origin is roughly the same for all foreign direct investment, however.

A recent Brazilian study, cited by Professor Stefan Robock, finds that of the 1,069 leading Brazilian firms in manufacturing, mining, construction, transportation, communications, electric energy, and agriculture, "foreign-controlled" firms accounted in 1974 for 27 percent of the number of enterprises, 22 percent of total net assets (book value), 38 percent of sales, and 29 percent of profits.[3] These findings, shown in Table 11, also illustrate the importance of government-controlled enterprises in Brazil's economy.

Robock observes that "within the private sector, foreign-controlled firms are significantly larger than Brazilian companies when measured by sales, profit and investment. Among the top 100 private firms in Brazil, multinationals accounted in 1974 for nearly 75 percent of sales, profits, total assets and equity investments." Government-controlled companies (11 percent of the 1,069 firms) account for almost 50 percent of the total book value. Because the Brazilian government bought out some of the major foreign-owned utilities and all of the foreign-owned petroleum refineries, the relative position of the multinational corporations in the total economy declined from the mid-1960's to the early 1970's, while the public sector increased at the expense of the private sector—foreign and domestic.

Data on the distribution of foreign investment in Brazil by country of origin clearly indicate the long-term decline of the British role; the shorter term (since 1950) relative reduction of the U.S. presence; and the recent in-

Table 11: Brazil: Relative Importance of State-controlled, Foreign-controlled, and Domestic Private Enterprises in 1974[a]

Enterprise under control of	Number of firms (percent)	Total book value (percent)	Total sales (percent)	Total net profit (percent)
Government..............	11.4%	49.5%	22.5%	32.9%
Foreign.................	27.4	22.1	38.2	28.6
National private...........	61.2	28.4	39.3	38.5
Total..................	100.0%	100.0%	100.0%	100.0%

[a]Based on 1,069 enterprises in manufacturing, mining, civil construction, transportation, communications, electric energy, and agroindustries.

Source: "Queme Quem na Economia Brasileria," cited in Stefan H. Robock, "Controlling Multinational Enterprises: The Brazilian Experience," *Journal of Contemporary Business,* Autumn, 1977, p. 58.

[3] "Queme Quem na Economia Brasileria," cited in Stefan H. Robock, "Controlling Multinational Enterprises: The Brazilian Experience." *Journal of Contemporary Business,* Autumn, 1977, p. 58.

crease of German, Swiss and Japanese investment as Brazil seeks to diversify its investment relationships (see Table 12).

Detailed information regarding foreign investment in Nigeria is far more limited than for the other two countries. Although the bulk of the economy has always been "Nigerianized"—since all peasant agriculture and almost all small trading are in Nigerian hands—the major share of commerce and industry, particularly the more modern sectors of the economy, is controlled by foreigners. It is loosely estimated that some 70 percent of industry in Nigeria is subject to foreign control.[4]

However, as a result of the indigenization decree of 1972 and the follow-up decree of 1976, the proportion of Nigerian ownership (if not control) in the economy must have increased in recent years.

Foreign investment in Nigeria is heavily concentrated in a single sector of the economy. The Nigerians are strenuously seeking greater investment diversification—into infrastructure (transportation and communications), vehicle assembly, and food production, for example. Before independence, more than half of the foreign investment in Nigeria came from Britain. (It has been estimated that one company—the United Africa Company, owned

Table 12: Percentage Distribution of Foreign Investment in Brazil, by Country of Origin, 1930-1976

Country	Year				
	1930	1950	1959	1972	1976
United States..................	21%	48%	38%	37%	32%
Federal Republic of Germany	—	—	9	11	13
Japan	1	—	2	6	11
Switzerland[1]...................	—	—	—	7	11
Other European...............	11	5	15	11	10
Canada......................	4	23	18	9	5
Great Britain	53	17	7	8	5
France	8	3	5	5	4
Other........................	2	4	6	6	9
Total	100%	100%	100%	100%	100%

[1]Included in "Other European" for 1931-1959.

Source: Adapted in part from Peter Evans, *Dependent Development: The Alliance of Multinational, State and Local Capital in Brazil.* Princeton, N.J.: Princeton University Press, 1979.

[4]Andrew Hilton, "Foreign Investment in Nigeria," unpublished dissertation, University of Pennsylvania, 1975.

by Unilever—accounted for a third of all non-mining foreign investment in the early 1960's.) U.S. investment, especially in petroleum, increased rapidly in the 1960's as the British share declined. The early 1970's brought a reduction in the amount of U.S. investment in Nigeria, mainly because the Nigerian government purchased 55 percent of the equity of the oil-producing companies and 60 percent of the equity of all oil-distribution activities (see Table 13). At the same time, however, the Nigerian government has urged American investors to take more interest in their country.

Table 13: Percentage Distribution of Cumulative Foreign Direct Investment in Nigeria, by Country or Region of Origin, 1962-73

(percentage distribution of paid-up capital including reserves and other liabilities)

Country	Year			
	1962	1966	1970	1973
United Kingdom	61.4	51.0	44.0	48.8
United States	8.8	17.3	22.9	17.5
Western Europe	21.2	22.5	22.4	23.5
Other	8.6	9.2	10.7	10.2
Total	100.0%	100.0%	100.0%	100.0%

Source: Thomas J. Bierstaker, "Multinational Investment in Underdeveloped Countries: An Evaluation of Contending Theoretical Perspectives," unpublished dissertation, Massachusetts Institute of Technology, 1976, table 4.2, p. 191.

Foreign Investment Policies

Each of these countries has its own set of national policies that impinge on foreign investment. In the Nigerian and Malaysian cases, both the conduct of policies and their application were influenced by post-colonial developments. Brazil is an older nation, with strong and complex aspirations about economic development. We will find there a recurring pattern of policies designed to encourage the foreign investor on some occasions, and to inhibit him on others.

Brazil

Brazil's policies toward foreign capital and the foreign investor have been and remain highly pragmatic. Brazil has welcomed foreign investment, even as Brazilians have been suspicious of foreign investors. The most extreme negative attitudes toward the foreign investor are found on the political left, a group which has been tightly controlled since 1964. Many of these individuals would opt for a policy of extreme independence—without outside assistance or interference. Some other Brazilian leaders articulate demands that foreign capital and foreign corporations be highly restricted and subject to comprehensive, stringent oversight and direction.

As political liberalization proceeds, the debate over foreign investment will surely become more heated. Persistently negative balance of payments, dangerously high cumulative foreign debt and debt-service ratios, and continued high levels of inflation will fuel the arguments on all sides. Multinational corporations, especially those headquartered in the United States, will inevitably be featured in these debates. For the first time since 1964, questions about appropriate policies for the country to adopt toward foreign investment will be more openly voiced by the mass media, trade unions, intellectuals, political parties, industrialists, and other interest groups—as well as by government officials.

Yet while many Brazilians fret about excessive profit remittances by multinational corporations, or about insufficient transfer of technology, they worry even more about the prospect that foreign capital inputs may dry up. Most Brazilians recognize that Brazil cannot become a major industrial power early next century without the active involvement of foreign capital, technology and management. The industrial history of the country since 1950 amply demonstrates this dependence, and developmental goals projected to the end of the century suggest that reliance on these outside inputs will be still greater in the foreseeable future, even if Brazil manages to resolve its enormously important and difficult energy problems.

If Brazilians differ regarding policies for the foreign investor, most still believe that the country should seek to obtain maximum benefits from the foreign investor at minimum cost. Increasingly, they feel that the structure of capital markets, the nature of competition among multinational firms, and the technical capacity of Brazil's leadership will enable them to approach this goal.

Brazil's policies toward foreign investment traditionally have been pragmatic and stable, but on occasion they have also shifted dramatically. Policy shifts can be explained in part by aspects of Brazil's history and development:

(1) Over most of its history, Brazil's linkage to the international economy was classically colonial. It produced primary goods (mainly coffee) for export, and consumed manufactured goods supplied by leading industrial powers. In good times these exports provided the income for industrial development, but because the world price of primary products fluctuated so widely, serious developmental planning was all but impossible. Worldwide economic disorder as well as the export, commercial and foreign investment strategies of Great Britain and the United States immediately affected Brazil's economic development, and led Brazilian governments to enact protective and other ameliorative national policies.

(2) Brazil's economic transformation proceeded at a dizzying clip once under way. Within a few decades, an overwhelmingly agricultural country produced most of its own manufactured products; and, in the late 1970's, these products themselves became the major factor in Brazil's export profile.

(3) During the course of this economic transformation, the United States replaced Great Britain as the major source of direct investment; foreign investment shifted radically from the nonmanufacturing to the manufacturing sector; and foreign direct investment from countries like Germany, Japan and Switzerland increased sharply. One consequence of these changes was that an increasing proportion of Brazil's exports were accounted for by the local subsidiaries of multinational corporations. By the 1970's, almost half of Brazil's manufactured exports were in the hands of multinational corporations.

(4) As in other countries, foreign direct investment is not evenly spread across the Brazilian economy but is highly concentrated in certain sectors. The foreign sector dominates the tobacco, pharmaceuticals, rubber and transportation equipment sectors. It is almost equally strong in electrical machinery, chemicals and heavy machinery, and has a marked presence in the textile, metal fabrication, and food and food processing sectors.

Compelled to make policy choices as foreign investment increased, Brazilian foreign investment policies have alternated between nationalistic restrictions on foreign investment and liberal encouragement of the overseas investor. Many of the policies and attitudes toward foreign capital crystallized in the 1930's are still central today in Brazil's relationship with foreign investors.

Getulio Vargas, during that period, adopted a highly nationalistic policy that advanced the development of a corporative state. Like Peron in Argentina, Vargas was committed to social reform, and sought to extend mass political participation. Between 1937 and 1945, Vargas opposed any policies—including those pertaining to foreign investment—that might erode his nationalistic plans. His successor, Enrico Dutra (1945-1950) is widely criticized for having invited the uncontrolled presence of foreign investment in postwar Brazil. Under Dutra, Brazil became one of the world's most liberal investment environments.

A combination of this wide-open investment climate and injudicious governmental economic policies produced severe disequilibrium. In 1950, Vargas was returned to office with an apparent mandate to reduce economic dislocation. He became openly incensed over the economically disruptive role of the foreign investor and equally critical of the alleged heavy-handed American government involvement in Brazil's economy. In particular, Vargas was angered by pressures emanating from the United States against Brazilian steps to expand the public-sector role in such industries as petroleum and electric power.

Vargas committed suicide in 1954, leaving behind a "testament" that Brazilian critics of foreign investors continue to cite. In it, Vargas explicitly accused foreign financial and industrial groups of collusion against his regime and the Brazilian economy.

The Vargas policies, which had led to the dramatic reduction of foreign investment in Brazil, were reversed by President Kubitschek, who felt that the decline of available foreign capital had severely impeded Brazil's economic growth. Within a few years the net inflow of foreign investment jumped 1200 percent. Kubitschek declared that Brazil could never achieve its rightful grandeur and destiny without massive participation of outside financial and industrial interests.

Kubitschek's policies were again reversed during the short-lived regime of João Goulart. Goulart's political rhetoric raised the spectre of socialism. Very much like the situation that was later to prevail in Allende's Chile, the political parties around Goulart became enmeshed in complicated wrangling and policy demands that led to economic chaos. Economic deterioration was reinforced by a precipitous decline in new foreign investments. The inflow of capital, having peaked at $150 million in 1957, fell to $28 million in 1964. Between 1962 and 1964, Brazil's economic growth was negative, inflation rates exceeded 100 percent, and the country reached the point of default on its foreign debt.

With the country at the brink of disaster, the military stepped in and installed General Costello Branco as President in 1964. Political parties were suspended, open politics severely curtailed, trade unions dismantled, and an authoritarian regime established. The "revolutionary" group insisted that Brazil's political and economic affairs be reordered to put the country back on an appropriate developmental trajectory, even at the cost of infringing on basic political freedoms.

Costello Branco established a new phase in Brazilian politics by bringing into the government and administration, individuals whose skills were primarily technical rather than political. On the ministerial side, these technocrats adopted the most severe orthodox economic policies to restore order and confidence. On the administrative side, they produced a pattern of finely tuned policies designed to encourage the foreign investor—without, however, making the kinds of concessions that prevailed under the Dutra and Kubitshek regimes. Indeed, these technocrats, however much they may be committed to the need for foreign investment, underscore that the good old days when the foreigner could have it largely his own way have irrevocably passed into history.

Economic policies following the 1964 "Revolution," rested on several basic assumptions. First, the economy was to be centrally directed. Second, both welfare outlays and wage increases were to be curtailed. Third, a strong foreign investment component in economic development plans was encouraged. Beginning in 1968, governmental policies regarding the public industrial sector, inflation, prices, wages, short-term public debt, and incentives to the multinationals created a launching platform for the spectacular growth that followed. In the next six or seven years of Brazil's "economic miracle," the economy literally exploded: Annual rates of new foreign investment increased 20 times; reinvestment increased almost 1,000 percent; the economy as a whole grew at annual levels around 10 percent. The foreign investment community, having shied away from Brazil in the early 1950's and again a decade later, now demonstrated seemingly unbounded confidence in Brazil's future.

This confidence is expressed notwithstanding the fact that Brazil's current policies toward the foreign investor are much less liberal than in the past. If Brazilian leaders are convinced of the need for foreign capital, and gratified when foreign investment in Brazil materializes, they are still convinced that they can avoid being steamrollered by foreign banks or multinational corporations. When they perceive a conflict between the so-called compelling logic of global business and the national interest, the former, not the latter, must give way. Believing this, capable officials drive tough bargains; they are formidable negotiators; they exploit competition among foreign banks and foreign corporations; and they effect closer supervision and control over the operations of the multinational corporations.

Brazilian policies toward the foreign investor, present and future, may appropriately be described as vigilant regulation. In summary form, the main outlines of these policies include the following:

1. Foreign investment will be courted on grounds that optimal, orderly, dynamic economic growth requires it. The preferred "model" of development will not exclude such inputs.

2. Foreign investors require political stability. The government will move cautiously to orchestrate a gradual "decompression" or opening up of the political system. In the short and medium term these steps may appear somewhat destabilizing; but they should not be mistaken as portending irrational or vindictive policies toward foreign investors.

3. Foreign investors require indigenous economic management capacity. Brazil has already shown marked ability to regulate market forces effectively, and generally to deal effectively with problems of central concern to foreign banks and corporations. Recent change in economic policies that range from regulations on import deposits, to economic development incentives and major reorientation of government investments in agriculture represent continuing evidence of such management skill.

4. Foreign investors require efficiency and rationality in public administration. Agencies exist and/or will be created that are staffed with competent personnel. Agencies will administer policies without prejudice to the multinational corporations. On the other hand, the MNC's will be held to full and open collaboration with these agencies in the administration of policies pertaining to the foreign investment community.

5. Certain industrial sectors are too vital to national security to permit much, or any, foreign investment presence. Public utilities, communications, banking and finance fall into this sphere. In addition, Brazil's natural resource sector is of prime concern. As much as circumstances will allow, this sector is to be owned and operated by Brazilians drawn from the private or public sector.

6. The public sector's presence in direct productive enterprise will remain at existing levels and perhaps even expand. Although individual governmental officials will pay lip service to the need for reducing state ownership of industrial enterprise, such a reversal of postwar trends is most unlikely. The military elite themselves are committed to existing arrangements. More important, Brazil's public administrative technocrats are deeply committed to assuring that the state will continue to play a direct role in the further economic development of the country.

7. Profitability of private enterprise is acceptable; fiscal arrangements, capital structures and flows, repatriation of income arrangements that are harmful to Brazil are not.

8. Investment flows will be carefully monitored. Intracompany loans will be restricted; other forms of repatriating capital will be regulated, as will corporate access to local capital markets.

9. The value-added consequences of existing and proposed investments and reinvestments will be regularly assessed. In particular, increased attention will be paid to technology transfer. Royalty payments for technology will be resisted. If Brazil must find ways to pay for managerial, manufacturing or scientific technology, it will do so only if maximum information about technology itself is disclosed, and only if it is clear that Brazil will pay for a given technology once and only once.

10. Diversification of foreign investors in Brazil will be encouraged wherever possible. A plurality of corporate nationalities is felt to be of benefit to Brazil, without prejudice to the multinationals of any given country.

11. Where factors of production and the nature of product and technology permit it, Brazil will seek to encourage national industries. Takeovers and acquisitions of local firms in such sectors will be carefully scrutinized and normally restricted. Joint-venture arrangements in sectors of potential national development will be encouraged.

12. Special incentives to multinational corporations are in keeping with the government's overall policies. As in the past, such incentives may range from tax exemption, quick-depreciation write-offs and exemptions from import deposits to local credit, special arrangements for capital financing, special concessions on import licenses, etc. However, it is a major tenet of current policy to reach a point by the mid-1980's where both incentives and restrictions are reduced to a minimum, with a more flexible, pragmatic, sector-by-sector and company-by-company approach at that time.

13. Although local equity participation is not mandated, it is en-

couraged. The government is concerned about the "denationalization" of the Brazilian private sector and recognizes that both state-owned industries and the multinationals have contributed to this unwanted, politically explosive development. Not only will joint ventures (with the public or private sector, sometimes with both in a triangular, or *tri-pé* arrangement) be encouraged; takeovers will be closely scrutinized. Where takeovers involve healthy Brazilian firms, or where they do not clearly involve the injection of new capital or technology, or encourage new exports, they are likely to meet with negative—even angry—government response.

14. Pressures for equity sharing and for increasing Brazilian shares in joint ventures are varied. For example, the government will not guarantee offshore loans where a majority of equity is owned by foreigners; wholly-owned subsidiaries face greater restrictions regarding the remittance of royalties or dividends; such subsidiaries will receive less favorable treatment in competitons for contracts let by government agencies.

15. Functional spin-off requirements are distinctly possible as future policy. Under such regulations, existing foreign firms would be required to permit capable indigenous firms to acquire manufacturing processes that are divisible. Rather than make a fetish of local equity ownership, Brazilians are likely to take a more sophisticated approach to bargaining with the multinationals in the interest of strengthening the Brazilian economy. This sophisticated approach is reflected in recent governmental decisions to place control of the minicomputer industry in the hands of local firms rather than major international corporations. This approach establishes national control while at the same time minimizing head-on collisions with foreign companies over divestiture of majority equity control.

16. The government will look with special interest to foreign investment plans that are explicitly directed to the resolution of the country's most nagging problems, the outstanding one being Brazil's balance of payments. The quadrupling of oil prices in 1973-1974, followed by the 60% run-up in 1979, have exacerbated Brazil's weak position in hydrocarbons. Those foreign investors who can help to alleviate the Brazilian energy and cost crunch, either through exploration and technology, or by rapidly increasing Brazilian exports to improve the balance of payments, will be warmly welcomed. Above all, the government will require that the foreign investor understand all aspects of Brazil's economic development problems, and take these problems, as well as Brazil's aspirations, into account in its planning, investment and operations.

To this end, Brazil increasingly demands that multinational corporations enter into negotiations and carry out dialogue through a single interloctor—not through individual product divisions operating in Brazil. Firms that are able to conform to this reqirement will be rewarded; others will not.

Malaysia

Malaysia is a small country, heavily dependent on international trade. It remains predominantly a producer of primary products which are sold on the world market. Because of this dependence on international trade and because of the traditional high demand for its products, Malaysia has been committed to an open, free enterprise economy. Foreign investment is welcomed. There is little hostility to foreign countries, and policy historically has tended to favor incentives rather than restrictions.

Since 1969, however, efforts to restructure the economy in a deeply divided : country have severely impinged on these policies. The New Economic Policy projects that both economic structural transformations and the ending of racial imbalances will be financed by economic growth. Since 1969, however, both domestic and foreign investment have fallen, in large measure because investors fear that the NEP will undermine economic growth prospects.

At independence, the new government of Malaya decided to maintain the same pattern of liberal economic policies that had prevailed earlier. The new government also launched a program of industrialization, based heavily on foreign investment. Tan Sri Mohar bin Raja, a prominent politician who served in the first Ministry of Commerce and Industry, observes: "As Malaya did not have the know-how and expertise the first logical reaction was to invite foreign manufacturers to establish factories in the country to produce at least some of the items which were then being imported." The Pioneer Industries Ordinance, which came into effect in 1958, provided tax-free facilities to selected foreign companies for up to five years and assured repatriation of profits and capital. The immediate objective of the pioneer legislation was simply to attract foreign investment and expertise. "There were no guidelines drawn up for foreign investment, there was no strategy, no direction or priorities as to which industries should be promoted," Mohar continues.

Between 1958 and 1968, the government gradually formulated a more coherent strategy for attracting foreign investment and for increasing the benefits the nation received from this investment. National goals to be served by foreign investment included development of local skills, job creation, export promotion, technology transfer, regional development, and local equity participation. Under the 1968 Industrial Incentives Act, a foreign investor could qualify for pioneer status if the investment project produced a priority product, was labor intensive, export oriented, utilized local raw materials, was capable of vertical or horizontal integration with existing Malaysian industries, or was related to agriculture.

Economic planners had begun to realize by 1968 that import-substitution industrialization was an inherently limited strategy. The desire to attract foreign investment in industry geared primarily to local consumption resulted too frequently in a multiplicity of competing firms and a loss of efficiency and of economies of scale. The Investment Incentive Act provided new incentives to export-oriented industries, and the Establishment of Free Trade Zones Act, which was passed in 1970, created areas in which factories producing goods solely for export could use machinery and equipment imported duty-free.

Job creation was a second, perhaps even more important, purpose behind the establishment of the free trade zones. After the 1969 riots, the government looked desperately for a way to absorb some of the growing number of unemployed whose discontent, it was felt, had triggered the urban rioting. Electronics factories seemed to be a realizable answer, and foreign companies were invited to establish manufacturing plants to produce components for their own domestic use. Exports from Malaysia increased and, more importantly, so did local employment.

The Malaysian government encouraged local equity participation without laying down rigid requirements. The government did indicate its preference for joint ventures; 100 percent foreign ownership would not be favorably considered. However, where foreign investments brought additional benefits (such as new jobs or increased exports), 100 percent foreign ownership might be acceptable.

The government also proceeded cautiously with "Malaysianization." All companies were exhorted, but not rigidly required, to employ Chinese, Malays and Indians in proportion to their numbers in the local work force. Companies employing more than 50 percent of any race might endanger their pioneer status. In addition, foreign investors were told that all joint-venture agreements and technical and management contracts relating to specific investment projects must be cleared by the government and must conform to standard rates for payment of royalties and management and technical fees. Malaysia encouraged investment from as many countries as possible to ensure that no foreign nation would assume too great a role in the domestic economy. Finally, Malaysia also signed the International Convention for the Settlement of Disputes, agreeing in advance to World Bank mediation in case of differences with foreign investors.

Political stability, a well-developed infrastructure, high levels of administrative honesty and competence, a conservative economic and fiscal regime, and consistent policies regarding foreign investment—together with the country's great natural wealth—made Malaysia a highly desirable investment object throughout the 1960's.

Although few people, Malaysian or foreign, faulted the aims of the NEP, these policies were the source of serious tensions and dilemmas for the foreign investor. First, while the government continued to emphasize that the 30-40-30 percent goals were general and global and were not necessarily applicable to any *individual* company, the relationship between global targets and particular companies was unclear. Second, although the need for foreign investment under the NEP was greater than ever, many investors continued to feel that the government's social goals would ultimately force foreign investors to divest a large segment of their existing equity, in one form or another. Third, the policy of increasing Malay participation in the economy, particularly their share of equity ownership, is perplexing because the Malay community lacks the necessary investment capital. Because this is the case, the public sector's share in the economy is increasing rapidly as equity is purchased to be "held in trust" for individual Malays or for the Malay community. Fear of government expansionism has increased, and confidence in the impartiality and competence of the administration has declined because of investors' perception of the growing militance and aggressiveness of the largely Malay cadres in the government service.

Vietnam and the world economic crisis formed the gloomy backdrop for still more alarming developments affecting investment. In April, 1975, two new acts of parliament seemed to confirm the worst fears of foreign (and many local) investors that aggressive state intervention would lead to erratic policies designed to further Malay interests at any costs. The Petroleum Development (Amendment) Act was passed in the midst of difficult negotiations between the government and the oil companies over the conversion of traditional concession and royalty arrangements to "production-sharing" along the lines initiated by the Indonesian national oil company, Pertimina. The amendment extended the powers of Petronas (the newly formed Malaysian national oil company) to include downstream activities such as the marketing and distribution of petroleum and petrochemical products. It also created a new class of equity shares— "management shares"—which were issuable (at a low price) only to Petronas. Each share would carry voting rights equal to 500 ordinary shares. Oil companies, critics and impartial observers all charged that the "management share" concept amounted to no less than effective nationalization without compensation of the oil companies in Malaysia.

The Industrial Coordination Act (ICA) was the second act passed in April, 1975. It required all manufacturing firms above a certain size to obtain a license, which could be revoked if the business failed to meet certain basic conditions—particularly those of the NEP. Although the ostensible purpose was to ensure the orderly growth of industry in Malaysia (and although it was modeled on existing Singapore legislation), the ICA appeared to confer vast discretionary powers on the Malaysian bureaucracy to influence business activities without provision for consultation or redress. In fact, the ICA seemed to be directed primarily at the Chinese community—to provide the government with the ability to enforce NEP goals on reluctant Chinese businessmen.

Although its impact on foreign business—particularly on business already in place as opposed to new investment—was uncertain, it signaled the last straw for many foreign investors. Domestic investment dried up as local, mainly Chinese, investors kept a larger portion of their assets in highly liquid forms. International investment fell far behind expectations. In 1976, manufacturing investment totaled less than 40 percent of the target laid down in the Third Malaysia Plan (1976-1980).

Under the leadership of the new Prime Minister, Datuck Hussein Onn, the government worked throughout 1976 and 1977 to restore foreign and local investor confidence. In November, 1976, Hussein intervened to force a settlement with the oil-producing companies, granting what many observers felt to be significant concessions. In December, the government repealed the management shares clause of the Petroleum Development (Amendment) Act. And in March, it introduced an amended version of the ICA.

Hussein, who was expected to be an interim Prime Minister, attempted to rein in both dissident politicians and over-zealous bureaucrats. He reaffirmed the need for foreign investment, and called upon the Malay community to work harder and to remember that the purpose of the NEP was to enable the Malays to compete fairly with the other communities, not to tilt the competition in their favor. He also sought to reassure the anxious Chinese population. The (then) Deputy Prime Minister echoed Hussein's views: "The government has answered by word and deed that new industrial investments are a matter of priority and investors can be assured that we certainly are not going to kill the goose that lays the golden eggs."[5]

Hussein's good intentions have not been questioned and his political skill is much admired, by non-Malay Malaysians and foreigners no less than by Malays. His government has reaffirmed its commitment to flexibility regarding the implementation of NEP goals. Leading members of the Cabinet decry the excesses of bureaucrats and promise redress. But there is no doubt that the country is considerably behind schedule for meeting the 1990 goals, nor that pressure continues to build up in the Malay community to ensure the NEP goals are met on schedule.

Nigeria

Foreign investors in Nigeria have been alarmed in recent years by what appears to be a severe outbreak of aggressive economic nationalism. Nigerian "indigenization" policies (which enforce local equity participation in foreign-owned enterprises) and pressures for "Nigerianization" (greater Nigerian participation in management and on boards of directors of foreign-owned companies), together with appalling infrastructure problems, have seriously inhibited investor interest. But compared with many other developing nations, Nigerian attitudes toward foreign investment are quite liberal. Nigerian leaders claim that their present policies do not mark any major alteration in their tradition of welcoming foreign investment and they feel that these policies frequently have been drastically misunderstood abroad.

Before World War II, foreign policies of the colonial government tended to displace indigenous Nigerian entrepreneurs while strengthening the position of expatriate trading companies. The objectives of foreign in-

<hr />

[5] Dato'Seri Dr. Mahathir Bin Mohamed, Deputy Prime Minister and Minister of Trade and Industry, quoted in *Far Eastern Economic Review,* April 7, 1978, p. 122.

vestment policy changed after the war: Instead of supporting the trading firms, foreign industrial and manufacturing firms were encouraged to establish operations in Nigeria. Until independence, policies were designed in particular to provide incentives and generous investment opportunities for British firms. Tax relief ordinances, aid to pioneer industries, and tariff protection all encouraged foreign (mainly British) investment. Rules regarding the repatriation of capital, nationalization and compensation were liberal and provided additional incentives.

Until the outbreak of the civil war, the policies inherited from the colonial administration remained virtually intact. The necessity for a continued inflow of large amounts of foreign investment was reiterated as a mainstay of government policy. If anything, incentives for investors were increased. The Constitution of 1963, which transformed Nigeria into a republic, granted the foreign investor "fundamental rights" and in a 1964 Statement on Industrial Policy, the government further assured foreign investors that capital would be secure against arbitrary interference and that foreign investors could continue to transfer their emoluments to any place of their choice.

Perhaps the only significant change in this period was a growing concern for the placement of more Nigerians in senior managerial and technical positions in the foreign companies. This concern was expressed in the Immigration Law of 1968, which established a system of quotas for expatriates. Nigerian leaders continued to feel that increased foreign investment was required for the realization of national development objectives, and on the whole, foreign investment policies embodied this outlook.

During the civil war, various short-term policies were enacted to halt the drain on domestic capital reserves and to exert control over prices and dividends. Most of these controls were relaxed by 1969. The development of petroleum policy during the war provided the first significant departure from the foreign investment policies laid down in the colonial period. This more militant approach to the petroleum firms was echoed in the 1968 Companies Decree. The Decree, requiring foreign subsidiaries operating in Nigeria to be incorporated separately from their parents, was still a cautious step in a more nationalistic direction, but it aroused considerable concern among foreign firms. Through 1970, however, as one student of Nigeria's foreign investment policies observes: "Outside of the petroleum industry...Nigerian foreign investment policy had not changed substantially and remained exceedingly conducive to the foreign investor. Even in the petroleum industry, the revised Nigerian policy was not yet oriented toward greater Nigerianization...but rather toward obtaining a larger share of the benefits."[6]

[6]Thomas J. Bierstaker, "Multinational Investment in Underdeveloped Countries: An Evaluation of Contending Theoretical Perspectives," unpublished dissertation, Massachusetts Institute of Technology, 1976, Table 4.2.

Beginning in 1970, policy became more militant, and the rhetoric surrounding the policymaking process more militant still. The experience of the civil war and Nigeria's new economic position, based on its great oil wealth, led the government to assert a more independent foreign policy and to emphasize Nigeria's leadership role in Africa. The objective of the Second National Development Plan (1970-1975) was to transform Nigerian society radically, to create:

"(1) a united, strong and self-reliant nation;
"(2) a great and dynamic society;
"(3) a just and egalitarian society;
"(4) a land bright and full of opportunities
        for all citizens; and
"(5) a free and democratic society."[7]

The Second and—even more so the Third—National Development Plans called for a dramatic expansion of the public sector of the economy. Nevertheless, the government emphasizes that it adheres to the notion of a "mixed" economy, depending on extensive participation by the private sector—both domestic and foreign.

Nigeria's foreign investment policies since 1970 have been shaped by the need to balance two overriding goals: independence and development. Nigerians are suspicious of foreign companies. Except for small, if vocal, fringe groups, however, most leaders agree that the contributions of foreign firms are crucial for economic development. Nigerians are concerned not to exclude foreign companies, but wish to ensure that their activities are consistent with the objectives of Nigerian development and benefit the country as well as the companies.

Nigerian policy is also aimed at increasing local participation in ownership and management. The "indigenization program" has two dimensions. In the first place, the government has determined that the state should control at least 55 percent of certain "strategic" industries (oil, mining, steel—the "commanding heights of the economy") and arrangements have been worked out with foreign firms in each sector to transfer ownership. Thus, the government acquired a majority share in the subsidiaries of all oil-producing companies operating in Nigeria, as well as a 60 percent share in all petroleum-distribution activities. Because of their size and importance, the government takes a direct role in these sectors, entering into a wide range of joint ventures with local and foreign partners.

[7]Central Planning Office, *Second National Development Plan 1970-1975,* Lagos, Nigeria: Federal Ministry of Economic Development, 1970, vol. 1, p. 32.

The government also seeks to increase private Nigerian participation in the ownership of enterprises. The first Nigerian Enterprise Promotion Decree, in 1972, created schedules that listed those enterprises reserved exclusively for Nigerian ownership (Schedule I) and those enterprises requiring 40 percent Nigerian ownership (Schedule II). Largely because of perceived inadequacies in the implementation of the first indigenization decree, a new decree was promulgated early in 1977: Additional enterprises were added to Schedule I; Schedule II now requires 60 percent Nigerian ownership; and all other industries were placed on a new Schedule III, requiring 40 percent Nigerian ownership. Firms were given until December 31, 1978, to comply with the decree, although the government directed that all banking institutions in the country should have 60 percent indigenous equity participation by September 30, 1976.

Almost all Nigerians emphasize the difference between "indigenization" and "nationalization." Nationalization indicates an outright takeover by government, while indigenization indicates a gradual process, enforced by the government, of converting to local ownership. Where the government has acquired equity ownership, as in the oil industry, compensation appears to have been reasonable and working arrangements with companies satisfactory. Foreign firms complain that the government's Capital Issues Committee set share prices far lower than their value. Nigerians respond that profits, even on sharply reduced equity holdings, are so high in Nigeria's booming economy that there should be no dissatisfaction. Many Nigerians also observe that the primary goal of the indigenization program—to spread equity ownership widely in the Nigerian community—is the best guarantee possible against expropriation. Many foreign businessmen agree, provided, they say, that they can be sure that a third indigenization decree will not follow the first and second. The current government's policy has been summed up by the Commissioner for External Affairs:

"Although our policy is now 60 percent participation in certain enterprises, the government still wants, and indeed expects, full involvement of foreign partners in these enterprises. No country can forever leave its economy solely in the hands of foreigners and no self-respecting government can afford to ignore its responsibility in this regard. Our policy on participation is not Right or Left, capitalist or Communist; it is purely and simply designed to benefit Nigeria and friends of Nigeria."[8]

---

[8]Brigadier Joseph Garba, speech, Lagos, Nigeria: Ministry of External Affairs, July 2, 1976.

Many foreign firms find the indigenization policy less onerous than pressure to "Nigerianize" local management. Firms that wish to employ expatriates must obtain a quota from the Ministry of Internal Affairs—a process normally involving lengthy and difficult negotiations. Quotas may be obtained for positions that are not reserved to Nigerians (accounting is a reserved profession, for example) if it can be proved that qualified Nigerian personnel are not available. Quotas, even then, are usually limited in duration and the government frequently reduces the number of expatriates foreign firms can employ. In addition, there are severe restrictions on the ability of foreign firms to dismiss Nigerian employees, and civil action brought by employees on the grounds of wrongful dismissal is common.

Nigerians are insistent that foreign firms show good faith in carrying out these policies. The government is determined to ensure that Nigerians are not hired as "window dressing," but are given meaningful responsibilities. It has announced that it will deal ruthlessly with cases of evasion by either Nigerians or foreigners.

Aside from these efforts to increase local participation, the framework of foreign investment regulation remains quite liberal. In general, although often subject to administrative delay, exchange controls on foreign business have been kept at a minimum. The transfer of profits and dividends earned during the civil war was blocked, but the backlog has been cleared and payments are normally made when due. Capital can now be freely repatriated with central bank approval, although recent measures, taken in response to sharply reduced oil income, may portend a more restrictive approach. Royalties, management fees, and consultants' fees are often more narrowly restricted. Both federal and state governments continue to offer substantial incentives to foreign companies, but the incentive program will probably be altered to emphasize greater value-added activities and the siting of enterprises outside major urban centers.

Part Two

Chapter 5
Perceptions of Multinationals: Contributions to National Development

THE CONVENTIONAL WISDOM about multinational corporations and developing countries is that leaders of the latter view the MNC's with fear and hostility. Evidence from the three developing countries included in this study establishes that this sweeping generalization is false.

Leaders in Brazil, Malaysia and Nigeria are quick to point to the positive contributions that MNC's have made to their national economic development. These leaders, including those who are more uneasy about the presence of large-scale foreign investment in their midst, are not alarmed about alleged corporate threats to their national sovereignty. They do not doubt that when corporate and national interests seem irredeemably in conflict, it is the nation—and not the multinational corporation—that will have the last word.

Of course, these leaders do not see the multinationals as benign, or entirely above suspicion. The same host-country elites who praise the MNC's for their fiscal rectitude will condemn them for clandestine forms of income repatriation or monetary exchange manipulations. If these leaders freely praise the tendency of the MNC's to create jobs, train workers, pay them well, and maintain high standards of industrial safety, they are equally ready to assert that the multinationals transfer less technology than they might. Host-country leaders are essentially unanimous in believing that MNC's out-perform indigenous business enterprises on many dimensions. But they believe, too, that MNC's do not always operate in their country according to the higher standards that are required of them in more developed nations.

Host-country leaders generally express well-balanced and realistic views. They recognize that most multinational corporations will have many alternative overseas investment opportunities and that a decision to invest in any given country must be based on a careful evaluation of costs and benefits on both sides. Far from repeating the slogans of those who are ideologically opposed to private enterprise and to the presence of foreign investors, they recognize that the name of the game is capitalism and profitability. They understand the meaning of the "bottom line" in this game, and they are essentially willing to play the game—as long as they see it to be essential to further national economic growth and development.

Above all, many of the host-country leaders are self-confident; they believe they have the skills to optimize the advantages that foreign direct investment may bring to their country. To achieve this goal, they say, they will rely not on corporate altruism or on corporate declarations about "social responsibility." Rather, they will rely on their own capacities to understand the complexities of banking and industry, and to develop coherent, reasonable and well-administered national policies toward the foreign investor. Their objective is to drive the best bargain possible for their own countries. If they are more skilled today than earlier in doing so, they say that they have learned these skills from the more developed nations.

Views such as these are becoming the norm throughout much of the Third World. Increased expertise and self-confidence in dealing with the multinational community will continue to spread, particularly in those developing nations that are most attractive to the foreign investor.

Far-sighted corporate response to these changes must involve not only recognition that they exist but also an effort to understand what brings them about. Creative response requires new efforts to develop corporate skills to "read" local environments more accurately; to pay more attention to local factors that are not, strictly speaking, economic; and to center greater analytical attention on patterns and changes in public policy and public administration that are likely to affect the overseas venture for good or for ill.

Key elements in the overseas environment are the attitudes, evaluations, demands and policy preferences regarding the MNC's held by the host-country's strategically placed elites. The Board's earlier study of Canada and Italy and this present study represent first efforts to get at this kind of information systematically, and to show how it may be profitably used by the multinational corporate community.[1]

In Brazil, Malaysia and Nigeria several hundred persons were interviewed, including 173 key national leaders: 50 in Brazil; 82 in Malaysia, and 41 in Nigeria. Of the 96 European and American MNC managers who were interviewed in these countries, 37 were nationals of the countries involved. In addition, 21 U.S. and British expatriates living in these countries and 15 U.S. government officers stationed there were interviewed. In reading and interpreting the quantitative evidence offered, it is essential to bear in mind that it reflects the coding scheme developed for this report and the authors' summary assessment of individual attitudes. The same

[1] Joseph LaPalombara and Stephen Blank, *Multinational Corporations and National Elites: A Study in Tensions.* The Conference Board, Report No. 702, 1976.

person who, in an overall sense, might be scored as highly favorable toward the multinationals may also have quite articulate reservations and criticisms to register regarding them.

General Orientations

Overall, the elite response to foreign investment in Brazil, Malaysia and Nigeria is remarkably favorable. Of the 173 elites interviewed, 112 (65 percent) feel that the advantages associated with MNC activities clearly outweigh the disadvantages. Almost 30 percent are more critical of the multinationals: They perceive more defects in MNC operations, but believe that, on balance, the host country benefits from their presence. Fewer than 4 percent of the total believe the disadvantages to be so great that the multinationals should be forced to leave the country (Chart 3).

Chart 3: Elite Attitudes to Foreign Direct Investment

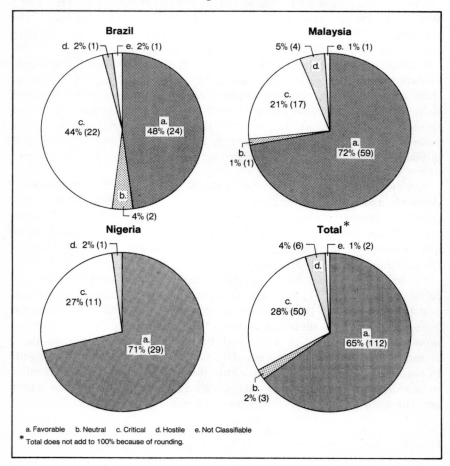

Brazil
d. 2% (1) ┐ ┌ e. 2% (1)
c. 44% (22)
a. 48% (24)
b.
└ 4% (2)

Malaysia
5% (4) ┐ ┌ e. 1% (1)
d.
c. 21% (17)
a. 72% (59)
b. 1% (1)

Nigeria
d. 2% (1) ┐
c. 27% (11)
a. 71% (29)

Total*
4% (6) ┐ ┌ e. 1% (2)
d.
c. 28% (50)
a. 65% (112)
b. 2% (3)

a. Favorable   b. Neutral   c. Critical   d. Hostile   e. Not Classifiable
* Total does not add to 100% because of rounding.

70

Most of the critics of the multinationals insist that the further economic development of their country is difficult to imagine without the continued— and even expanded—MNC presence. Many of these same leaders dismiss as demagogic and irresponsible the kinds of criticisms and demands regarding the MNC's that emanate from some international bodies, or from radical groups and organizations in their own countries.

There are variations in elite attitudes to the MNC's as Chart 3 indicates. For example, the Brazilians are more polarized than the others in their evaluations. Why should this be so?

Although Brazilians are often vehement in demanding that they not be indiscriminately lumped with the other "Latino" countries of South America, they share some of the hostile attitudes toward the MNC found in other countries in this region. These are countries where the extensive political influence of the United States has often been resented. As in Canada and Italy, deep feelings of anti-Americanism are readily directed toward the American corporate affiliate, the most tangible local evidence of the international power and the influence of the United States. Thus, although Brazilians (unlike, say, Canadians or Mexicans) are not seriously concerned about being overwhelmed by the U.S. colossus, a certain amount of antagonism toward the U.S. Government finds its way into their attitudes toward the multinationals.

More important in interpreting Brazilian attitudes is the country's higher level of industrialization and its longer experience with a variety of international industrial enterprises. Brazilians can argue that their early industrialization proceeded on a boot-strapping basis, with limited assistance from industrial countries other than Great Britain. Having achieved considerable momentum in industrialization and general economic growth, and having developed an impressive indigenous industrial class, Brazilians may agree less than either Malaysians or Nigerians that continued growth requires the presence of the multinationals. Brazil's industrial class, centered in São Paulo and the Southeast, manifests mixed feelings about the MNC's. In general, representatives of the groups interviewed in this study say that the MNC's are needed for continued growth. On the other hand, they find this need to be greatly diminished in those sectors where their own enterprises are located.

Ebbs and flows in foreign direct investment often served to trigger or to intensify periods of economic growth, or of economic disequilibrium and turmoil. Brazilian regime changes, themselves, at least since the days of Vargas, have generally been characterized by abrupt changes in the treatment of foreign enterprise. Foreign enterprises responded to these changes by equally abrupt increases or reductions of the net flow of foreign investment into the country. In view of all this, it would be astonishing if Brazilian attitudes toward the multinationals were as homogeneous as those found in Malaysia and Nigeria.

These differences in national attitudes are reflected in Chart 4, which summarizes respondents' opinions about the importance of MNC's to further economic growth efforts. From two-fifths to almost one-half of the Malaysian and Nigerian respondents define the multinational role as *essential;* but less than 20 percent of the Brazilian responses fall into this category.

Chart 4: Role of MNC's in National Economic Development

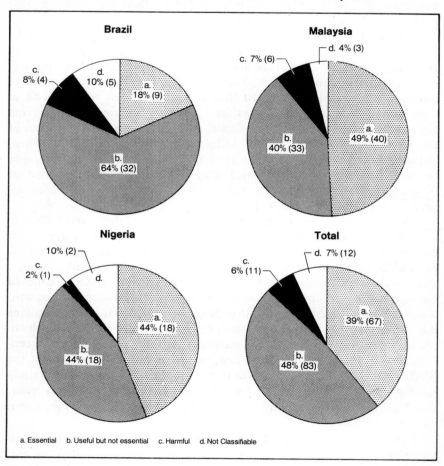

a. Essential   b. Useful but not essential   c. Harmful   d. Not Classifiable

On the other hand, in all three countries, more than 80 percent of those interviewed believe that the multinational presence is either *useful* or *essential.* In contrast, a mere 6 percent of the total sample (and only one respondent in Nigeria) conclude that the presence of MNC's is basically unessential, or even harmful, to national development.

The three countries are, of course, not typical of the Third World. Indeed, they were selected for analysis in part because certain aspects of their atypicality make them particularly attractive to multinational corporations and, therefore, germane to any discussion about the MNC's and the Third World. These are, after all, *major* developing countries where the prospect of large-scale multinational investment is more than purely academic, and more than marginally important to the investor. They are likely to become leaders and exemplars in their respective parts of the world. Their views of foreign investors are much more relevant, therefore, than those of leaders of countries where there is not likely to be very much foreign direct investment.

Specific Benefits and Advantages

Respondents were asked to specify the kinds of benefits and advantages associated with the presence of the multinationals. Of the 173 respondents, 41 percent mentioned only one advantage; these first (or only) specified advantages or benefits that are summarized in Chart 5. Many respondents mentioned more than one advantage or benefit. The cumulated first and second benefits and advantages mentioned by all respondents are shown in Table 14.

Looking at these data, the great importance respondents place on the transfer of technology, and the relatively minor importance they ascribe to managerial skills, training of indigenous persons and new forms of industrial organization is surprising.

Elites clearly see the multinational corporation as a necessary instrument for reducing the technological backwardness of their countries. The most striking aspect of elite responses across the three countries is their uniformity. Nevertheless, it is apparent that emphasis on technology transfer as a principal advantage is most marked in Malaysia and Nigeria, countries which, by comparison with Brazil, are not so far along the path of industrial development.

The interviewers sought to find out whether either a person's specific occupation, or location in the private or public sector, is significantly associated with attitudes about the benefits and advantages brought by the multinationals. Occupation as such was not found to be significant. For the effect of association with the private or public-sector on basic attitudes, see Table 15. As can readily be seen, respondents in the public sector are more likely than those in the private sector to emphasize technology transfer as the most important advantage deriving from the multinationals, while private elites tend to put greater stress on general aid to economic development. Although the evidence is not conclusive, it is in keeping with what was expected. It was anticipated that the public-sector elites would have had more direct experience with the MNC's; that they would be more acutely aware of the relationship of the multinational corporations to national development plans; and their sense of principal contributions (as well as principal criticisms) would be much more specific than those of local respondents in the private sector.

Chart 5: Advantages of Multinational Corporations by Country

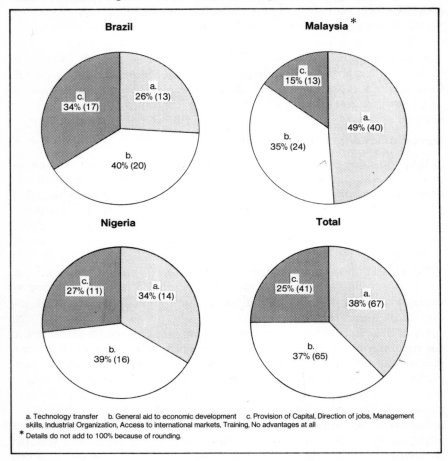

Brazil

a. 26% (13)
c. 34% (17)
b. 40% (20)

Malaysia *

c. 15% (13)
a. 49% (40)
b. 35% (24)

Nigeria

c. 27% (11)
a. 34% (14)
b. 39% (16)

Total

c. 25% (41)
a. 38% (67)
b. 37% (65)

a. Technology transfer   b. General aid to economic development   c. Provision of Capital, Direction of jobs, Management skills, Industrial Organization, Access to international markets, Training, No advantages at all
* Details do not add to 100% because of rounding.

When analyses were made by countries, it was found that the stress on technology was particularly associated with public-sector respondents in Malaysia and Nigeria. Public servants in these less-developed countries, where an indigenous private industrial sector is only beginning to emerge, are likely to be acutely conscious of the technology gap as a key factor in their underdevelopment. Acquiring technology is seen by these respondents as the key means of closing the gap between themselves and more developed economies. This also suggests that the public sector in these countries will take greater responsibility for facilitating the inflow of technology and for making this new technology available to the local private sector—or in developing the entrepreneurial application of the technology itself.

What about respondents' contacts with, or knowledge about, the MNC's? These factors were correlated with their evaluations of foreign

Table 14: Advantages of MNC's: Cumulative Frequency of First and Second Items Mentioned, 173 Respondents

Advantage	Number of mentions	Percent of mentions[1]	Percent of sample mentioning (N = 173)
Technology transfer.........	99	39%	61%
General aid to economic development	81	32	47
Provision of capital..........	22	9	13
Creation of jobs.............	18	7	11
Management skills	15	6	9
Access to international markets	14	5	8
Training	6	2	4
Industrial organization.......	2	1	1
Total....................	257	100%	

[1]Details do not add to 100 percent because of rounding.

direct investment. Chart 6 shows that more frequent contact seems to produce somewhat more favorable attitudes toward the multinationals. About 75 percent of those individuals with "great" contact with MNC's express favorable attitudes toward them, in contrast to some 44 percent of those with "scarce" contact. More than 50 percent of the elites with "scarce" contact are either critical or hostile to the multinationals, as compared with 26 percent of those with "great" contact who are critical—and none who are hostile (see Chart 6)

Turning to the question of how frequency of contact is associated with elite assessment of the role of MNC's in national development, the distributions are again in the expected directions (see Chart 7). Clearly, whether contact is great or scarce affects the proportions of the elites found in the "essential" and "negative" categories. However, irrespective of degree of contact, about half of the respondents believe the role of the MNC's in national economic development to be useful—even if not essential. If the two positive categories are combined, over three-quarters of those with even "scarce" contact give a favorable response.

The highest incidence of "scarce" contact with the multinationals is registered by those in our surveys who are classified as "intellectuals" and "mass media" representatives. Of the 18 persons in this category whose contacts with the multinational community could be assessed, almost 80 percent fall into the "scarce" category. Thus, it appears that the most sweeping and stringent criticisms of the MNC's tend to come from those respondents who have had the least contact with them and, therefore, probably have the least information about them.

Table 15: Advantages of MNC's by Occupational Elite Category[1]

Advantages	Public Sector		Private Sector		Intellectuals, Mass Media and Other	
	Number	Percent	Number	Percent	Number	Percent
Technology transfer	36	43%	18	33%	13	37%
General aid to economic development.	29	35	27	49	9	26
Provision of capital	8	10	2	4	3	9
Management skills	3	4	2	4	1	3
Training.	0	0	0	0	1	3
Industrial organization	1	1	1	2	1	3
Access to international markets	1	1	1	2	0	—
Creation of jobs.	3	4	2	4	3	9
No advantages at all	2	2	2	4	4	11
Total	83	100%	55	100%	35	100%

[1]Percentages may not add to 100 because of rounding.

Chart 6: Elite Orientation to Foreign Direct Investment, by Degree of Contact with MNC's

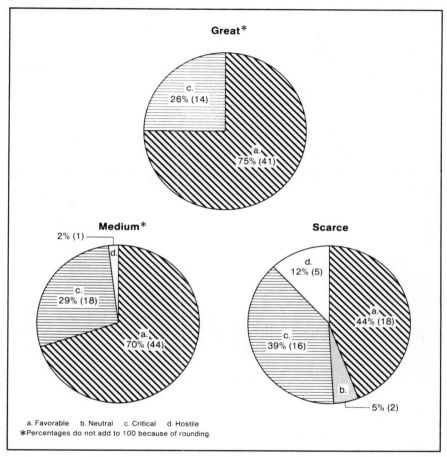

a. Favorable   b. Neutral   c. Critical   d. Hostile
*Percentages do not add to 100 because of rounding.

Interview protocols were analyzed to discover how much actual information or knowledge the respondents seem to possess about MNC's. Of the 171 persons who were rated on this question, well over three-quarters were considered to possess "medium" or "great" knowledge; about one-fifth were classified as having "scarce" knowledge, or none at all. Level of knowledge seems not at all significantly associated with the respondents' general orientation to the foreign investor (see Chart 8). The idea that great knowledge might lead to significantly more favorable orientations toward foreign investors is only weakly supported.

Qualitative Evidence

The qualitative responses underscore the general acceptance of multinationals, even when there are some doubts. A leading Brazilian technocrat says: "We know we need foreign capital and are prepared to accept it." The same idea is echoed by a Malaysian civil servant: "We need the MNC's to help in our economic development—to achieve more rapid economic growth." An American-trained Nigerian economist, working in the government, underscores the multinationals' association with a wide variety of values associated with economic development: "A developing country like Nigeria cannot purchase these values. They are brought in by the multinationals and provide an absolutely essential element for economic development and modernization."

Chart 7: Role of MNC's in National Economy, by Degree of Contact with MNC's

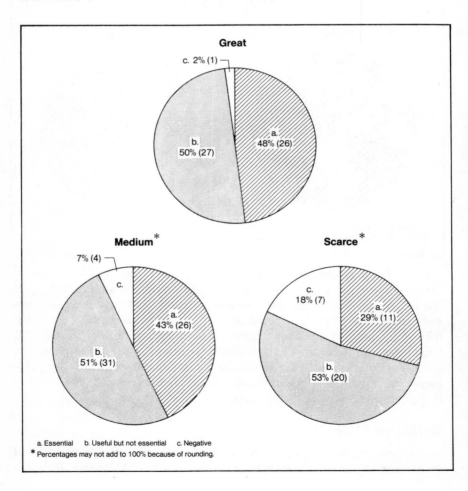

Great

c. 2% (1)

a. 48% (26)

b. 50% (27)

Medium*

7% (4)

c.

a. 43% (26)

b. 51% (31)

Scarce*

c. 18% (7)

a. 29% (11)

b. 53% (20)

a. Essential   b. Useful but not essential   c. Negative

* Percentages may not add to 100% because of rounding.

Chart 8: Orientation to Foreign Direct Investment, by Respondent's Knowledge of MNC's

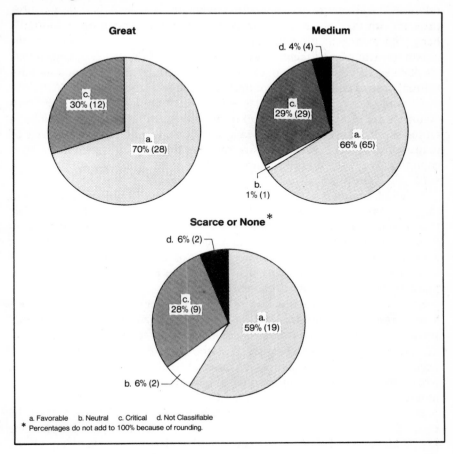

Great

c. 30% (12)

a. 70% (28)

Medium

d. 4% (4)

c. 29% (29)

a. 66% (65)

b. 1% (1)

Scarce or None *

d. 6% (2)

c. 28% (9)

a. 59% (19)

b. 6% (2)

a. Favorable   b. Neutral   c. Critical   d. Not Classifiable
* Percentages do not add to 100% because of rounding.

The ubiquitous stress on technology transfer is noteworthy. A Brazilian planner, for example, says: "It is possible for this country to do research on new technology, but it would take too much time." The issue of time is fundamental for many of these leaders: They have neither the opportunity nor the inclination to wait until indigenous research and development capability makes it possible to achieve industrial efficiency and modernization.

A former top Nigerian civil servant sums up the view of many elites in the less-developed nations: "Looking at the next stage of development which we are trying to achieve in Nigeria—moving from a primitive, precapitalist economy to a middle-level modern economy—involves extensive inputs of modern technology, often in areas in which technology is improving from day to day. For this reason, present-day Nigerian needs require very close cooperation with foreign firms, no matter what other concerns that relationship gives rise to. No matter what the internal rhetoric may be, progress can take place best to the extent that Nigeria can make mutually beneficial arrangements with foreign multinationals that provide for the maximum transfer of technology.'' He concludes that such arrangements ''will have to recognize that to achieve this transfer of technology substantial returns will have to be permitted to the foreign companies.''

To some extent, national elites will tend to emphasize what their own countries are most in need of, and to downgrade what they believe to be in ample supply. Thus, a Chinese Malaysian businessman echoes the views of many others there when he stresses the primacy of technology over capital: ''We really do not require foreign capital. The local supply will be sufficient if the political and racial climate is right.''

Nigerians, in an era of superliquidity, also rate technology transfer and the potential importance of the MNC's to general development much higher than capital inputs. These attitudes are in marked contrast to findings in Brazil, where indigenous capital is in much shorter supply. There the leaders emphasize the need for greater net inflow of capital in the form of new investment—not intracompany debt, long-term borrowing in local capital markets, or reinvestment of retained earnings.

Some respondents are quick to recognize that technology transfer covers a wide range of corporate activities, from organizational and managerial formats to the most basic level of training rural workers for places in industry. Thus it is acknowledged that the transfer of ''soft technology'' occurs when an indigenous person goes abroad for an advanced degree; when new corporate organizational modes are learned and adopted; and, indeed, when expatriates posted to a host country teach by example. In this regard, the observation by a Nigerian is noteworthy: ''The attitudes of the expatriates affect the attitudes toward work of the indigenous people. One expatriate accomplishes more than several indigenous workers, simply by sheer work, even when no special skill is involved. Devotion to work, the satisfaction gained from work completed, and the discipline in doing work—all of these are scarce in developing countries. Much can be learned from foreigners in this way. This is a reason why it is good to send people away from their country for several years for training, even when the possibility to develop the skill is available here. It is important to acquire not only the objective skills but the attitudes toward work.''

Many elites are strongly dedicated to the idea that their nations must develop with the most deliberate speed. They tend, rightly or wrongly, to believe that the more traditional aspects of their own societies are incompatible with developmental goals; consequently they welcome ideas and institutions that will help them to break down tradition and to introduce the ideas, values and methods of work of modern industrial society. Given this, it is understandable that the multinational corporation, one of the most visible symbols of advanced industrial society, should generally be welcomed as a potential catalyst of change.

A Malaysian lawyer and political leader puts the matter of the MNC fomenting change quite concretely: "When a foreign MNC hits Trengganu, the whole state will be transformed. People who work for the company will demand better surroundings. Once the electric cables are laid, the government might as well supply current to all the people in the area. It is the same with water. And once roads are built, everybody will be able to use them. A lot of changes will take place as a result. The local people will demand these amenities. Things will not be the same again."

The respondents are also aware of the degree of interdependence found in the world economic system in which the multinationals are prime actors. The need to make realistic appraisals generally supplants ideology—or what might be the understandable preference of most elites to have their nations develop without benefit of outside help.

Thus, a Nigerian banker says: "Foreign firms are indispensable to us. No matter what else we may think, that is a stark reality." A Nigerian lawyer, once active in politics, comments: "I can't see any developing country opting out of the operations of multinational corporations. Like it or not, they will be involved." A senior Brazilian official in the planning ministry echoes this thought: "Unless we want to disassociate ourselves from Western civilization, the only thing to do is to negotiate a modus vivendi with the multinationals."

An underlying theme in many of the responses is that the multinationals are needed in these three countries precisely *because* they are underdeveloped. This less-developed status refers not only to the rural and traditional sectors of society but to the indigenous business and industrial communities as well. A Brazilian industrialist remarks: "The Brazilian businessmen have not yet achieved a capitalist mentality. They do not know how to plan. Therefore, the multinationals will continue to have a predominent role for years to come."

It was anticipated that the most radical and nationalistic sentiments about the multinationals would be found in the academic and intellectual communities, and this proved to be the case. In the universities, outspoken and sweeping criticisms are directed not merely at the multinationals but at the capitalist system itself. Indeed, some of the critics have a vested interest in having existing national developmental plans fail—on the calculus that economic stagnation is a necessary, and perhaps sufficient, condition for bringing about political turmoil, upheaval and change.

But a sharp sense of nationalism can also be detected among members of the local business communities. Business associations in Brazil, for example, have pressed the government to restrict further expansion of foreign direct investment unless the foreign companies bring in more net capital from abroad, or unless they can show that they will actually transfer technology that is not locally available. In Nigeria, local business groups have urged the government to increase local equity-sharing requirements of foreign companies that wish to establish new businesses or continue operating there. A Nigerian who holds a key position in a British-based firm notes that many Nigerian businessmen see the presence of multinationals as an obstacle to their own growth, and many would like to see still higher requirements for local equity sharing for foreign companies.

A Malaysian businessman is more outspoken. He emphasizes the global benefits MNC's provide and then continues: "As far as I am concerned, we started with nothing. Now, we have factories and are better off. At least, most people think so. People who argue about exploitation do not see the point of progress. There are others who argue about pollution and the environment. But they do not understand the problem of unemployment. I must emphasize that I am talking about the present. If we have the technology, capital and local expertise, then I will say, 'to hell with the MNC's'."

Interviewees were asked to assess general attitudes in their country toward the "multinationals," defined to mean the large-scale American, European or Japanese companies with affiliates in their country. These respondents perceive the attitudes of their countrymen toward the multinationals to be more favorable than their own. Thus, an overwhelming 96 percent of the Malaysian and 75 percent of the Nigerian elites estimate that people in their respective countries are favorable toward MNC's.

Brazilian respondents are clearly less sanguine—only 44 percent believe that general attitudes are favorable (see Chart 9.) The size of the country, the fact that the elites interviewed were located in three different cities, and the fact that the presence of foreign direct investors in the economy has more than once caused acrimonious political controversy there help to explain why respondents were somewhat more hesitant to speculate about the views of their countrymen toward the multinationals. In São Paulo, for example, some of the social costs of rapid industrialization are dramatically visible—not merely in the kind of traffic jams that also beset a city like Lagos, but also in the glut of over 10 million people, the stepped-up tempo of daily living and, perhaps above all, the green cloud of smog that perpetually looms over the city.

The Malaysian response to this question is particularly intriguing—96 percent of the respondents perceive the attitudes of their countrymen toward the MNC's to be favorable. A wide array of explanations was provided.

Some Malaysians, for example, pride themselves on being more realistic and pragmatic than other people. One says: "We are more confident in our abilities to govern. The others are incompetent and corrupt. Because of their own errors, they have to blame someone else for their failures and difficulties. It is very easy for them to blame the multinationals."

The sense of governmental competence, of ability to deal effectively with multinationals, and of the need to avoid confrontation and crisis with the

Chart 9: Perceptions of National Attitudes Toward MNC's

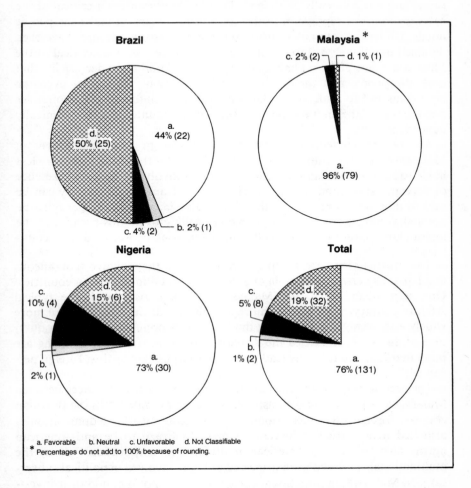

Brazil

d. 50% (25)
a. 44% (22)
c. 4% (2)
b. 2% (1)

Malaysia *

c. 2% (2) — d. 1% (1)
a. 96% (79)

Nigeria

c. 10% (4)
d. 15% (6)
b. 2% (1)
a. 73% (30)

Total

c. 5% (8)
d. 19% (32)
b. 1% (2)
a. 76% (131)

a. Favorable   b. Neutral   c. Unfavorable   d. Not Classifiable
* Percentages do not add to 100% because of rounding.

multinationals that are so essential to economic growth emerge from other responses. Competence to keep the MNC's within bounds is said to grow with experience. Furthermore, since the country itself is relatively conservative, since it is strongly committed to free enterprise and the open economy, it is logical that there should be basically favorable views toward the foreign investor. Another respondent adds that the evidence suggests that the multinationals represent a real bonanza. As long as the country is thriving and the economic pie continues to grow, there is little reason for thinking that the attitudes toward the MNC's will turn negative.

One Malaysian makes the observation that in Malaysia political divisions are so deeply centered on ethnic problems that most people are sidetracked from thinking about the multinationals. He says: "The local people see each other as the enemy." "The people," another Malaysian respondent says, "are not politically conscious. That is why they are not critical of the MNC's. Political repression in the country also helps to make the people docile. Under the Internal Security Act, many opposition leaders have been detained indefinitely without trial. Left-wing leaders who are critical of the MNC's are not given a chance to organize." Another leader argues that both the people and their present leaders are naive, and that even the politicians fail to understand the complexities of international economics and the role of the multinationals in keeping the country in an economically dependent state.

Another respondent adds that much of foreign direct investment in Malaysia emanates from Singapore and, because of this, Malaysians are less likely to see the multinational phenomenon as involving the heavy presence of foreign capital and managers. He says: "If any single country can be said to dominate foreign investment in Malaysia, then the finger must be pointed at Singapore. But few people are willing to do this because of the interlocking nature of social and family relations between the two countries."

Two further views are worth reporting, in that they involve spontaneous comparisons between Malaysia and African and Latin American countries. One respondent notes that Malaysia, by comparison with the typical African country, not only has more amenities, but the amenities are more widely and evenly shared among the indigenous population: "It is a question of disparity. In Africa the disparities between standards of living are more marked, and this may lead to stronger resentment against foreign personnel."

The second respondent calls attention to important differences between Malaysia and Latin America, using Brazil as an example: "In the Brazilian context, foreign investment dominates the economy. That domination is also tied to a particular foreign country. In Brazil to be anti-American means also to be anti-American multinational corporations. Also, the multinationals in Brazil were suspected of being involved in political subversion. In Malaysia, multinational corporations are not big, and their investment is a drop in the ocean of world multinational investment. They are not doing big things in Malaysia, so we escape many of the ill feelings associated with large multinational corporate investment and domination."

The visibility of the multinationals, their role in the economy, and their specific nationality, all make a difference. Some supporting evidence along these lines is provided below.

Chapter 6
Multinationals: The Negative Views

A FEW RESPONDENTS in this study are extremely hostile to foreign corporations. Some feel that the disadvantages for host countries associated with MNC operations far exceed the advantages. One Nigerian official, well-acquainted with MNC's, says he believes that "foreign corporations make enormous profits in underdeveloped nations because they vastly exaggerate the risk of doing business there. The companies are often better informed and organized than governments are, but they still complain that their profits are insufficient." A Brazilian bureaucrat casts a similar argument in more ideological terms, stressing the social disruption caused by the multinationals. "MNC's are the primordial agents of international capitalism. Their negative effects are very numerous, such as fraud and corruption. This happens because they operate in very vulnerable societies. Their presence disarticulates a lot of things in the economic system; it destabilizes the system." These individuals would like the multinationals out or, at very least, subject to stiff restrictions.

A few respondents reject prevailing models of economic development. They question the wisdom or necessity of industrialization as the basis for development. A Malaysian official, for example, urges the exploration of alternative modes of economic development, other than industrialization. "What do we want in development," he asks. "Will industrialization alleviate our rural-based problems? Do we want industrialization at all?" Other respondents emphasize the need for greater national autonomy—for development without *external* assistance.

Sentiments like these make the headlines; they are the stuff of which ringing speeches are made at international gatherings. Given the prominence such utterances are accorded by the mass media, it is difficult to get across the point that they represent a tiny minority view, even among the severest critics of the multinationals. Yet, if the data from three developing countries are taken as reasonably representative of the attitudes of strategic elites in these countries, it is clear that few of these persons would actually move to bar the multinationals and opt for a "Chinese" model of economic development. It should be added that "strategic elites" are not simply the so-called Establishment, or the power-holders in society. They include as well those host-country elites whose positions or occupations in society place them in the opposition to the status quo and whose views of foreign investment and investors are highly skeptical.

If there is an alternative model of national development that appeals to some respondents, it is the Japanese. The crux of the Japanese approach is the careful control of external inputs into economic development. The basic argument is that a developing nation must accurately assess its needs for foreign capital, technology and expertise; it must carefully control and supervise the means whereby these inputs are transferred to the domestic economy; and it must always seek to maximize the overriding goal of national self-determination.

This chapter is not concerned with the relatively tiny group of extreme MNC detractors who would exclude them. It is primarily concerned with those who acknowledge and accept the inevitability of multinational participation in national economic development but, who nevertheless, are critical of certain MNC policies and practices and demand changes in government policies that pertain to the foreign investor. For the multinational community itself, it is essential to know which modes of operation give rise to suspicion and anger, or what causes consternation even among those who want to see the multinationals remain in their countries.

Disadvantages of Multinational Operations

The disadvantages associated by the respondents with MNC activities are much more diffuse than the advantages. While three-fourths of those interviewed cite the transfer of technology and general assistance to economic growth as the prime advantages, nothing like that number agree as to the major disadvantages. Thus, the most frequently mentioned *specific* defect noted by respondents (i.e., financial practices) is cited by only 14 percent of the group. Moreover, the six defects cited most often are mentioned by barely half of the total.

At the most *general* level, we find the mirror image of the advantages discussed in Chapter 5: The presence of multinational corporations is said to distort national development by creating structural or sectoral imbalances in the economy. One form of distortion, it is claimed, is simply that of making the local economy overly dependent on external forces over which local officials and organizations have little or no control. In the case of Brazil, allegations about distortion often turn on the "denationalization" of the local economy. Denationalization has a quite specific meaning: It refers to the gradual but progressive squeezing and contraction of the domestic private sector. But the broader criticism is that the multinationals increase the unevenness of economic development, giving rise to "developed industrial enclaves" that favor a small proportion of the local population and greatly aggravate geographic economic disparities. In a few instances, respondents echo the argument that the multinationals create a demand for luxury goods, cater to the indigenous middle classes, and, therefore, simultaneously put the local economy out of kilter and contribute to aggravated income inequality.

A second general criticism refers to harmful aspects of corporate philosophy. While it is acknowledged that corporate managers have to be governed fundamentally by questions of profitability, it is also added that some corporations become obsessed with the "bottom line" at the expense of everything else, including the interests of the host country. Thus, local perceptions of corporate philosophy are frequently summed up in the sentence: "They are only interested in the profits they make here."

Disquietude about corporate philosophy is widespread. It is not readily dispelled by corporate philanthropic activity—however visible it may be—or by the adoption and publication of corporate codes of conduct. Respondents more often refer to corporations that never really settle into a local economy and culture; to corporate managers who make brief stopovers overseas on their way to better assignments at headquarters; to corporate overreactions to what they consider unstable local conditions—in a word, to the evidence that suggests a single-minded corporate philosophy designed to maximize return on investment regardless of the costs to the local economy or society.

The more specific corporate defects cited by respondents are heavily concentrated on the transfer of technology and on financial practices. Given the findings in Chapter 2, the frequency of reference to technology is not surprising. Most frequently, MNC's are criticized for resisting transferring technology; respondents also claim that inappropriate or outmoded technologies are often transferred; that unwary host countries wind up being charged more than once for a given technology; and that on at least some occasions the "black box" that presumably contains some costly technological innovation or process is empty.

Criticisms of financial practices are another matter. On the one hand, elites give the multinationals high marks when it comes to financial and fiscal rectitude, especially when compared with local business practices. This impression is marred, but certainly not seriously eroded, by infrequent (even if sometimes spectacular) examples of "unusual" corporate payments.

On the other hand, many respondents feel that whenever the multinationals can engage in one form or another of transfer pricing they do not hesitate to do so. Indeed, transfer pricing is far and away the most frequently cited example of unacceptable corporate financial practice. Where transfer pricing is almost impossible for local government to police, the suspicion, frustration and anger expressed by host-country elites is that much higher.

The various criticisms made of the MNC's are aggregated into six major categories in Table 16. Brazilian complaints that the MNC's are involved in the "denationalization" of the Brazilian private sector are coded as "hinders or destroys local development." "Other adverse economic practices" includes claims that the multinationals dry up local capital markets, or cause inflation, or create balance-of-payments difficulties. The category "other harmful corporate practices" is essentially residual. It represents a long and diverse list of claims, including corporate resistance to local participation in management, undesirable industrial practices, too much control of local affiliates from headquarters, efforts to influence local governments, and so on.

In addition to what has already been said, the most striking aspect of Table 16 is the differences among countries. Brazilians, for example, are deeply concerned with the possibility that the MNC's do, in fact, distort the nation's developmental aspirations. This possibility is continously raised by opponents to the present regime; it has been reiterated insistently in recent years as the remarkable growth rates of the late 1960's and early 1970's have slowed down, and as Brazilian officials come increasingly to associate their balance-of-payments problems not only with the petroleum crisis but also with the operations of the multinationals.

Brazilian allegations about distortions of national economic development

Table 16: Disadvantages of MNC's (aggregated by general category)

Criticism	Brazil	Malaysia[1]	Nigeria[1]	Total[1]
Hinders or distorts national economic development	38%	22%	5%	23%
Other harmful corporate practices	10	17	39	20
Corporate philosophy harmful	6	20	17	15
Financial practices harmful	14	15	12	14
No (or inappropriate) technology transfer	14	12	7	12
Other adverse economic effects	10	2	7	5
No disadvantages	6	2	5	4
Not classifiable	2	11	7	8
Total	100%	100%	100%	100%

[1] Details do not add to 100 percent because of rounding.

example of nationalization

derive from two additional structural factors. One is the concentration of the developed sectors of the economy in the southeastern portion of the nation. The rapid development of industry there—in which foreign direct investors have been prominent participants—tends to accelerate the economic and related amenities gap between the Southeast and the rest of the country.

As for the other, there is no doubt that the private Brazilian sector has been progressively squeezed. A significant proportion of the pressure comes from an aggressively expansive public productive sector—not primarily from the multinationals. Nevertheless, when Brazilian elites discuss this problem, they usually refer not to state corporations but to the multinational firms. Protests and criticisms of this kind often emanate from leading Brazilian industrial families even though they, themselves, frequently participate in joint ventures with the MNC's.

Malaysian and Nigerian respondents place greater stress than Brazilians on the harmful aspects of corporate philosophy. This is to be expected in less-developed countries where the possibility of getting to and staying beyond the take-off point in sustained industrial growth appears much more difficult. In these countries, where well-developed indigenous industrial capacities and communities are still markedly lacking, it makes an enormous difference whether the MNC's come and go, as if through a revolving door; whether expatriate managers are viewed as short-termers; and whether the multinational firm is seen as making a long-term commitment to the host country.

In the Nigerian case, it is essential to comment on the heavy concentration of responses in the "other harmful corporate practices" category. For a variety of reasons, including their colonial heritage and the issue of race as well as the history of foreign economic involvement there, Nigerians are particularly suspicious of corporate practices. Recent experience in the oil-boom climate has not diminished this suspicion. Nigerian feelings are often expressed by allegations of extensive transfer pricing, of corporate efforts to slow down or to sabotage demands that more local managers be Nigerians rather than expatriates, and of lingering colonialism expressed in corporate efforts to influence decisions of the Nigerian government. *— corruption*

In considering the specific disadvantages respondents associate with direct foreign investment, it is arresting to note how infrequently they mention the kinds of multinational shortcomings that are typically alleged by those who write disapprovingly about MNC's. What often exercises the critics of a multinational presence in Third World countries does not necessarily arouse the ire of the residents of these countries. Interview protocols of the 173 host-country elites were analyzed for the first and second mentions of disadvantages associated with MNC's. Table 17 shows the number of times some of the typical allegations and criticisms cited in the literature were actually mentioned by respondents.

Table 17: Disadvantages of Foreign Direct Investment, by Frequency of Mention by Host-Country Elites

Disadvantage	Frequency	Percent of Total Mentions (N = 267)	Percent of Sample Mentioning (N = 173)
Little initial capital invested	3	1.1	1.8
Exploitation of local resources	3	1.1	1.8
Excessive profits to MNC	3	1.1	1.8
Excessive central corporate control...............	9	3.3	5.3
Excessive export of capital...............	10	3.7	5.7
Undesirable or inappropriate technology....	15	5.6	8.5

Specific Criticisms of Multinationals

Having examined the defects respondents allege to be associated with MNC operations, it is now appropriate to take a more qualitative look at several of the key issues raised by the critics.

Distortion of Local Economy

The most difficult and politically volatile issues are claims that the multinationals distort local economies and keep host countries in a state of permanent and increasing dependence. They are neatly summarized by a Brazilian businessman who says: "We've always been dependent as a country on foreigners. Our economic growth has been a function of the foreign economy, and this orientation has dominated all of our economic and financial policies." Another Brazilian industrialist picks up the theme: "The negative aspect of the MNC's operations in this country is the influence they exert on our economy, increasing the already existing gap between them and the capacity of national firms to compete with them." A Brazilian banker adds: "The national enterprises are reduced to the position of mere productive departments of the multinationals."

As one listens to the Brazilian respondents with care, it is apparent that the most severe criticism is leveled against their own national government. Knowledgeable Brazilians know, for example, that it is the Brazilian public sector, hard at work promoting and implementing governmental policies, that represents a major factor in the "denationalization" of the indigenous private sector. Respondents recognize that many of the disadvantages associated with the MNC presence in that country refer less to multinational behavior than to unsatisfactory governmental policies.

The distorting economic impact of the multinationals may, in fact, be the fault of the national government. A young Brazilian economist underscores this point: "It is the lack of control over the MNC's actions that generates the problems. The MNC's are not the villains of the scene. What must be checked is the economic system itself. The type of capitalist system that was implanted in Brazil after the 1950's is what should be discussed." Elite perceptions and criticisms of their country's policies toward foreign investors are dealt with in detail in Chapter 8.

Technology Transfer

As indicated above, the issue of technology is central in all three countries. Simply, the dilemma is this: Whereas host-country leaders identify technology as the most important contribution the multinationals can bring to their countries, the reluctance of MNC's genuinely to share and transfer technology bothers these leaders most.

A Malaysian bureaucrat claims that a common trait among all multinationals is their zeal and preoccupation in keeping control over technology: "The MNC's never tell us the knowledge in their technical recipe books. We receive the so-called packages that do not tell us anything beyond how to utilize the equipment—when they actually tell us that. These packages do not provide the conditions for us really to absorb know-how, which is what matters."

While Brazilians are more likely to rail at the reluctance of foreign firms to share advanced technology, Malaysians complain more frequently about fragmentation of production processes, of the creation of enclaves of higher technology production—what Canadians describe as "truncation."

The electronics industry in the Free Trade Zones is cited by several Malaysians as an outstanding example of the lack of diffusion of technology. A Malaysian businessman, referring to the electronics industry, says: "Three thousand people were trained but all three thousand cannot make a complete computer circuit. They each can only make certain parts. If the MNC's were to pull out, we would still not be able to make a complete unit on our own."

Another Malaysian, a more radical critic of the MNC's asks: "Where is this technology transfer they talk about? How does having a few electronic factories here help improve our technological capacity? All they do is bring in the parts for people to wire together. When they leave, our workers will be unemployed because the skills are not transferrable. We do not have the capacity to set up an electronic factory on our own."

There is a discernible correlation between the content of the statements about technology and the existing level of industrialization of the host country. This is likely to be dramatically the case where, as in Nigeria, underdevelopment is *not* accompanied by shortage of local capital. As an expatriate manager of a major British firm puts it: "Nigeria is unique among the developing nations in that Nigerians don't really care about foreign investment for the sake of foreign capital. What they want is skill, technology and know-how. And this makes it very easy for the sharp operators to take advantage. The Nigerians are frequently taken to the laundry because the foreign investor has so little at risk, and simply does a job on them."

The oil-rich Arab states also have an abundant supply of local capital, and are also deeply suspicious about the quality of technology that goes into major infrastructural and industrial projects they are financing. Whereas the Arab states are willing to employ skilled and semi-skilled workers imported from abroad, the Nigerian situation is fundamentally different. Nigerian complaints abut the lack of technology transfer are more frequently directed at the failure of foreign companies to develop indigenous skills—particularly technical skills. This is a galling problem for the largest and potentially the richest African nation. Thus, a senior official of Nigeria's Central Bank says: "Nigeria's primary problem at the present time is its failure to make use of its human resources, and foreign-owned firms must take a heavy responsibility in this failure."

A national government official claims that the multinationals "do not provide meaningful employment that would introduce Nigerians into the real operation of a modern company. They do not entrust Nigerians with the secrets of the organization." Like so many other respondents interviewed there, he sees the problem of technology as extending from the highest levels of management to the lowest level of technical training in production.

What about allegations of undesirable or inappropriate technology? The range of criticism is quite wide, and almost everyone has a favorite horror story to tell. Intellectuals are inclined to be prescriptive about what should or should not be produced. They also want more labor-intensive industries in countries like Brazil and tend to believe that even high-technology industries can be adapted abroad to take better account of the need to absorb large numbers of workers on urban labor markets.

Alleged failures of foreign corporations to worry more about adaptation, or about the appropriateness of products for given overseas climates, are embedded in an observation by a Brazilian manager of a state-owned enterprise: "MNC behavior has nothing to do with our national reality. They apply technological models here developed for other situations. One sees a company producing oil for a freezing point of -30° in a tropical country. We cannot expect adequate technology. The MNC's transfer obsolete technology, which they account for as capital. They bring ready-made products and want the market to adapt to their conditions."

Some Brazilians blame the indigenous business community for not paying more attention to adaptation and other nuances of technology transfer. Indeed, as one official of Brazil's National Bank for Economic Development (BNDE) describes the local business community: "The local entrepreneur does not have the mentality for technology transfer. The government has to force local business to be more concerned about technological development. Only the government is interested in technological transfer." The point is that the problem of technology transfer may well involve a lack of interest on the part of both the multinationals and members of the local business community. It is recognized, however, that technology transfer does occur, particularly if technological adaptation is a necessary condition for operating successfully in an overseas market. This is acknowledged by a Brazilian critic of the MNC's, who says: "In general, MNC's are not interested in doing research here. They bring technological black boxes. But it is also true that they are sometimes led to develop technology adapted to our particular circumstances. In this sense, we have a positive aspect of the learning process."

The Brazilian Situation

The Brazilian government has traditionally sought to exercise rigorous control over transfer and payment for technology. It has imposed strict registration requirements for licensing agreements and severe limitations on the remittance of royalty payments abroad—especially between related companies. All patent and trademark licenses and technical-assistance agreements must be registered with the government (with the National Industrial Property Institute, INPI), which carefully analyzes each agreement to ensure that there will be a maximum of technological transfer at lowest cost to the host country. Although some nationals—as well as many foreign businessmen—feel that Brazil's policy is too strict, every indication is that it will become still more severe in the future.

Early in 1978, after much negotiation, the Brazilian government finally decided not to grant contracts to foreign companies to produce minicomputers. Instead, contracts were given to four local companies. The key issue was obviously the willingness of the foreign companies to transfer the technology that the Brazilians wanted. *The New York Times'* correspondent in Rio commented on the decision: "The direction Brazil is now taking seems clear. It wants to own its modern technology. If foreign companies don't want to go along, the market will be reserved for national companies." And the president of CAPRE, the government agency empowered to control the import of all computer equipment and to determine policy for the industry, added: "Brazil is changing from a mere spectator to a principal actor conscious of her ability and future."[1]

---

[1] David Vidal, "Brazil Declares Computer Independence," *The New York Times,* February 19, 1979.

A statement by a top government leader, former Commerce Minister Calmon de Sa, affirms the same principle: "We want to give priority to projects that contemplate greatest Brazilian participation, and we want the technology to be developed here."[2] And a statement by a group of prominent Brazilian business leaders urging reform in Brazilian business also demands the "selective regulation of the influx of foreign capital"—to ensure, among other objectives, that technological benefits are adequate. Some government officials have taken much more radical postures. The head of Telebras, the state telephone holding company, recently stated: "When Brazil possesses its own technology in an area, foreign companies will not even be considered."[3]

Statements such as these could easily be read as an expression of growing ideological rigidity in Brazil or, even more mistakenly, as a Brazilian policy designed to drive out the multinationals. Neither interpretation could be farther from reality. Brazilian leaders are certain to drive harder bargains and, as part of a process in which they are recognized as unexcelled, government officials will use various ploys to keep the multinationals off balance. Because the issue of technology transfer is a burgeoning one, and because the government itself cannot behave as if it were unconcerned about it, considerable rhetoric and even seemingly stringent policies will focus on this area. Nevertheless, it is overwhelmingly apparent that the Brazilians want the MNC's to stay, and that they assume the managers of the multinationals will learn the Brazilian way around problems that may appear absolutely insurmountable to a non-Brazilian.

Corporate Financial Transactions

The issue here is neither profitability nor financial rectitude. Respondents are certain that multinational business in their countries is profitable—often very profitable. If not, they ask, why would the MNC's be here? Furthermore, most of them recognize that rates of return on investment are likely to be higher overseas than in the MNC's home countries. Why else would there be strong inducements to go abroad?

If profitability—even at high levels—is acceptable, distortions of profits and losses and hidden forms of repatriating capital and income are not. Critics overseas, including those who are fundamentally favorable to the MNC's, are convinced that the multinationals utilize a wide range of devices to remit profits at levels beyond what is fair and reasonable and, in some cases, prescribed by local laws.

[2]"The Brazilian Gamble," *Business Week,* December 5, 1977, p. 76.

[3]Diana Smith, "Call for reform in Brazilian business," *Financial Times,* London, July 7, 1978, and Sue Branford, "Problems with overseas connections," *Financial Times,* London, July 21, 1979.

As was said earlier, the bête noire is transfer pricing—not only over- and under-invoicing, but essentially all forms of intracompany transactions that permit the MNC's to distort the real profit and loss profiles of their overseas affiliates. A much-criticized practice, and one which is certain to come under much closer scrutiny and regulation, is intracompany indebtedness. Many Brazilian respondents insist that these loans work against the Brazilian economy in several ways. First, they say, the interest charged (particularly when no liquid capital itself has necessarily been transferred to the affiliate) is a form of disguised income repatriation. Second, designated locally as a cost of operations for the affiliate, interest charges serve to reduce profitability. Third, the double effect of this is to reduce the taxable income of affiliates and to defeat local laws that heavily tax the open repatriation of income above certain prescribed levels. Last, these intracompany loans are included as a portion of Brazil's foreign debt and, therefore, aggravate the balance-of-payments problem.

Nigerians are exercised about this issue, too. A Nigerian public official decries "the use of company accounting systems that enable international corporations to perform financial manipulations to the detriment of the host country." Another Nigerian—much more moderate in his view of multinationals—says: "The difficulty Nigeria faces is to properly assess the true costs of the inputs provided by the foreign firms. The danger is that they will encourage substantial overpayment for these benefits by removing wealth from the country.

A second financial practice noted in all three countries involves capitalization. On the one hand, it is acknowledged that the investor will try to get started overseas with a minimum in hard capital outlay brought in from the outside. On the other hand, examples of clever manipulations add up to yet another list of local horror stories about foreign investors. One of them, from a former Nigerian diplomat now in business, goes like this: "A foreign company will invest a million Naira, make a profit of 100 million, and declare a dividend of 15 million of which they repatriate 15 percent. Not bad!"

Another Nigerian businessman, extensively involved with the multinationals, puts the issue less dramatically: "By far the main defect of these companies is the insufficiency of their own capital. They come in with only a small amount of their own capital and expect it to be matched by local funds. They have a better credit rating and are known to the foreign banking community here, so they have favorable access to local funds, too. They use little of their own money and could keep 100 percent of the ownership of the business they set up here—and management control, too, with little outlay of original capital."

Multinational executives make exactly the same complaint—in reverse. Expatriates in Nigeria argue that it is difficult to find local partners who will (or can) put up the 40 or 60 percent of the initial capital required by the Indigenization Decree. Similar views are found among multinational managers in Brazil. They are echoed by technocrats at Brasilia who indicate that even the more powerful local industrial interests are sometimes unable to come up with needed joint-venture capital, or to produce accurate estimates of eventual levels of capitalization that large-scale ventures may require.

Host-country elite concerns about corporate financial practices reveal tensions and some ambivalence about the presence of multinationals. The same Malaysians who are critical about some corporate financial practices will express bewilderment and fear when levels of foreign direct investment fall off. When this occurred recently, Malaysians argued among themselves whether the decline of FDI was due primarily to the international economic situation or to governmental policies toward the MNC's. Although some Malaysians condemn past practices that permitted a multinational to enter with very limited capital and to take a great deal of it out, there is growing confidence that this sort of practice can be controlled in the future. A senior officer of the Malaysia Central Bank says: "Formerly the multinationals came into this country with very little capital. They borrowed heavily locally, they built up their assets here, and then they repatriated their profits. But this can not happen again. We have learned our lesson."

All three governments intend to monitor incoming investments carefully. The Brazilian and Malaysian national banks have specifically designated departments and officers entrusted with this responsibility. These institutions are also responsible for monitoring currency transactions and enforcing foreign-exchange controls. This second function may not be as vital in Malaysia, however, as it would be in many other places, including Nigeria and Brazil. A Malaysian Central Bank official, reflecting on his country's very liberal foreign exchange regulations, remarks that the multinationals do not take advantage of this. He says: "They behave themselves very well. We don't see foreign firms playing games against the currency. Don't forget, we have little inflation and a currency that is more stable than the U.S. dollar. There is no reason to hedge against it."

Brazilian banking and other officials see the picture quite differently. High levels of inflation, an unstable currency, and a massive foreign debt are known to create considerable nervousness in the multinational community there. The Brazilians pride themselves on having devised one of the most complicated—but, they argue, effective—systems of mini-devaluation in the world. Nevertheless, Brazilian banking and administrative officials point out that they confront a major problem in multinationals using a wide variety of devices designed to reduce their exposure whenever they develop fears about inflation levels, debt-service ratios, or massive devaluation of the local currency. Many of them express astonishment and chagrin over the apparent inability of some corporate central financial managers to recognize that a large-scale devaluation in Mexico does not mean that one will follow in Brazil. Corporate financial officers who watch the soaring inflation that Brazil began to experience again in 1979 take a more skeptical view.

A senior government economist in Brazil aptly summarizes the problematic aspects of multinational behavior in this area:

"A large portion of our debt in the balance of payments is related to captive financial markets. The MNC's do not bring risk capital. The MNC's, in addition, are given a lot of incentives to establish here. Instead of bringing risk capital (and, therefore, implying an inflation in our foreign debt) the firms seek financing at very high interest rates. This aggravates our balance-of-payments problem. I see this basic problem: In a market economy the MNC's do not cover the risks. By rejecting the risks they follow a short-run accumulation pattern. The social costs of the risks are then transferred to the community without transferring the private benefits. From the point of view of foreign loans payable in foreign currency, the MNC's account for two-thirds of the Brazilian total."

Brazilians add that this problem is compounded whenever MNC's go into the local currency market as a hedge against devaluation, and thereby help drive up the cost of money astronomically. In any event, leaders in both the public and private sectors are agreed that the need for governmental oversight and controls is very great. A high-level technocrat in Brasilia notes: "Only by exercising controls over foreign exchange can we facilitate living with the MNC's. It's not possible to have total control. But exchange and investments, export and import prices are controllable. With these measures, it is easier to deal with the companies. You can't have absolute control; but I would say that this kind of problem is not difficult to manage."

A businessman in Sao Paulo objects, claiming that the Brazilian system is wrongheaded. "Our legislation on foreign capital is very bad. One basic mistake is that it is not concerned with capital entrance but very much so with profit remittance, royalties and such things."

A senior official in Brazil's central bank agrees but he believes that things are changing, and quite rapidly:

"Companies can get around this 12 percent limitation (on nontaxed dividend or income repatriation) by various alternative schemes. We could inquire whether the debt-versus-equity situation of a given company has gone up. Maybe it has. I would not affirm that this is the method always used because I don't have the data. I have no estimate as to the magnitude but it is large. We are now establishing a computer program that will give us this kind of information accurately and instantaneously on a large number of companies here in Brazil.

97

"We are going to take a close look at companies that come here to expand their investment in Brazil. In the past, there has not been a close questionning to discover what proportion of this new investment would be in equity, what proportion in debt—and whether to the parent company or other (external) loaning agencies.

"We do not formulate policy here; the Committee for Industrial Development (CDI) establishes policy. CDI now has an internal policy to convince the multinationals to balance their export-import situation if they want fiscal incentives. They are going to make it a condition, too, that two-thirds of any new investment must be brought in from abroad as equity."

If Brazilians are most concerned about improving their national administrative capability to negotiate with, oversee and regulate the multinationals, Nigerians are more concerned with reducing the alleged ability of the MNC's to influence both government and administration. Nigerians are more likely than others to see the MNC's as directly involved in the political process. They view foreign firms, and especially American firms, as overseas extensions of their home governments. They worry about tendencies of some multinationals to engage in corrupt practices within administrative agencies. On the other hand, many Nigerian respondents realistically, even if unhappily, acknowledge that there is corruption in sectors of the civil service that not only permits—but sometimes compels— companies to buy contracts, permits, visas and so on. A prime goal for Nigerians is to improve administrative capability at this very basic level.

Local Managers: Criticisms of Multinational Corporations

Among the 96 affiliate managers interviewed in Brazil, Malaysia and Nigeria, 37 were natives of their respective countries. This makes them particularly interesting not only to other elites in these societies, but also to parent companies that find themselves under increasing pressure to incease the proportion of indigenous managerial personnel. The attitudes of these managers regarding the costs and benefits associated with MNC operations provide an illuminating counterpoint to the criticisms reviewed so far in this chapter.

Indigenous managers of foreign-owned firms have particularly difficult situations in Third World countries. They labor at times under severe cross-pressures of loyalty to country and to company. They frequently find themselves defending their companies to fellow nationals who are critical of foreign businesses, and defending their countries to unsympathetic and sometimes insensitive business associates. Being the defender of an unpopular cause—twice over—can be exceedingly disturbing, particularly in countries like Brazil and Nigeria where nationalistic feelings run high.

Indigenous managers are much more articulate and specific in their evaluations and criticisms of multinational practices and policies. These criticisms were drawn on heavily in an earlier report.[4]

If complaints from affiliate managers about overcentralization at corporate headquarters are universal, they are particularly intense, and have much more profound long-term corporate implications when they come from host-country natives. Not only do these managers complain bitterly about their company's lack of autonomy, they add as well an impressive list of additional policies they insist are in the real interest of neither the parent company nor the host country. These policies include the rapid turnover of expatriate managers; rigidities and insensitivities in dealing with host-country nationals and mores; excessive legalism; and lack of confidence in indigenous managers reflected in frequent visits from headquarters, excessive central financial control, and the exclusion of locals from certain functional sectors of management.

Local managers frequently allege that the worst offenders are American firms. Managers of both U.S. and European multinational affiliates say that American firms are less flexible, more aggressive, and tediously legalistic.

Most managers, local and expatriate, believe that U.S. firms are tightly controlled at the center and that this represents a major difference between American and other multinationals. There are a few dissenters from this view, who hold that central control is not really that different. Some note that frequent visits to the field by managers from headquarters may nevertheless create this impression. On the other hand, the observation that U.S. managers move in and out of overseas assignments so quickly that they are never really able to get a real feeling for the local situation is essentially universal.

A more telling lament from local managers is the difficulty of getting an understanding and sophisticated hearing at headquarters, given the relatively scarce number of headquarters personnel who have had in-depth overseas experience, and the relatively low level of headquarters' interest in the international side of business. Linked to this complaint is another: Corporate headquarters' vision in the United States is often blinkered by rigid expectations regarding return on investment. Among the problems this creates is failure to make optimal overseas adaptations, as well the failure to identify and exploit wider business opportunities that exist in host countries.

Equally pervasive among indigenous managers is the conviction that their colleagues at headquarters often lack acute understanding of the political and social environments of host countries. They are too easily worried, or panicked, by what appear to them to be dangerous local political ten-

---

[4]Joseph LaPalombara and Stephen Blank, *Multinational Corporations in Comparative Perspective*. The Conference Board, Report No. 725, 1977.

dencies. Above all, they manifest an excessive preoccupation about leftist tendencies in local politics, failing to recognize that these tendencies are almost always less pernicious to international business than is assumed or feared.

The fear of communist insurgency, a Malaysian executive observes, grows exponentially with the distance of headquarters from the local scene. A Brazilian working for a U.S. corporation sums it up: "There will *always* be incentives and opportunities down here. It is a very important job to convey that message to you Americans. Brazil can and will solve its problems. We have often thought of what is to be communicated to corporate headquarters. We have to have some feeling for when the people in New York are beginning to get too nervous."

As already noted, these local managers are frequently nationalists, and they strongly believe that this posture is not inconsistent with their responsibilities and loyalties to the parent company. Indigenous managers decry their companies' failure to understand the developmental aspirations of host countries. A Nigerian manager believes that headquarters executives often underrate the desire of former colonies to be independent in the economic as well as the political sense. They complain that headquarters does not give enough thought to aligning their company's business to national objectives, programs and plans.

An answer to headquarters' complaints that local plans are often incoherent, contradictory and chaotic is provided by a Brazilian. The multinationals can make a major contribution and win a lot of local respect if they do not wait to say this after the fact but rather offer their technical services to host countries as the planning and the program-setting process is under way.

The charge that multinationals are not really interested in transferring technology is echoed by indigenous managers. Nigerians, more than any others, tend to be suspicious in this area. But in all three countries, for example, managers were encountered who believe that their own companies are not sufficiently committed to encouraging local industrial development—by every effort to use local suppliers, for example, or by exploring in greater detail how to increase value-added activities. These managers, of course, are also more aware than many other local elites of the benefits brought by international business. But they are clearly cross-pressured and perplexed, as indicated in the comment by a Nigerian manager: "At this point in time, given the level of development in Nigeria, we desperately need the support of our international organization. We could not operate without the support of the company's purchasing agency. Until the Nigerian economy is more developed, we cannot look for more advantages. We are lucky to be part of this MNC. Of course, this relationship can be used to our disadvantage by unscrupulous firms."

These managers are often fighting on two fronts—headquarters in one direction; critics of multinationals at home in the other. Brazilian managers, for example, are well aware that the private sector there is being squeezed at least as much by the public sector as it is by the MNC's. They also know that the problem is frequently the mentality and the corporate work habits of local businessmen. In the words of a Nigerian manager, the local businessmen "want to reap where they have not sown." Nigerians agree with their Brazilian and Malaysian counterparts that local entrepreneurs lack experience and management skills; that their demands regarding return on investment are often rapacious. A Brazilian executive adds that even when the multinationals are interested in joint ventures it is difficult to find a local partner willing to put up capital—to take a long view about profitability rather than choosing to sell outright to the MNC. As for social responsibility, these managers overwhelmingly agree that the local firms and business community do not hold a candle to the behavior of the typical multinational firm.

But social responsibility is not to be confused with fine-tuning of overseas investment to local needs or aspirations, or to something as basic as technology transfer. Local managers allege that multinationals, including their own companies, are lacking in commitment to training locals and to providing them with optimal employment assignments and opportunities for advancement. It is no secret, for example, that in many U.S. companies overseas, some managerial positions (especially the managing director or chief financial officer) do not often go to the locals. Nigerians go beyond this to claim that the multinationals have been more successful at "Nigerianization"—placing Nigerians in senior corporate positions—than in insuring that these locals are adequately trained to do the job. The irony in Nigeria is the possibility, noted by many, that the local firms prefer to hire expatriate managers, while the foreign firms will eventually be forced to hire Nigerians exclusively. If this goes hand in hand with inadequate management training, the implications down the road are quite clear.

Nigerians are also hyperconscious about racism, subtle or otherwise. Whereas Brazilians allow that local managers demand and get the very highest salaries, Nigerians allege the existence of a double standard, even within one company. Nigerians say they are not accorded sufficient authority and respect, and that expatriates "who are no more than supervisors and have no management skills feel superior to Nigerians, even to Nigerian managers. They are often ignorant and prejudiced, and the companies tend to side with the expatriates."

But, again, these highly pressured indigenous managers are not unsympathetic to problems faced by the multinational firm. They agree with their expatriate colleagues that the worst local problem faced by the MNC's is uncertainty—especially with regard to the timing, content and administration of public policies affecting international business. One way out of this dilemma, they claim, is for the parent company to become more intimately involved with the local business and governmental communities. If this is not the habitual way of the multinationals, it will have to become so in the future. And there are potential rewards in doing this. For example, a young Nigerian manager of a British-based firm says: "If our company were here on a longer term basis, in partnership with Nigerians, there would be no reason to fear nationalization. It is the present corporate policy that makes the worst outcome more likely. By refusing to invest and develop a greater stake in the country, the company makes the possibility more likely that it will be badly treated here."

Sentiments such as these suggest that the multinationals should reexamine both basic corporate philosophy and operating modes as they pertain to overseas investment environments. One of the pressing and intriguing problems in this reappraisal is that of equity sharing.

Chapter 7
Joint Ventures, Equity Ownership, and Control

THERE IS STRONG EVIDENCE that 100 percent equity ownership of overseas multinational subsidiaries is rapidly becoming a thing of the past. Professor Richard Robinson of the MIT Sloan School has made a survey of entry policies for foreign firms in 15 host countries which reveals "almost universal pressure to force the spinoff of foreign ownership into domestic hands." In certain cases, "fadeout" requirements mandate majority local ownership after a specified number of years if incentives are sought, if the firm seeks to manufacture new products, to locate on new sites, or to establish new branches. In certain countries tangible rewards are also made available to firms that sell specified portions of their equity to the general public.[1]

A United Nations' survey of national legislation and regulations relating to transnational corporations also draws attention to the growing movement in developing countries in favor of increased local equity participation—although it finds that a relatively small number of countries sampled—six out of thirty-seven, including India and Mexico—actually *require* majority local ownership.[2]

Chart 10 shows that fully 75 percent of the respondents in this study believe that joint ventures between local companies and foreign firms and increased local equity holding in local MNC affiliates are desirable; almost half feel that these arrangements are not only desirable but essential.

---

[1] Richard D. Robinson, *National Control of Foreign Business Entry*. New York: Praeger Publishers, 1976, p. 320.

[2] Centre on Transnational Corporations, *National Legislation and Regulations Relating to Transnational Corporations*. New York: United Nations, 1978, p. 8. Required local equity participation was a key provision in the Andean Pact. See Robert Black, Stephen Blank and Elizabeth Hanson, *Multinationals in Contention*. The Conference Board, Report No. 749, 1978, Chapter 8.

Differences among the national groups are striking. Nigerians, for example, are much more likely than Malaysians or Brazilians to view joint ventures as both desirable *and* essential. Indeed, the first and second National Enterprise Promotion decrees described earlier form a cornerstone of Nigerian policy toward MNC's that makes levels of local ownership ranging from 40 to 100 percent a matter of firm public policy.

Chart 10: Joint Ventures and Local Equity Participation

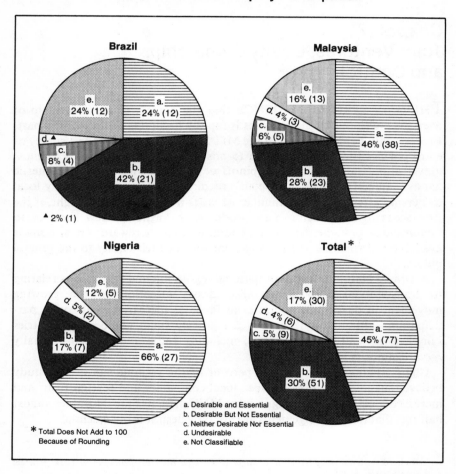

In Malaysia, equity-sharing requirements are critical, too, not only in terms of the regulation and control of multinationals but even more importantly as a means for helping to resolve basic racial tensions in Malaysian society. Brazilian respondents, although agreeing that increased joint ventures and local equity sharing are desirable, are less likely to believe that they are essential for national development. Few Brazilians feel that these arrangements are undesirable, but more than in the other countries, are aware of the potential disadvantages for the host country.

Brazil

Brazil—unlike Malaysia and Nigeria—does not mandate local equity participation in multinational ventures. Nevertheless, the Brazilian government, conscious of extensive criticisms regarding the "denationalization" of the private industrial sector, is clearly interested in encouraging more joint ventures and is stepping up pressures in this direction.

As is typical of host countries everywhere, certain sectors of the Brazilian economy (e.g., airlines, shipping, the mass media) are closed to foreign capital. Beyond this, the government is interested in protecting majority Brazilian ownership in key sectors such as mining, steelmaking, banking and insurance, and telecommunications. Indeed, the extractive sector is one where major Brazilian public corporations, like Petrobrás and CVRD, control all—or very large proportions—of existing enterprise. In the petroleum sector, for example, only very recently, and reluctantly, have the Brazilians issued a number of "risk contracts" permitting a few of the major oil companies to explore for offshore petroleum deposits. Where natural resources are involved, governmental policies are spurred not only by economic nationalism but also by the belief that past policies in this sector have encouraged exploration by foreign investors.

Concern about "denationalization" leads the Brazilian government to be acutely interested in the mode of foreign investment and reinvestment. Thus, while takeovers are not prohibited, they are severely scrutinized and generally frowned upon. Where takeovers involve healthy local companies—or where they do not clearly result in the injection of new capital or technology or encourage new exports—the government is likely to react negatively, perhaps by utilizing the wide array of instruments at its command to make life more difficult for that company.

The pressures for more joint ventures—with either private or state-owned local enterprise—are increasingly expressed in terms of the incentives or disincentives that the government will offer the foreign investor. For example, the government will not guarantee offshore loans where a majority of equity is owned by foreigners; wholly owned subsidiaries face greater restrictions regarding the remittance of royalties or dividends; they may not be permitted easy access to local funds; more important, they will receive less favorable treatment in competiton for contracts that are let by agencies of the national government. The other side of this posture is that multinationals willing to enter into joint ventures will sometimes be accorded unusually attractive incentives and benefits.

The Brazilian government is deeply concerned with the export-import profile of multinational enterprises located there. Thus, "functional" spin-offs may become even more important than equity spin-offs. The Brazilians have emphasized the "law of similars," which requires that preference be accorded to local components or products whenever they reasonably approximate what might otherwise be imported. As Robinson, in the study cited earlier, observes: ". . . it might come to pass that foreign-controlled firms could find themselves under considerable pressure to spin-off all divisible manufacturing processes for which competitive local subcontractors could be found. In this way, no ownership spin-off of the original firms might be required, but its functions would be transferred increasingly to national industry." (p. 321)

This underscores a point made earlier: The Brazilians do not make a fetish of local ownership, but cast the issue in the broader framework of national objectives. These objectives include strengthening the national economy in designated sectors, accelerating technology transfer, reducing imports in manufacturing, and expanding exports across the board.

Most respondents believe that the Brazilian government will *not* make equity sharing the prime issue for asserting its authority over the multinationals. The Brazilian approach is reflected in recent governmental decisions that place control of the minicomputer industry in the hands of four local firms as opposed to major international corporations that sought these contracts. Proponents of this solution argue that it should serve as a model for other Third World countries. They say that the decision establishes "national control yet minimizes the risks of showdowns with foreign companies over their divestiture of majority control. Instead of seeking control of the companies, Brazil has in effect set out to control the market"[3]

Brazilian government leaders are aware that the major impediment to joint ventures is often not so much the reluctance of the multinationals as it is the lack of local entrepreneurs who are willing or able to enter into such relationships. The locals may lack the expectations and expertise that large-scale corporate enterprise requires. They may be short on modern managerial talent, or lack adequate access to capital. Their demands regarding return on investment may be unrealistic. Their ability to hold up their end during periods of cash-flow crises or required capital expansion may be limited. In some cases, the local entrepreneurs may actually prefer selling out to the MNC to becoming associated with it.

In addition, some of Brazil's largest and most well-established industries—dominated by the leading Brazilian industrial families—may simply prefer not to enter into a joint venture with any foreign firm. Although this attitude has been changing in recent years, it remains a factor that has helped to produce fewer joint ventures than one might otherwise have expected.

---

[3]David Vidal, "Brazil Declares Computer Independence," *The New York Times,* February 19, 1978.

The government's awareness of this problem has led it to encourage a triangular system of joint ventures called *tri-pé* (tripod). This involves bringing a foreign company, a national company, and a public-sector company (or financial institution) into a triangular joint venture. The model presumably provides advantages for all sides. From the standpoint of the foreign investor, state involvement offers certain guarantees regarding the degree of local commitment to such enterprises and the readiness of the government to go to considerable pains to assure that they will not fail. Where the government is involved in *tri-pé* through one of its public corporations, this can mean considerable stability for the multinational partner in the provision of capital and raw materials. It can also mean built-in marketing opportunities in the form of guaranteed government purchases.

Private-sector partners offer the foreign investor knowledge of the local culture, and presumed expertise regarding the best way of dealing with often very complex relationships with the government. Furthermore, private-sector participation in joint ventures should serve to mute criticisms that the multinationals are hard at work "denationalizing" the indigenous industrial structure. Private-sector partners, in turn, are assured that the national government itself will guarantee that the hardest possible bargain is driven with the multinational partner and that there will be continuing interest in and oversight of the venture by the government.

For the government, the multinational brings in needed capital, technology and managerial know-how. The arrangement also answers the private-sector criticism that it is the public sector, much more than the multinationals, that has been squeezing out the national bourgeoisie in recent years.

Although the *tri-pé* formula seems to be ideal, actual experience with it has not been entirely satisfactory. In the first place, aggressive public-sector policies designed for further *tri-pé* are viewed by some critics as just another example of either further expansion of state capitalism or further concessions by Brazil's technocrats to the multinational community. Those who fear and oppose the further extension of state capitalism are quick to note that, since around 1967, state enterprises have increased their capital and reserves at a pace that dwarfs the progress registered by the multinationals. In fact, if the state sector is added to the private industrial sector in Brazil, it can readily be shown that the multinational share of Brazilian industrial investment has declined in *relative* terms over the last decade, even as MNC investment has grown *absolutely*.

In the second place, some *tri-pé* ventures foundered. Failures were usually associated with the inability of the Brazilian private sector to provide its share of capital requirements, or to a lack of sustained entrepreneurial interest in pushing an enterprise to the point of self-sustaining growth. Where the private-sector partner falls short, the result in Brazil tends to be that the public sector increases its share of the joint-venture holding.

Nevertheless, earlier failures have not been entirely useless. Some of Brazil's public corporations, having learned the necessary lessons, have proceeded to set up other *tri-pê* arrangements on a more careful basis. In Brazil's underdeveloped Northeast, for example, a number of the most challenging and ambitious industrial development programs involve the *tri-pê* scheme.

Although many multinational companies are uncomfortable in joint-venture arrangements in which one partner may be a gigantic public corporation, there is little reason to expect that this tendency will be reversed. Indeed, if the Brazilian private sector is unable to remain viable within the *tri-pê* format, pressures for more joint ventures will spawn more bilateral partnerships between the MNC's and the Brazilian public sector.

In the long run, Brazil will also pursue other means of encouraging local equity sharing. For example, legislation on the so-called "open-capital company" (a special form of limited company) provides some fiscal advantages for those who pursue this way of broadening local ownership in corporate stock. The intention of the law is not only to encourage wider equity participation but also to spur the development of domestic stock exchanges.[4]

Malaysia

Local equity sharing was not required by the Malaysian government in the early post-independence years. By the early 1960's, however, the government "expressed its preference" to foreign investors for greater local equity participation. Its policy was to encourage this by negotiating with foreign firms on an individual basis. But other goals, such as increased employment, were paramount and no rigid requirements regarding joint ventures or equity sharing were imposed.

Foreign firms are restricted in certain sectors. In agriculture, fishing and mining, for example, 51 percent local ownership is usually required. There is also growing pressure to ensure that all plantation and extractive companies are headquartered and controlled in Malaysia.

The NEP altered this approach. Restructuring equity ownership became a key dimension of the government's effort to reduce the economic imbalances among the ethnic groups.

The exact nature of the equity-sharing requirement—especially as it affects local and foreign companies already in Malaysia—remains unclear. Are the two goals of economic growth and restructuring actually compatible? Executives in companies operating in Malaysia wonder whether a 30 percent share to be made available to the Malay community, either

---

[4]One study of this arrangement concludes that the incentives are quite limited, and that the benefits apply to the MNC affiliate but not to the parent company. See Walter L. Ness, Jr., "Local Equity Participation in the Subsidiaries of Multinational Corporations: The Case of Brazil," unpublished paper, November 1973.

directly to individuals or "in trust" through various public or semi-public agencies, would fulfill their obligations, or if they would be forced ultimately to divest 70 percent of their equity to Malaysians. The Malaysian government emphasizes that no existing capital would be divested and that only new or expanded activities would be subject to these guidelines. But many query how "expansion" is to be defined in a fair and reasonable fashion.

Who does a foreign firm take as a partner? Individual Malays have little capital for investment. The most likely partners or purchasers of equity capital are government-sponsored corporations or trusts. The rapid expansion of government corporations like Pernas raise many questions about the role of the state in Malaysia—particularly about the role of the bureaucrats who run these agencies—and about the relationship between the public and private sectors of the economy. For some, at least, efforts to achieve the goals of the NEP are leading quickly to a form of "state capitalism." Widespread consternation about the expansion of state capitalism, noted in Brazil, can be seen emerging here.

Concern, as indicated earlier, reached new heights with the passage of the Industrial Coordination Act (ICA) and the introduction of "management shares" in the amended Petroleum Development Act. Local Chinese businessmen complained bitterly that the government was seeking to bring about the wholesale transfer of assets to the Malaysian community. Foreign investors were fearful of the government's new aggressiveness and rigidity. Some Chinese, seeking to fend off ICA pressure, urged the government to turn its guns on the foreign investor and concentrate on reducing the foreign-owned share of the economy rather than trying to force a Malay partner into a family-owned Chinese laundry or restaurant.

At the end of 1976, however, there were clear signs of a shift in government policy. Key civil servants now emphasized that the Ministry of Trade and Industry would exercise extreme flexibility in implementing and administering the ICA. For example, all manufacturing activities in existence when the ICA was enacted would automatically be granted a license. Similarly, neither new nor existing manufacturing operations would be required to meet equity or employment requirements before being licensed. The license would be issued first, and conditions would have to be met within a reasonable time.[5] To ease pressure on Chinese-owned businesses, small companies were exempted from equity-participation requirements.

Flexibility in implementing NEP and ICA goals should not be confused with retreat from the original NEP objectives. Somewhat to the surprise of local and foreign observers, Prime Minister Hussein Onn—who had pressed for less rigidity in implementing NEP goals—told delegates to the July, 1977 annual assembly of UMNO (United Malays National Organization) that he was staking his political future that the promises of the Third

---

[5] See *Far Eastern Economic Review,* May 6, 1977, pp. 38-40.

Malaysia Plan would be carried out. But as the country continued to fall short of interim Third Plan objectives, many observers wondered whether key NEP goals might be revised—particularly after the 1978 national elections provided clear evidence of Hussein's authority in the country.

Nigeria

Nigeria also requires local equity participation but, unlike Malaysia, its approach is inflexible. This is so in part because the influx of foreign companies into Nigeria makes lengthy negotiations impracticable. It also results from lack of experience and skill in the Nigerian civil service, which makes it difficult for the Nigerian government to carry on tough negotiations with many foreign companies simultaneously. Nigeria, however, is also deeply politically committed to local equity participation. If Malaysian policy is an instrument for coping with racial fragmentation, Nigerian policy is a dimension of deeply held convictions of economic and political nationalism. Nigerian nationalism—the desire for self-determination in every aspect of national life—is closer to the surface than in Malaysia, and at the same time less deeply implanted than in Brazil. Nigeria's indigenization policy is central to this nationalistic commitment.

One of Nigeria's leading statesmen, Chief Simeon Adebo, describes the equity-sharing policy as the logical and necessary culmination of an indigenization process that predates independence.

"What Nigeria has embarked upon is a voyage more hazardous than the Nigerisation of the civil service; it requires from all of us much greater faith than that earlier experiment. Decolonization involves not only the taking over of the political government of the country, the civil service, and the management of public boards and corporations, but also the indigenization of the public sector of the economy. Without this last development, independence would remain very much a shell without the substance. Both historically and by the nature of the case, the takeover of political control comes first, and then that of the civil service. Economic decolonisation is last and toughest of all."[6]

By the mid-1960's, the government's pioneer legislation for foreign companies was coming under increasing criticism. Opponents argued that it was too liberal, provided too many advantages for the foreign companies, and guaranteed too few benefits for Nigeria. The 1968 Companies Decree was seen by many as the first step in the direction of a more nationalistic policy. This was followed in 1972 by the Nigerian Enterprise Promotion Decree (NEPD).

[6]Chief Simeon Adebo, "The Challenge of Indigenization," unpublished speech delivered to The First National Conference on Management Development, Lagos: Nigerian Institute of Management, March 1974.

110

An American political scientist suggests that the NEPD was basically a highly conservative policy—a response by the government to the fear that it might be preempted by political and economic nationalists demanding a more radical policy. He notes: "The NEPD, therefore, can be seen—not as a significant shift of policy away from partnership towards nationalization—but as a means of maintaining the momentum of foreign investment in those areas where it was still deemed essential while at the same time avoiding the alienation of those sectors of the relevant Nigerian public which had come to associate foreign investors, rightly or wrongly, with economic exploitation and concomitant social ills."[7] In Nigeria, as in other countries, some of the seemingly most aggressive government policies may actually constitute a form of defense against more radical demands and policies.

One respondent, a prominent civil servant active in this era, suggests that the origins of the 1972 NEPD lay in the government's need "to respond politically to the feelings of the growing Nigerian business class—feelings that all business carried on in Nigeria was controlled by foreigners and that the government was not helping to change this situation." He observes that the government believed that if this feeling continued to grow, it might upset the entire development process which rested ultimately on expanding the indigenous Nigerian business sector. Thus, "the government had to take steps to secure and enhance the role of the Nigerian entrepreneurs, *without* damaging the overall investment climate."

According to this respondent, the task for the government in 1972 was to enable the Nigerian business class to own shares in foreign firms and to acquire a say in management, and thus to quicken the pace of training, skill development, and Nigerianization at senior management levels. Yet it did not want to prejudice the overall growth of the economy or injure the development of critical sectors where foreign participation was absolutely necessary. In addition, the government also wanted to encourage foreign firms to move from less to more technical concerns. The first indigenization program was designed to achieve all of these aims. The respondent concludes: "It reserved certain sectors exclusively for Nigerians; it was moderate enough so that the overall investment climate would not be injured; and it provided a substantial premium for foreign firms on increasing the technological level of their activities in Nigeria."

The NEPD must also be placed within the wider context of evolving Nigerian economic policy at this time. The NEPD should be seen as a complement to the Second Plan providing the nation with the means to realize many of the Plan's goals. Nigerian leaders were determined to enhance Nigeria's autonomy and its role as the leading Black African nation. Nationalism not nationalization: that was the key theme in Nigeria's economic policies in the early 1970's. It is a nationalism, however, not bent

[7] Andrew Hilton, "Foreign Investment in Nigeria," unpublished dissertation, University of Pennsylvania, 1975, p. 54.

on "going it alone" but on preserving good relations with foreign corporations while altering the balance of control in the economy.

Various observers suggest that the 1972 Decree was directed primarily against the Lebanese, Syrian and Indian traders who monopolized much of the smaller scale commercial life in Nigeria. These groups, who competed more directly with Nigerians, were the ones dispossessed by the demand for 100 percent Nigerian ownership in Schedule I of the 1972 Decree.

The 1972 Indigenization Decree established two categories of enterprises for local equity participation. The first category (Schedule I) reserved 22 types of enterprises exclusively for Nigerian ownership. These ranged from assembling radios to hairdressing, candlemaking, breadbaking and tire-retreading. Schedule II listed 33 types of enterprises that were to have 40 percent Nigerian ownership. Among these were department stores, real estate agencies, shipping and many lower level technology manufacturing industries. Most businesses requiring higher technology or elaborate organization were not included in either category and thus could remain wholly owned by foreign parents.

The government of Brigadier Murtala Mohammed, which replaced that of General Gowan in July 1975, was highly critical of what it saw as the failure of the Gowan regime to establish the domestic bases for the assertion of Nigeria's presence in Africa. The new leaders were deeply concerned about the seemingly pervasive corruption in the Nigerian civil service, and about the alleged failure of Gowan's government to secure greater benefits from the exploitation of Nigeria's vast, but wasting, oil wealth.

In November, 1975, an Industrial Enterprise Panel was set up to examine the Enterprise Promotion Decree, to report on its implementation, and to assess the extent to which the aims and objectives of the Federal Military Government in establishing the scheme had been achieved. The panel was also instructed to recommend amendments to the Decree with a view to expanding the enterprises affected by it, as well as increasing the level of indigenous participation in such enterprises. The panel's report, together with government comments on its recommendations, was published early in 1976. The report was highly critical of the implementation of the 1972 Decree: "The 1972-74 Indigenization exercise succeeded in a limited way only in the narrower and short term objectives of the scheme. In respect of the wider national policies and objectives of the Federal Government as spelt out in the Second National Development Plan and which formed the basis for the indigenization exercise, it is the considered view of the panel that the achievement of the scheme as implemented to-date fell short of expectations."[8]

[8]*Federal Military Government's Views on the Report of the Industrial Enterprises Panel,* Federal Ministry of Information, Lagos: 1976, p. 4.

The panel stated that only about a third of the firms affected by the Decree had fully conformed to its provisions; it called particular attention to cases in which the intent of the Decree has been circumvented, frequently with the active connivance of "misguided Nigerians." One result was that many fewer firms than expected had actually sold shares publicly; many more had placed 40 percent of their equity privately, often in the hands of only a few (or even one) Nigerian partners who, for their part, had often pledged to refrain from involving themselves in the management of the business. The result was the creation of a new class of "Mr. Forty Per-centers"—of "Lagos millionaires"—whose new wealth rested not on productive involvement in these businesses but on their willingness to serve as "fronts" for their foreign associates.

Although the published comments of the Government were much more moderate than the conclusions and recommendations of the Indigenization Enterprise Panel, the new enterprise promotion program announced in June, 1976 marked a significant escalation of the terms of the in-digenization program. This time, no exceptions were to be granted. The government moderated many of the panel's harshest recommendations. It also sought immediately to reassure foreign investors that the extension of the indigenization program did not represent a radical change of direction, but rather the continued and gradual assertion of Nigerian control over its own economy.

The government did accept one of the panel's most important recom-mendations—that future indigenization regulations should impose an upper limit to the amount of shares a single Nigerian can own in an individual enterprise. The limit was placed at 5 percent, thus building into the new indigenization program a strong commitment to the democratization of share ownership in the country.

Foreign investor reaction to the new program was mixed. Many were surprised at the severity of the new Decree and most felt that the panel's findings were—at least—unbalanced. One U.S. bank departed precipitously when it decided it could not meet the new equity-sharing requirements; other companies continued to negotiate with the government for an ex-ception. At least one of these, a U.S. company, left when it became evident that satisfactory arrangements could not be worked out. Most, however, stayed, although all worried about the prospect of a third round, especially following the promised return to civilian rule and open politics.

Elite Responses

How do the elites in each of these countries feel about these official policies? How do those individuals who are influential in the policy-making process assess current requirements regarding joint ventures, equity par-ticipation and control?

Nigerians, Indigenization and Local Control

Nigerian elites participating in this study strongly support the indigenization program. Only two Nigerian respondents claim that they are opposed, although several others wonder whether the government made a tactical error in raising the requirement for local equity ownership to 60 percent in Schedule II in the second indigenization Decree. One, a government planner, observes that 51 percent "might have accomplished all of the desired goals without appearing to be so radical."

But these views are definitely in the minority. Few individuals express any serious reservations about the accuracy or the interpretation of the Industrial Enterprise Panel's data, and few seem to question the contention that the second Decree was necessary because the impact of the first had been undermined by the collusion of foreign firms and corrupt civil servants. Few perceive the indigenization program in narrowly economic terms, or feel that the capital spent to purchase equity in foreign subsidiaries might be better invested in other ways.

Nigerian elites see the indigenization program in essentially political terms, as an assertion of Nigerian nationalism. Yet almost none of them wish to see the multinationals leave Nigeria. They are more likely to express anger and exasperation at those firms that complain about the terms of the program or threaten to pull out of Nigeria unless they get special treatment.

There is a very severe lack of consensus among Nigerian elites with respect to the objectives of the indigenization program. And even among those who agree on the desired ends, there is argument that the program as currently conceived does not provide the most suitable vehicle for achieving these goals.

The most serious differences exist between those who see the objective of the indigenization program primarily as enhancing Nigerian influence within foreign companies and those who seek to extend equity ownership more widely in Nigerian society. This disagreement emerged most clearly in the debate over the government's decision in the second Indigenization Decree to limit to 5 percent the equity any individual could own in a single foreign corporation. The most vociferous opponents of this proposal were local business leaders who urged the extension of the indigenization program but who wanted no limitation on individual Nigerian equity holdings. They argued that the 5-percent limitation would prevent Nigerians from increasing their influence in the foreign corporations by forcing the dilution of local equity holdings into tiny parcels.

Some civil servants take an opposing view. They contend that the growing inequality of wealth in Nigeria, which was increased by the implementation of the first Indigenization Decree, constitutes one of Nigeria's most urgent social and political problems. For them, the primary objective of the indigenization program must be to secure the widest possible distribution of ownership and wealth within the Nigerian community.

A few respondents argue that there is no necessary conflict between these goals. A banker observes that "one is really a shorter and the other a longer term goal. The egalitarian goal takes longer to achieve. It is more a residual effect of achieving greater influence and participation in the first place." However, more respondents see a clear trade-off between the two objectives. Another businessman admits that widening the base of ownership is an important aim. "But when it comes to a particular company, it would be foolish to spread the shares so widely that Nigerians would have no possibility of exercising influence on management. In fact, the 5-percent regulation ensures that the existing expatriate management will be cemented in power."

Others, more frequently in government or the academic community, say that Nigerian businessmen have not shown nearly as much interest in corporate decision making or management as in collecting dividends and serving as silent partners for foreign companies. They fear that further concentration of wealth and power might lead to severe social conflict.

Some who oppose the 5-percent limitation speak of the longer range need to create an indigenous business class that would provide the foundation for a capitalistic society. A certain level of economic inequality is necessary, they say, for that class to develop. A manager in a major multinational affiliate emphasizes this: "If we are going to have a capitalist system, we must—at least until the economy becomes crystallized in Nigerian hands— have the financial capacity to engage in entrepreneurial activities. This means that shareholding and wealth must be sufficiently concentrated to provide for the development of an indigenous entrepreneurial class."

These differences appear to exist in the highest levels of the Nigerian government. None of the participants in the study feels that the government has yet come down definitely on one side or the other. The 5-percent limitation was put into effect in the January, 1977 Decree, but government spokesmen continue to emphasize the need to stimulate local entrepreneurial development. An official in the planning ministry says that the government remains uncertain whether it should push for more rapid entrepreneurial development or for a wider distribution of ownership. "The government is aware of these conflicting goals but at the present time a 'government view' does not exist." A senior adviser to the cabinet takes the view that outside observers are attempting to read too much into the government's policies, and that the government's aim is simply to aid Nigerian business. He says: "The primary goal of the program is to give the local economy, the local producer, a boost. It is to give the indigenous entrepreneur an advantage to the extent that this can be done. The program's motives are not nearly as complex as people are trying to make them out to be. Our aim is to encourage Nigerian entrepreneurial development. That is the primary goal of the program."

In the view of several local businessmen, the essential aim of the indigenization program is to put more Nigerians into senior management positions in MNC affiliates. "Shareholding is relatively meaningless," one notes, "unless Nigerian ownership can be translated into a real part in decisions."

While almost all Nigerians feel that local control of the economy is insufficient, few feel that this can be remedied by increasing the government's role in corporate affairs. Only one respondent says that the goals of the indigenization program might be better accomplished if the government purchased equity shares in foreign companies (as in Malaysia) and held them in trust for individual Nigerians. Few suggest that more extensive government control and regulation is an acceptable alternative means of heightening local interests in these companies. For the most part, Nigerians seem to be as reluctant as foreign managers to encourage greater government involvement in the private sector—although an emerging generation of politicians may have different ideas.

Requirements for greater equity participation and increased local involvement in corporate decision making raise a problem for one group of Nigerians—those who are managers in the foreign firms. All want to see greater local equity participation, but several worry about the consequences in the shape of outside influences on corporate policy and decisions.

Thus a senior Nigerian manager in a major British-owned firm, who strongly supports the indigenization program, says: "At the same time, we as staff are also concerned about the possibility of undue influence being exercised on our management as a result of the indigenization program. We see that wholly indigenized and publicly owned companies in Nigeria do not do so well. They are much less efficient than we are, and they are more subject to political pressures. We feel that indigenization could lead to this, depending on the political situation."

Another Nigerian manager of a foreign company stresses that Nigerian managers inside these firms will behave more responsibly than outside shareholders, or new indigenous members of the board of directors. He wants to see the influence of Nigerian managers inside these firms increase, but fears that outsiders—local shareholders or new members of the board— will only be interested in increasing their dividends. "It is the Nigerian managers inside the firm who will want to see these changes through. I will want our board of directors to reflect the balance of equity ownership *eventually,* but I don't want a crash program for more indigenous control that might ruin our business."

Malaysians and the NEP

Malaysians universally applaud the goals of the NEP, including the provisions for local equity participation. Almost everyone interviewed agrees that the equity-sharing policy is designed primarily to widen the base of ownership in the Malaysian economy and not to undermine existing management control. Malaysians make a clear distinction between ownership and control. A European manager stresses the point: "What the Malaysians want now is ownership, not control. They wll be quite happy to have the foreign firms' management and control for the foreseeable future."

Malaysians are, of course, interested in greater local control, but this is seen as a longer term goal. A top civil servant acknowledges that the Malaysian government is well aware that foreign investors want to maintain control. "But in terms of our global targets of 30-40-30, there must be some firms that have less than 50-percent ownership in their operations here. We realize that this might make Malaysia less attractive for foreign investors. That is why we tell the foreign investors that they have to gear themselves to a situation in which the professional managers run their companies, not the shareholders—at least in the foreseeable future."

Malaysian elites may stress both flexibility and the longer term, but the foreign investor wants to know what the longer term will be, and what equity arrangements will then be preferred. Well-informed Malaysian respondents predict that the MNC's will have to accept minority status sometime in the future. A Minister in the Malaysian government says: "Yes, the foreign investor will *ultimately* play a minority role. I cannot see that this country will continue to have its economy dominated by foreign companies. We will say 'Good luck to you. You have done well, but now it's time for local firms.' Maybe foreign firms will not even hold a minority interest in time."

For the present, the Malaysian approach is summed up in the words of a top civil servant, with responsibilities for working with foreign investors: "We try to be very flexible. We particularly want to know what the foreign company can do in five years and what it projects for ten. We do not ask the impossible. We recognize that no single rule can apply. But we want to know the method that will be undertaken to comply. We recognize that the method may well be complex—because the situations are often complex. For example, we might permit restructuring at the holding level rather than at the subsidiary level—or vice versa. But we want to be sure of the company's commitment to the overall objective."

Unlike the Nigerians, Malaysian elites seem to agree on the objectives of the NEP. There is much more disagreement among the Malaysians, however, with regard to the implementation of NEP policies. Many see a different type of trade-off: not between two different objectives of the indigenization policy, but between NEP goals for social change and economic goals. Malaysians worry that the commitment to restructure the economy might defeat plans for more rapid economic growth. A Chinese Malaysian businessman voices these concerns: "Without growth you can't restructure. But some companies may not be allowed to grow unless they restructure. There is a clear danger in this. If government policy is interpreted rigidly, the end result may be stagnation."

In this regard, who will own the local equity is clearly a vital question. The issue is salient in Malaysia, as it is in Nigeria. The difference between these countries is that government corporations, semigovernmental agencies, cooperatives and trust funds play a far greater role in Malaysia— acting in trust for the Malay population—than in Nigeria.

The rapidly expanding role of the public sector in Malaysia disconcerts many, Malays as well as non-Malays. A leading Malay banker, for example, expresses a strong preference for equity participation by Malay cooperatives and trusts over public corporations acting in trust for the Malays. "It is essential that the government mobilize Malay capital, rather than using public funds from tax revenue. In the cooperatives, all of the money is truly Malay money. On the other hand, Pernas's money comes entirely from tax revenues. If the government uses these funds—that is, revenue from all of the Malaysian communities—in order to buy shares for just the Malay community, we don't know what will happen in the future. The government could say Pernas is holding shares it had purchased for the Malays. But by 1990, it might revoke this mandate." And a senior member of the government echoes this concern: "We are really conning the Malays," he says, "into believing that all of this is Malay money, when it is actually government money raised through taxes from the entire Malaysian community."

Even Malays are fearful of the government's empire-building tendencies and are concerned about the government's ability to control the various semi-public agencies and corporations that act as trustees for the Malay community. Some feel that the government has already gone into competition with individual Malays to purchase shares in foreign companies and local businesses.

Disinvestment raises many problems, too. When will the shares now held in trust be made available to individual Malays? How will this be done? What guarantee is there that it will ever be done? The same member of the government quoted above observes: "I am very much concerned about the distribution of these shares to individuals. Can the government really *sell* these shares to individuals. Will we? It will not be easy to get around the vested interests. And I think that mass participation by Malays also poses dangers. We cannot just turn over all of these shares to Malays. That will not help our economy. What we need is a period during which business-minded Malays will emerge—from the bottom, not from hothouses like Pernas."

There is widespread agreement among Malaysian elites that the government has been too rigid and too zealous in interpreting NEP objectives. A leading Malay politician states that: "Thirty percent is not a magic figure. It is more of a guideline. At times, even 20 percent would be enough if the investments are strategic ones." Not everyone believes that the government can achieve this flexibility. A Chinese businessman is afraid that "the leaders of the government have made so much noise about 1990 as the target date that the goals are possibly inflexible."

Malaysians, like Nigerians, also fear that the equity participation program will accentuate economic inequality among the local population. This may become a particularly severe problem within the Malay community. The program designed to alleviate economic inequality *among* the racial communities may wind up creating much greater inequalities *within* these groups. One local Malay businessman says: "Suddenly, the Malay community possesses a huge chunk of wealth, and the extremes of rich and poor within the community are as great—and probably more extensive—than in the other Malaysian communities."

As in Nigeria, some respondents say that the equity-sharing program encourages Malays to act as fronts for their foreign, or even Chinese-Malaysian, partners. Tales of "Ali Baba" partnerships are commonplace. With limited skills and experience, the temptation is strong for any Malay who can get in on the ground floor to capitalize on government patronage. Many observers feel that this situation is changing. A recent report quotes one Malay millionaire as saying: "The process tends to breed Chinese multimillionaires, but no matter, more and more we find that there are Malays who can handle the complex businesses that they would not consider even 10 years ago."[9] And, as in Nigeria, the belief that development requires the emergence of an indigenous entrepreneurial class leads many to accept greater inequalities of wealth, even within the Malay community. Many acknowledge the dangers inherent in this approach, but believe that development cannot proceed in any other way.

For Chinese-Malaysians, the equity-sharing program in the NEP poses both risks and opportunities. The most serious risk is that demands for restructuring will be extended to the vast number of smaller Chinese businesses. (Malays are quick to point out that "small" refers normally to the amount of paid-up capital, not to the actual business carried out so that "small" Chinese businesses may actually be quite large.) Many Chinese businessmen worry that they will not be able to expand their businesses—for, if they do, they will then fall under NEP provisions and be required to take in Malay partners and employees. On the other hand, equity-sharing requirements for foreign companies raise the possibility that much of the locally held equity will ultimately fall into Chinese hands. This has happened in the past, according to respondents.

The dilemma faced by the Chinese-Malaysian community is becoming more complex than this, however. The Chinese have been smugly certain that the Malays would not adapt successfully to modern economic life, and that the Chinese businessman would retain his leading position in the Malaysian economy. Malays, however, have proved to be capable of participating in the most technologically sophisticated and complex sectors of the economy and, with the aid of the government, have, in fact, leap-

---

[9]"Outgrowing their proverbs—the Bumis can do it," *Far Eastern Economic Review,* September 2, 1977, p. 57.

frogged over the Chinese, who remain locked into the least modern and dynamic sectors of the economy. So the Chinese face what a senior civil servant, an Indian-Malaysian, terms a "terrible dilemma." "The Chinese can keep hold of what they have now. However, the Malays are taking over all of the modern sectors of the economy—those that will grow in the future—and the Chinese are locked into sectors that cannot grow. The alternative is to participate much more actively in the NEP, but this means handing over initially 30 percent of the ownership of their businesses to Malays. If they do this, then they might not have anything left. If they do not, they might not have anything left. So it is all a terrible dilemma."

Brazil and Joint Ventures

Brazil stands in sharp contrast to Nigeria and Malaysia on this issue. Because it is much more industrialized, because it has a fairly strong indigenous industrial base, and because the Brazilian public sector is already heavily involved in industrial production, national policies on equity sharing are quite different.

Brazilian policy stresses joint ventures between the multinationals on one side and Brazilian firms—privately or publicly owned—on and the other. Indeed, from the standpoint of control over local corporate decisions, the Brazilian formula would be much more restrictive of parent-company freedom than either the Nigerian or the Malaysian approach. The Brazilians do not want just a piece of the financial action; they want control of the company as well.

It is significant that Brazilian elites who comment on joint ventures express considerable interest in assuring that these arrangements are more than a sham, that they will give local interests more control over MNC affiliate activities as they affect benefits and the overall direction of the Brazilian company. A wide range of Brazilian elites interviewed for this study favor more joint ventures, but also express skepticism and reservations, particularly with regard to the present joint-venture policies and strategies of the Brazilian government. Their doubts can be summarized as follows:

(1) Local firms involved in joint ventures get into lopsided relationships they cannot adequately control—or sometimes even understand. Thus, a well-informed Brazilian economist says: "Joint ventures may be utilized as a mechanism of control in favor of the interests of the host country. In practice, however, it has not worked well. There is a tendency for the stronger partner to bring along a conception of how the deal should be defined."

(2) Even where local entrepreneurs are in a majority equity position, they do not really control corporate decisions. A Brazilian businessman contends that many joint ventures with an ostensible Brazilian majority frequently involve other agreements that restrict the powers of the majority partner. The

joint venture itself does not resolve the enormous differences in the wealth, experience and power of the partners.

(3) Joint ventures are not necessarily an adequate technique for assuring the transfer of technology. Technology transfer is one area, a Brazilian bureaucrat comments, where foreign MNC's often refuse to provide Brazilian majority partners with real equality. Prior accords tend to establish guidelines acceptable to the foreign company. Several Brazilian respondents also complain that typical joint-venture arrangements can tie their country to an outmoded or inappropriate technology and thus limit its longer term growth potential. In the words of one government official: "The advantage of the joint venture is that it allows us to produce here what would otherwise be imported. The disadvantage is that joint ventures generate dependence in other areas."

(4) The cost to Brazil of some joint ventures is considerable because the arrangements permit the MNC's to receive substantial incentives for which they would not otherwise qualify. A technocrat—whose responsibilities cover petrochemicals—says that in his experience the multinationals gain more from joint ventures than the local partners. He says: "I'm not all for joint ventures. The capital that foreigners bring is actually very small, if you consider the total amount of capital involved in a given project. In general, it boils down to 10 to 17 percent of the total costs and, because of this, the foreigners are entitled to benefit from goverment incentives."

(5) Respondents argue that because the private entrepreneur is normally the weakest part of the *tri-pé* system, the state enterprise will inevitably expand into the vacuum on the Brazilian side. An economic planner notes that while the MNC brings technology and foreign markets into the deal and the state enterprise provides capital, the private company frequently represents only weakness. In this sense, the private entrepreneur can serve as a "front" for the expansion of state enterprises. A local businessman says that the MNC's are jeopardizing their own longer term interests by taking part in these arrangements: "The MNC's are making a mistake. Even though they gain a larger space to maneuver in by associating with state enterprises, they are diminishing the possibilities of developing private initiative in Brazil."

Several respondents suggest that, as in Nigeria, the greatest long-term value to Brazil from joint ventures with foreign companies is the pressure these arrangements enable the Brazilian side to apply with regard to the placing of locals in top management. A former senior member of the Brazilian cabinet underscores these sentiments: "If I were the Minister of Finance in Brazil, I would send the MNC's a list of qualified Brazilian managers and ask them to choose those who will run the local operation from this list. I would compel them to do this. The best way to nationalize the multinationals is not nationalization. It is not to take it over, but to make sure that the local managers are Brazilians."

Chapter 8
Elite Evaluation of National Policies

LEGISLATION and regulations about equity sharing constitute only one aspect of a host-country's policies toward multinational corporations. Views of host-country leaders are likely to affect broader policies related to foreign investment. For the firm seeking to get its bearings with regard to the nature and level of risk to its overseas investments, it is crucial to know how these individuals feel about existing foreign investment policies in their countries, and what new policies they would like to see put in place.

About 50 percent of all those interviewed say that their government's policies dealing with foreign investment and MNC's are "about right"—although this figure includes significant national variations. Three-quarters of the Nigerians and almost half of the Malaysians—but only a third of the Brazilians—characterize their country's policies in this fashion (Chart 11.)

A large number of Malaysians—mainly Chinese businessmen and government officials—say that their government's policies are too restrictive. About one-eighth of the Malaysian respondents believe that policies are too liberal—a view shared by twice this proportion of Brazilians.

About one-fifth of all of the elites interviewed say that national policies are confused. Most of this group feel that benefits for the host country arising out of MNC operations are limited or inadequate because government policies are not well-conceived, are not implemented effectively, or are mutually contradictory. In actual numbers, half of these are Brazilians.

A closer look at these responses by elite category—especially when public- and private-sector elites are separated—reveals certain interesting, although not entirely unexpected, findings (see Table 18). A larger proportion of public-sector than private-sector elites in all three countries affirm that FDI and MNC policies are about right, although the difference is substantially greater in Brazil and Nigeria than in Malaysia.

Brazilians in both the public and private sectors are much more likely than Malaysian or Nigerian elites to be critical of their country's policies regarding foreign investment and foreign firms, and, in particular, to insist that these policies are confused. Most interesting, however, is the very substantial proportion of *private-sector* leaders—more than a third of all the Brazilian businessmen and bankers interviewed—who say that government policies are *too liberal.*.

Malaysian and Nigerian private-sector elites are much more likely than their Brazilian counterparts to support government policy as it now exists. In Malaysia, however, a substantial segment of elites complain that government policies are too restrictive: Some 40 percent of the private-sector leaders and about one in seven of the Malaysian public-sector leaders are of this opinion. A surprisingly large proportion—about one-sixth—of Malaysian public-sector elites complain that their government's policies with regard to foreign firms are confused. This may reflect the communal tensions within the civil service, and the cross-pressures felt by non-Malay officials more than anything else.

Chart 11: View of Own Country's Policy Toward MNC's

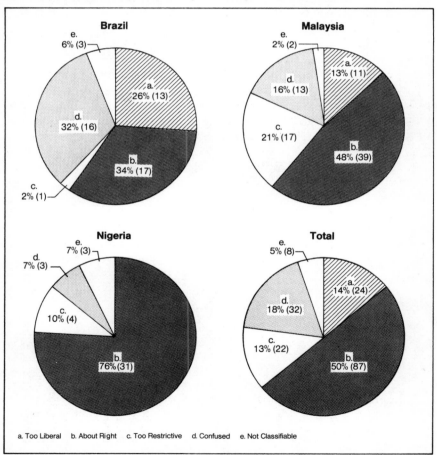

a. Too Liberal   b. About Right   c. Too Restrictive   d. Confused   e. Not Classifiable

Table 18: Elite Perceptions of Their Country's Policies Toward MNC's

Elite Category	View of Policy				Total	
	Too Liberal	Too Restrictive	About Right	Confused	(Percent)	(Number)
All Respondents:						
Public Sector	10%	7%	63%	20%	100%	81
Private Sector	9	22	50	19	100	54
Intellectuals	46	23	23	8	100	13
Mass Media	20	0	30	50	100	10
Trade Unions	60	0	40	0	100	5
Other	0	50	0	50	100	2
						N = 165
Brazil:						
Public Sector	16%	0	52%	32%	100%	25
Private Sector	35	0	29	36	100	14
Other	50	12%	0	38	100	8
						N = 47
Malaysia:						
Public Sector	10%	14%	57%	17%	100%	42
Private Sector	0	42	50	8	100	29
Other	50	7	14	29	100	14
						N = 80
Nigeria:						
Public Sector	0	0	100%	0	100%	14
Private Sector	0	12%	69	19%	100	16
Other	0	25	75	0	100	8
						N = 38

The respondents were also asked what direction they preferred to see policy take in the future (Table 19). A third of all respondents (and particularly, those in the public sector) want to see their government conduct tougher negotiations with multinational corporations in the future, even though almost all of these individuals value the MNC's and want them to stay. They are convinced that benefits can be enhanced by harder bargaining on the host-country's side, and they urge their government to pursue this strategy.

What benefits in particular are sought by this group? Interviews confirm that technology heads the list. One-half of those who want a tougher bargaining stance rate technology as the key input that the multinationals can provide. It is likely, therefore, that the prime host-country goal in future negotiations will be greater technology transfer.

A smaller group of respondents (13 percent of the total and mainly Brazilian) emphasize the need for their governments to ensure that multinational programs are more closely integrated into national development plans. A similar size group (13 percent), primarily Nigerians and Malaysians, want policies that produce greater local equity participation. And a slightly smaller group (11 percent)—mostly Nigerians—feel that indigenization of local management should be the primary goal of national policies.

Brazilians are particularly insistent about better integration of the MNC's into their planning schemes. To further this goal, considerable research has been conducted by the Brazilian government on the role of the MNC's in the Brazilian economy. This has led, for example, to growing pressures on the MNC's to spell out their medium-term plans—and how these plans (as articulated or modified) can be made to dovetail with overall national planning targets.

Table 19 shows that only one person of the 173 interviewed feels that the first task of government in dealing with foreign firms should be to cooperate with other Third World countries in creating better balance of power in the world economy vis-á-vis the multinationals. The stress is not on benefits to the Third World as a group but, rather, on benefits to their own country. Not even the intellectuals, who might be expected to take a broader view of the "collective interests" of the Third World, place any stress on this point.

Elite Responses

These statistical summaries can be fleshed out by a careful sampling of what the respondents from each country actually say.

Brazil

Respondents in Brazil are least happy with existing policies. While only one respondent evaluates policies as too restrictive, a quarter say they are

Table 19: Preferred Future Policies—Primary

Policy	Brazil		Malaysia		Nigeria[1]		Total[1]	
	Number	Percent	Number	Percent	Number	Percent	Number	Percent
Harder bargaining..............	16	32%	31	38%	10	24%	57	33%
More equity sharing	4	8	8	10	10	24	22	13
More indigenization[2].........	3	6	6	7	10	24	19	11
Integration of MNC's into national plan	11	22	7	9	4	10	22	13
Exclude all or sectors; takeover MNC's	6	12	4	5	2	5	12	7
Less rigid policies	—	—	12	15	1	2	13	8
More emphasis on private sector	3	6	5	6	—	—	8	5
More Third World cooperation...	—	—	1	1	—	—	1	1
Other......................	—	—	2	2	1	2	3	2
Indeterminate or none.........	7	14	6	7	3	7	16	9
Total.................	50	100%	82	100%	41	100%	173	100%

[1]Percentages do not add to 100 because of rounding.

[2]In Nigeria "Nigerianization."

too liberal, and fully a third feel that current Brazilian policies are confused (Table 18). It must be stressed again that this latter group is anything but hostile to the presence of MNC's. Indeed respondents often underscore their beliefs that confused and incoherent policies are in themselves frequently the reason for some of the misunderstandings and frustrations that characterize relationships with the foreign investor.

There is fairly widespread agreement among the Brazilian respondents that where objectives are clear and agreed upon, their government's policies are usually effective. A young technocrat reflects this: "Some controls are effective, others are not. In the case of projects in which the government is the purchaser, either the multinationals associate with national groups or they do not do business here. In all areas in which the government is a purchaser of goods or services from the multis, our policy is one of gradual national control, starting with the production of components. Thus, there is a series of mechanisms to control the MNC's activities. Even though these mechanisms are not entirely cohesive internally—there are breakdowns here and there—as a whole there is coordination."

Brazil has traditionally preferred to deal with foreign investors on a case-by-case basis, relying on flexible policies rather than comprehensive laws or codes. It is precisely this approach, respondents say, that has contributed heavily to the failure of the government to define more clearly its basic goals, and the role it wants the foreign investor to assume. According to a Brazilian civil servant, the failure of government to define sectoral goals adequately is a major reason for "denationalization" of the private sector: "The government doesn't have a position on the role of foreign companies in various sectors of the economy, or the proportion each of the main actors—state firms, national firms and foreign firms—should have."

Other government officials frame the problem more broadly. One observes: "We don't really have legislation on foreign capital. We have a very open economy and, from the legal point of view, we are not prepared to face the problems that multinationals bring. Many of the defects, I have said, are not theirs. They are ours; the government's." Another adds, "We still do not have the legal instruments to regulate the multinationals. This country is still like grandma's backyard. And, since we don't know how to organize, and have no clearly defined goals on our agenda, we don't tell them what we want them to do, and they do whatever they want."

Lack of coordination and competition among government departments and agencies is said to constitute a major hindrance to more effective regulation of foreign firms. A banker says: "A global policy dealing with foreign investors presupposes coordination among all organs of economic policymaking. Such a thing does not exist! It is even difficult to establish a coherent policy in Brazil for one sector of the economy."

Relations between the federal and state governments is just one dimension of the problem, but one of particular urgency. A federal bureaucrat observes that the federal government has adopted a more selective policy toward multinationals than have the states. He complains: "At the regional level, they give everything they can to the foreign companies, thus breaking through the federal system of control." A businessman adds that, because the government does not yet have a clearly defined regional policy, there is competition among the states and between the states and the federal government. "The result is that the state governments have set up their own mechanisms to attract foreign investment. This is the case of the state of Minas Gerais, where the government offered a lot of incentives for several major projects. Minas totally broke with federal policy. The state government was right from its own point of view. If there is no definition by the federal government, the possibility is open for the states to offer incentives of their own."

Some feel that lack of administrative and negotiating skills within the government are a critical weakness. "From the point of view of establishing firmer government control, it is necessary to improve our human resources in the bureaucracy so that our people can carry on a dialogue at the same level as the 'foreign invaders.' We, too, must have the capacity to negotiate and, if necessary, to confront the other side. The multinationals have far greater capability in their ranks: They not only absorb people with higher qualifications but also people who have access to the upper decision-making levels. They offer better working conditions—higher salaries, for instance." Another Brazilian comments: "It is possible to live with the MNC sector. But the state enterprises have to be prepared to carry out a dialogue with them. And for that they need good technicians, well-prepared engineers, economists, lawyers, and so on. There is no argument against know-how."

In the end, several respondents come back to the initial problem—the failure to define policy objectives clearly. This leads, some say, to severe conflicts among the government's most urgent economic objectives. A young banker makes the point that a very critical issue is raised by the government's determination to utilize foreign investment as a main driving force for economic growth and, at the same time, to tighten its control over MNC activities and operations: "I don't see how the government will ever be able to impose stricter control over profit remittance, royalty payments, sourcing and so on when the government itself is committed to a policy of increasing the involvement of foreign companies in many sectors of the economy." The result of these conflicts, respondents say, is that the government has failed to adopt more selective or rigorous criteria for evaluating proposals made by foreign companies. And foreign firms are found in sectors where their participation is no longer justified—where there is no lack of local technology or capital.

Members of the local business community echo these conclusions, if not the analysis leading up to them. The continuing "denationalization" of the Brazilian private sector causes bewilderment and anxiety not only among Brazil's smaller producers but also among the "multibillionario" families that are themselves very large-scale industrial and financial operators in the country. Some of these families already have extensive joint ventures with foreign firms; but this does not keep their leading spokesmen from condemning governmental policies that appear to be squeezing out the local private sector. This situation leads one industrialist to say: "Because we are a national enterprise, the government fails to help us as it should. There is no disposition in the government to support national industry. Such support is essential in terms of making the Brazilian entrepreneurs more conscious of their role and more capable of acting to defend their interests. Up to now, we have had a totally unrealistic policy toward national industry."

Allegations of this kind bring members of the indigenous industrial community closer to critics on the political left, who argue that the policies of government create greater and unwarranted Brazilian dependence on outside nations and their financial and industrial organizations. The overwhelming support for the Brazilian Democratic Movement (MDB) registered in the state of São Paulo in the elections of 1978 reflects a confluence of anti-government feeling among industrial as well as intellectual and working-class groups in that important part of the country.

Government officials who are the objects of these changes question their validity. They insist that the years since 1964 cannot be described objectively as an era of increasing governmental permissiveness toward the foreign investor, and they add that the managers of the MNC's are entirely aware of this. These officials insist the government has moved slowly but resolutely in the direction of rationalizing policies and procedures pertaining to the MNC's, but without arousing fears that Brazil is bent on making the country a problematical or unattractive environment.

An officer of the Bank of Brazil says: "We have an investment policy; it is not true that we lack one. We let foreign capital come in here and choose for itself the best field to enter. We said that we would establish new policies later. Now it is time to do this; from now on we will have tougher policies here. No more letting people in automatically."

A technocrat responsible for monitoring the export profile of foreign firms indicates that the government will proceed with kid gloves, but that the gloves will cover an iron fist:

"We are going slowly with the foreign firms. We can't just say to them: 'Look, you're simply going to export.' But the government has enough power to make life miserable if they do not export. If the multinationals are responsible for one-half our trade deficit, they will hear the following message from us: 'If you help us, we will help you. If you do not help us, then it is the market law for you, with no help from us.' We will say you can import all you like, but there will be no incentives given. We cannot deny any of these companies the right to grow, but we can make the process of growing more expensive."

Brazilian civil servants say that they will remember which of the foreign companies operating in Brazil were willing, at critical junctures, to aid the government and to take some risks with the government. They will be especially friendly toward those companies that are willing, to the best of their ability, to assure that their overall trade balance will be positive each year, and that loans the companies incur outside of Brazil will be paid off entirely in the course of the special program they have contracted with the government.

While most Brazilian respondents express concern that their government is not yet negotiating forcefully enough with foreign companies, many expatriate managers in these firms see definite signs of change. A top executive in a British-based company says: "So far, Brazil has been a very easy country to operate in. There are few restrictions, and the political climate is very friendly to international investors." But, he adds: "The situation is beginning to change. There is pressure on foreign exchange. I would expect pressures for Brazilian participation in new ventures. And nationalism is sweeping all over the developing countries. There is a growing realization of the strength—and the potential strength—of Brazil as a nation."

An American expatriate in Brazil agrees that the multinationals will come under much additional pressure: "I'm sure the multis will have to duck. They will also have to play by the rules that the government makes." He adds: "I don't think the multinationals can ever be stronger than the government. They will be less and less so. So, decision making and profitability will be based more and more on the conditions and restrictions in the host country. More and more, production will have to be brought here."

A second American businessman expresses his expectations summarily: "The Brazilians are not going to run out the multinationals. But they now know where and how to put on the pressure." And a U.S. government official reports hearing a senior Brazilian administrator say: "We are squeezing the multinationals very hard now, especially on export-import. I want you to know that we will continue to do this. We cannot permit the MNC's to ease off. After a time, it is necessary to call in the managers of these companies and give it to them right between the eyes. The MNC's will accept it. We are going to tell them that incentives now are going to be based on cooperation and compliance."

If Brazilian officials appear tough-minded, they are also respected as fair and, above all, as extremely competent. Most expatriates affirm this high quality. One, a Swiss, observes of the federal agency that deals with export incentives: "CACEX over the years has mounted an information system that's as good as the CIA. They have full information on prices—the international prices, the prices of pirated materials, the prices in Italy, everything. They keep pushing the prices down. CACEX is very much in the saddle. They know what they are doing."

Few foreign businessmen believe that Brazilian governmental policies and administration suggest abandoning that country. "From a business or U.S. government point of view, there's nothing wrong with these laws. It is no more than the U.S. government would insist on. The Brazilians want foreign investment to be consistent with their economic plans and goals. But their laws should not discourage the foreign investor."

The expatriate managers interviewed in this study acknowledge that Brazil's posture toward the foreign investor will become more severe in the future. They quickly add that they believe the MNC's will have to learn to cope with more insistent pressures—for more joint ventures, greater exports, higher levels of technology transfer, and so on. They feel it is highly unlikely, however, that the Brazilian government, even a civilian government, will adopt a radically different "model" of economic development than the one that has prevailed since 1964.

The changes already in process will present new challenges for all multinational firms, and for American firms in particular. Firms will have to be more knowledgeable about Brazil if they are to participate successfully in tough-minded bargaining and negotiations with Brazilian officials. It will be essential to gain greater understanding of the developmental goals of Brazil, as well as of the conflicts and tensions, inside and outside the government, that the setting and implementation of these goals entails.

As one American puts it: "The bureaucracy here is a monumentally difficult thing to deal with, but it can be done. Typically in the United States you will fill out the forms and you will send them in and you will expect that, if you have done it correctly, you will get what you have coming and in good time. Here the bureaucracy has tremendous power to deal with you personally. They can make exceptions and they can give exemptions. They do not necessarily follow their own guidelines. What it boils down to in the end is a negotiation inside the government. It is difficult to describe this to a management at home that wants it all laid out in advance. They want to know from us what are the rules—what the rules mean for the company. It is very hard to tell them that what the rules are and what will happen in negotiation are not necessarily the same thing."

Malaysia

The communal issue in Malaysia makes the assessment of local attitudes toward government policies regarding foreign investment more complex than elsewhere. For example, many Chinese in both the public and private sectors would not mind seeing tougher policies directed toward foreign companies, especially if this took some of the heat off them. But most fear that such policies might serve as all-too-convenient levers for Malay administrators to intervene in Chinese businesses. Some Malay officials may, in fact, be more concerned with increasing pressure on the Chinese community than with restricting the activities of foreign companies.

These Chinese fears may well be unfounded. By the end of 1976, Malaysian leaders representing all ethnic communities had come to feel that the government had gone too far in its effort to implement NEP goals. A third of the private-sector elites who express views on the future direction of national policy would prefer government policies to be less rigid in the future. Just under 15 percent prefer future government policies that place greater emphasis on the private sector of the economy. The majority of these individuals—most of whom are Chinese businessmen—say that they are reacting to what they see as the excesses of the Industrial Coordination Act (ICA). Even so, about half of the public-sector and almost a quarter of the private-sector leaders who commented on this issue urge tougher bargaining with foreign firms.

One official, who has experienced a long and arduous negotiation with foreign firms, highlights this demand for a tougher posture: "We must acquire more knowledge. We must use information sources that are not affiliated with the MNC's. We must not be made fools of. If necessary, we must spend money to acquire more knowledge. The posture to be adopted from now on is to take an extreme stand first because the multinationals also take extreme stands. Never agree with them on the first negotiation. They talk of all sorts of things—use all sorts of figures to try to overwhelm us. But they cannot wear us out if we are patient."

This degree of suspicion and hostility is unusual. Many more respondents talk about longer term trends in which changing needs and capacities give rise naturally to new policies toward the foreign investor. Thus, two ministers in the current government separately note that while Malaysia found it necessary at the beginning of the process of industrialization and development to accept any investment, the situation is now changing. One of them says: "If you look at the First Plan, you see that we tried to get anyone and everyone in. But things began to change in the second half of the Second Plan and in the Third Plan. We began to look for smaller companies: medium-sized companies. We tried to diversify our involvement with foreign investment to avoid depending on a few large companies or on a few parent countries."

The second minister emphasizes the role of the public sector: "During the period of the First and Second Plans, the government felt that the roles of the private and public sectors of the economy were distinct. It was the role of the public sector to provide the infrastructure for economic activity and then to stand back and allow the private sector to come in. But is is clear that this cannot continue for too long. Our early policies led to rapid but inequitable growth. We now have a mixed policy, with more deliberate public-sector intervention, particularly with regard to the structuring of ownership and employment. In this atmosphere, multinational corporations find certain difficulties in meeting our aspirations."

A pattern emerges in Malaysia not unlike that in Brazil. As the host country develops greater administrative capability, its self-confidence grows. That self-confidence is inevitably reflected in a greater propensity on the part of public-sector technocrats to intervene in all aspects of direct foreign investment.

On the other hand, regulatory tendencies, as in Brazil, are neither irrational, excessive nor rigid. Typically, demands for tougher bargaining are coupled in Malaysia with a commitment on the government side to maintain responsiveness and, above all, to ensure that the investment climate remains favorable. A top-level technocrat, charged with heavy responsibility for economic planning, represents this approach very well: "Even when foreign investment does pick up in Malaysia, we should bargain much harder at the beginning of the negotiations than we have in the past. We can determine the terms of investment at the beginning. But once we have agreed on terms, we should not change the rules in the middle. What foreign firms want most is certainty. They don't mind harder bargaining, but they really object to changes in the rules. They want to have confidence that the rules will remain stable."

Malaysian elites, like those in Brazil, are careful to note that many of the problems regarding the foreign investors lie with the indigenous national governments and not with the multinationals. Thus an elder statesman in the civil service notes that the country has never clearly defined the role it wants the multinationals to play because it has no focused industrial policy. Where expectations are unclear, it is always easy to argue that the benefits that the MNC's bring are insufficient.

In Malaysia, as in Brazil and Nigeria, the federal system of government often inhibits more coherent and effective policies. Thus, some Malaysian respondents note that the lack of understanding and coordination between the federal government and the states undermines more effective foreign direct investment policies. In the words of a regional bureaucrat: "The federal boys do not understand the states. They treat all of these states alike—lump them all together. The same regulations are applied to rich and poor states. As no two states are alike, policy must be adjusted to each particular situation." The other side in this debate is equally pointed. Federal officials often have little patience with regional leaders who appear entirely self-serving, or who are incapable in any case of incorporating the national view in their thinking. These federal officials complain that the states compete with one another for foreign investment and undercut federal policies designed to control the multinationals.

Other Malaysians, especially those who are the most dissatisfied with government policies toward the multinationals, emphasize the heterogeneity of Malaysian society, and particularly the racial cleavages that continue to distract the attention and sap the energies of national leaders. According to many expatriate managers, as well as Malaysians themselves, Malaysia's racial heterogeneity gives rise to conflicting objectives regarding the multinationals. Foreign direct investment is perceived as an absolute requirement for continued economic growth; at the same time, the multinationals are required to share their equity locally. Critical economic objectives are thus dependent on continuing foreign investment and on maintaining a favorable investment climate; at the same time, the quality of the investment climate may well be sacrificed, at least to an indeterminate degree, in order to achieve critical social goals. A top government official observes: "These are very legitimate issues. The Plan *is* very woolly. What does it mean to say that we will implement the goals of the Plan within the context of growth? What is growth? Who defines it? And how? As long as these things are not well articulated, we are forced to work on a case-by-case basis. To me, it is all very confusing."

Considerably more frequently than in Brazil, Malaysian elites emphasize the problem of policy implementation. The governmental administration remains sufficiently compact so that coordination within the policymaking process does not pose such enormous problems as in Brazil. In addition, rather more than in the other two countries, Malaysia's political leadership has retained comprehensive control over policymaking. But how is policy finally delivered? This is the point that draws the critical attention of Malaysians and non-Malaysians.

A leading member of the government, when asked how he feels foreign investors view Malaysia today, responds: "The major concern of the foreign investors here is with *predictability*. They say: 'We accept the goals of the NEP and equity sharing. But what about the different interpretations of these goals? What are we actually required to do? Will the rules change in years to come? Is there one uniform interpretation or can every minor bureaucrat make his own?' "

Many respondents continue to worry about the ability of the government to control the civil service, and about the politicization of the bureaucracy along ethnic lines. Some of these comments reflect a major change in the role of the public administration in Malaysia. At independence, Malaysia inherited an administrative corps closely patterned on the British model. A key norm of this model is the concept of neutrality—the idea that administrators steer clear of open political involvement and use their professional skills to set policy alternatives for their political leaders, and then administer those policies as they are chosen. Much of this, many respondents observe, has changed: The British model is no longer the ideal. New, younger administrators have adopted instead the norm of "guardian bureaucrats": They see themselves as guiding Malaysian development and exerting a much greater influence on the course of policy development. Several respondents take the view that these younger officials were responsible for pushing the ICA, and say that senior officials and political leaders are loath to tangle with them because of their influence in Malay communal politics.

Some respondents disagree strongly with this diagnosis, however. The real problem, they say, has to do with the quality and experience of the bureaucracy—not with new norms or ethnic politics. The fact is that post-colonial developments brought new administrative problems unheard of during the colonial days. Ambitious, complex programs of economic development and management confront inexperienced administrators with unprecedented challenges.

Multinational corporations, as a major factor in these developmental schemes, pose extremely difficulty administrative problems. The importance of the issues at hand, the sheer difficulty of working with such complex organizations as the multinationals, and the relative inexperience of local officials, create a situation in which passions rule and policies are made without adequate thought for their consequences. A member of the Malaysian government observes: "When you sit across the table from these people, who represent the largest and most powerful firms in the world, you feel that you are dealing with such expertise and knowledge that you are automatically on the defensive. Yet you represent the host country and you must defend what belongs to that country. Thus, there is a tendency for the host-country bureaucrats, who are often young and inexperienced, to over-react."

Another official, who has a broad responsibility for dealing with foreign companies, disagrees with the idea that the civil servants are overzealous in their efforts to implement NEP goals. Bad management skills are much more of a problem than political commitments, he says. The civil service has not kept pace with the economic development of the country or with the growing complexity of public policy. He adds that if there is a problem of "overzealousness," or something like it, it should *not* be blamed on the younger and more junior officials in the ministries. If such problems exist, it is because members of the government push lower-level administrators in this direction.

Some expatriate MNC executives feel that the impact of new norms and patterns of administration in the civil service is entirely pernicious. An American executive, for example, observes: "We see a new breed emerging, more nationalistic and more Malay oriented. It all changed during the previous administration. From our point of view, we are dealing with new faces and new attitudes. Our initial negotiations were tough, but very pragmatic. The corporation felt comfortable with those people. Now there is a whole new ball game. The people on the other side and their attitudes are all very different now." Others say that, from their point of view, the changes in the civil service have been more rhetorical than real. A British manager says: "If you didn't *hear* what they were saying, you would never think that this was a bad place at all. They make very tough statements, but the practices are really not that difficult to get along with."

For foreign firms just coming into Malaysia, there is less uncertainty. Requirements are reasonably clear and the two sides can bargain within this framework. A Malaysian involved in this process insists: "They must play poker with us and we can bargain with them." The situation of firms already sited in Malaysia may be more problematic. Here, many respondents emphasize, there is greater uncertainty as to what the rules are, how they are going to be interpreted, and what are the responsibilities on both sides. Firms in different sectors also get different messages. The extractive sector will almost always be treated more severely than manufacturing companies, particularly those with higher value-added export potential.

Almost every expatriate manager in Malaysia agrees that the danger of communist insurgency is overrated by headquarters executives. They strongly disagree with the idea that Malaysia will suffer seriously from communist guerrilla activities. Few, however—at least at the time the fieldwork for this study was carried out in 1978—had much sense of the possible consequences of the revival of Islamic militancy in Malaysia, although many of the signs of this were already highly visible. Most were reassurred by Hussein Onn's administration and felt that the Prime Minister had recognized their complaints and was seeking to improve the investment climate.

Nigeria

Nigerian elites are significantly less likely than those in the other countries to criticize their government's policies regarding foreign investment and multinational corporations. Three-quarters of the Nigerians who respond to the question about government policy (31 out of 41 interviewed) say that these policies are "about right." This includes all of the public-sector elites. About 12 percent of the private-sector leaders say that government policies are too restrictive, and almost 19 percent complain that policies are unclear. On the whole there is strong approval of the direction of national policy, moving (at least in Nigerian eyes) gradually but firmly to assert local control of the Nigerian economy, while at the same time preserving good relationships with those foreign investors who are prepared to adjust and adapt to the Nigerian environment.

Nevertheless, a number of respondents express concern at the lack of clarity of policy objectives. This is most consistently expressed with regard to the indigenization program, but the concern is directed to other governmental policies as well. The fear is not that restrictive policies, but that confusion and lack of coherence regarding them, is causing extraordinary difficulties for foreign investors.

For example, a leading economist now active in business, says that many Nigerians in the private sector feel that the government has failed to assign meaningful priorities to the various objectives it hopes to achieve in dealing with foreign firms. He asks: "What is the goal of the indigenization program? Is it control of the economy? Certainly the program has resulted in more indigenous ownership. But it has produced no more control over the economy or over foreign firms than there was in the past. Are the purchasers of the equity shares of the foreign firms really entrepreneurs? Not at all. What must be done is to stimulate Nigerian *entrepreneurship,* not just ownership. What is the relationship between the government's commitment to greater equality of wealth and more rapid economic development? Greater equality is obviously an important goal. But should it be given the same priority at this moment as more rapid growth?''

Several respondents in the public and private sectors relate this lack of clarity to a more general problem of goal setting in the Nigerian economy as a whole. A former civil servant takes reinvestment as an example. Many Nigerians, he says, feel that foreign firms do not reinvest a sufficient amount of profits made there. He argues, however, that reinvestment is actually more a problem of the way in which the Nigerian government manages its own investment policy and, in particular, the investment policies of those key industries in which it exercises primary control. If the government encourages sufficient investment in such state-controlled industries as steel and petroleum refining, the private sector—and the foreign sector within it—will take its lead from the public sector. If the Nigerian government's efforts at economic management are unsuccessful, if overall economic objectives are confused and contradictory, if the public sector itself is poorly managed, then, he says, the government's policies with regard to the foreign sector cannot be much better.

For many Nigerians, criticisms of foreign firms represent failures in government policies. Foreign firms are scored, for example, for their reluctance to devote greater effort and resources to upgrading indigenous skills. These companies, it is said, are more willing to give Nigerians top positions than to help them acquire meaningful skills. But the failures on the government side are also well-recognized. A leading business consultant and former senior government official observes that the Nigerian government has made no systematic effort to develop a more active manpower training program. "Whatever can be said about the multinationals," he concludes, "they are still doing more than the government itself."

Nigerians are also well aware of how severely problems of infrastructure and lack of skills in the civil service can impinge on policy implementation. If the most elementary forms of communication are faulty—or lacking altogether—even among ministries and agencies of the government, the policy process is bound to be in frequent disarray. Similarly, while Nigeria boasts of relatively large numbers of highly educated and trained personnel, at least by Third World and African standards, the drain of top manpower out of the federal government and into the newly created state administration has been severe, and the flow out of public-sector service and into the private sector is perhaps even more serious. Few Nigerians interviewed failed to place corruption high on the list of severe problems, too. All of this imposes an enormous burden on the government in carrying out even those policies that are well-conceived to begin with.

The problem of governmental shortcomings can be delicate and volatile, especially when they are indiscriminately voiced by exasperated multinational managers. Nigerians are not unwilling to discuss these matters, but they are deeply resentful of what they feel are one-sided or sensationalist renderings of "horror stories" about life in their country. Nigerians, they say, do not have to be told—especially by a foreign businessman—that the telephone system is unreliable at best and that mail simply vanishes into a void. Most Nigerians interviewed feel that the foreign media have made little effort to present a "balanced" picture of the country and have often dramatically overstated its problems. A Harvard-educated Ph.D. in economics, now in the planning ministry, comments that U.S. newspapers are "illiterate about foreign countries and completely uneducated about Nigeria."

The perception that foreigners fail to comprehend what is happening in Nigeria today, and the demand that foreigners deal with Nigeria much more on Nigerian terms in the future, motivate the attitudes toward government policy of many of the respondents in this study. A senior official in the Central Bank emphasizes: "Nigerians realize that they need the cooperation of the multinational corporations, but this must take place on a truly cooperative basis. Nigerians are aware that companies must have the opportunity to make profits, or else they will not stay here. But it must be clear that Nigerians will set the priorities for economic development. Foreign companies can come into Nigeria to help realize the objectives established by Nigerians."

If public-sector elites press for tougher negotiations with the MNC's, private-sector leaders more often express preferences for policies to increase still further required levels of local equity participation and local participation in management. Many leading Nigerian businessmen want the government to ensure that they—and not the MNC's—will be in the driver's seat in the economy. They do not want government to preempt that seat, however. Thus, they tend to seek government policies that will speed the development of an indigenous entrepreneurial class. Highly individualistic and aggressive, the Nigerian business community is fighting to avoid being ground between the public sector and the foreign corporations—what has happened, in the view of many observers, in Brazil. The problem is that the local business community simply lacks the necessary resources to accomplish this task and is required to rely increasingly on public-sector funds and government policies. The same pressures that make the private sector vulnerable in Brazil are clearly at work in Nigeria.

How do expatriate managers, in and outside Nigeria, assess all of this? Multinational managers participating in the study underline the uncertainty of the current environment. Some insist that Nigeria is totally erratic in terms of policy affecting foreign firms. Most foreign businessmen with greater experience in Nigeria, however, point to the longer term development of current policies and suggest that the trend of government policy toward foreign investment has been fairly steady, and moving gradually in a nationalistic direction. But the upcoming transition to civilian rule causes even many of the wisest of Nigerian hands to hedge their bets, at least for the moment.

Basically, many expatriate managers echo the comment of a manager of a British-based firm. It is quite simple, he says: "The price of entry has increased. If you want to come in now, you have to pay the price." Whether a foreign company is prepared to pay the price depends largely on its estimate of its economic potential in the country, the impact of government policy, and the likely result for the foreign sector of the return to civilian rule (or, indeed, the impact of the failure of that process.)

Corporate Policy and Practice: More Stringent National Requirements

A clear conclusion emerges from the data treated in this chapter: While multinational corporations are viewed in fairly positive terms in these three developing countries, they will be subject to increasing demands by host-country governments to increase the benefits they provide for these countries.

Asked: "Who should control multinational corporations?", the overwhelming reply of respondents is that this is a task for host-country governments. Only Malaysian respondents suggest that self-regulation would provide an appropriate form of control—and fewer than 3 percent of the entire group of respondents say that home-country governments should have the primary authority for controlling their multinationals. For more than 80 percent of the respondents, there is simply no question that host-country governments should exercise this responsibility, or that multinationals should look primarily to the host-country for guidance (Table 20).

In these three countries at least, multinationals will live to an ever greater extent in an "environment of negotiation" in which increasingly active, skillful and aggressive host-country leaders (mainly but not solely in the government administration) offer a wide range of benefits and threaten an equally wide array of penalities for corporations that do—or do not—conform to host-country policies, programs and aspirations.[1]

The elites interviewed in the study do not, however, anticipate radical alterations in their governments' policies toward foreign investment and MNC's, at least not in the foreseeable future. The issue of technology transfer is fundamental, everywhere, and, despite its recognized complexities, it will remain high on the agenda of host-country leaders who bargain,

---

[1]These conclusions are similar to those drawn by Professor Richard Robinson in his examination of the entry policies of 15 developing nations: "It became clear in the course of our study that national goals imposed on the entry of foreign business were becoming increasingly sophisticated, pragmatic, honest and effective." Richard D. Robinson, *National Control of Foreign Business Entry*. New York: Praeger Publishers, 1976, p. 320.

Table 20: Attitudes on Control of MNC's

Source of Control	Brazil		Malaysia		Nigeria		Total	
	Number	Percent	Number	Percent	Number	Percent	Number	Percent
Home country	—	—	3	4%	1	2%	4	2%
Host country	47	94	55	67	38	93	140	81
Self-regulation	—	—	15	18	—	—	15	9
Indeterminate	3	6	9	11	2	5	14	8
Total	50	100%	82	100%	41	100%	173	100%

Table 21: Probable Future Policies Toward Foreign Investment

Likely Future Policies	Brazil		Malaysia[1]		Nigeria		Total[1]	
	Number	Percent	Number	Percent	Number	Percent	Number	Percent
Favorable, more moderate	3	6%	14	17%	2	5%	19	11%
Favorable, more restrictive	5	10	10	12	—	—	15	9
Favorable, more predictable	1	2	12	15	—	—	13	8
Unfavorable, in general.	—	—	—	—	—	—	—	—
Unfavorable, by sector	—	—	—	—	—	—	—	—
Unchanged.	33	66	34	42	34	83	101	58
Indeterminate	8	16	12	15	5	12	25	15
Total	50	100%	82	100%	41	100%	173	100%

[1] Percentages do not add to 100 because of rounding.

negotiate and deal with multinationals. It is also reasonable to expect that as host countries like Malaysia and Nigeria reach higher levels of industrialization—like Brazil—they will get touchier about profit remittances. Corporate financial practices constitute a third area in which more stringent requirements can be anticipated, although this study suggests that there is substantially less concern among host-country elites about these matters and that they are quite confident that they understand these practices and, within reason, can control them.

It is important to underline that in one of these three countries, Malaysia, a substantial number of respondents—mainly in the private sector—would like to see less stringent requirements on foreign companies. Finally, about 10 percent of all respondents feel that no additional requirements are necessary.

About 58 percent of all respondents say that their government's policies are not likely to change in the foreseeable future. More than 27 percent expect that future policies will be more favorable to foreign firms, although almost a third of this group feel that these policies will also be more restrictive. (Greater stringency in requirements for foreign companies is *not* necessarily equated with hostility, and host country leaders indicate that in many cases foreign companies can gain substantial benefits by conforming to more stringent requirements.) Not one person anticipates that foreseeable policies will be relatively more unfavorable to foreign investment (Table 21).

National variations, once again, are interesting if not conclusive. More than 82 percent of the Nigerians (34 of 41 interviewed) say that future policies will be unchanged; 66 percent of the Brazilians say this, too; but only 42 percent of the Malaysians make the same statement, although it is the most frequent response from each country and from the total. Almost 44 percent of the Malaysian respondents indicate that future policies toward foreign investment will be relatively more favorable, although a substantial number of these individuals say that these policies will also be more restrictive.

Part Three

Chapter 9
Overseas Investment

THIS PART OF THE STUDY deals with the operational side of MNC's in developing countries. It constitutes a more detailed discussion than one provided in an earlier report.[1]

Investment Strategies

Viewed from multinational corporate headquarters, investment in the less-developed countries implies a significant allocation of capital and high-talent manpower. However, these are not among the advantages of foreign direct investment most frequently singled out by host-country leaders. These persons suspect that even initial multinational investment rarely involves a significant inflow of new capital. Where required financing is generated in local capital markets, governments are accused of failing to ensure an adequate flow of capital to indigenous entrepreneurs. Where financing is in the form of external debt, the consequences to the host country (for example, debt-service ratios) are frequently viewed as troublesome.

Increasingly, host-country governments set limits to external financing as well as to multinational access to internal capital. They typically require foreign firms to obtain prior authorization to raise capital locally. In addition, these governments will scrutinize intracompany financial arrangements with a view to increasing the proportion of an overseas investment that is registered as new equity rather than as intracompany loans. Income- and investment-repatriation plans that turn on intracompany debt service are scored more and more often as involving double losses to the host-country—first by adding to the balance-of-payments deficit, and, second, by reducing the level of corporate profits subject to local taxation.

More stringent regulations reflect a general desire to tighten control over the national economy. Exactly what form such controls should take, and precisely what effect controls will have on net inflow of foreign capital are

[1] Joseph LaPalombara and Stephen Blank, 1977.

144

matters widely debated among host-country leaders. Resolution of these issues inevitably turns on structural and environmental considerations that are not only economic but, more often than not, political as well.

Brazil provides a striking example of how economic and practical considerations interact. The petroleum crisis of 1973 greatly exacerbated Brazil's balance-of-payments difficulties. Even at sharply reduced levels of economic growth, dependence on petroleum imports pushed the nation's cumulative foreign debt to disturbing levels. Debt-service ratios that consume half or more of the country's foreign exchange earnings are alarming not only for the international banking and corporate community but for those who hold political power in Brazil as well. Where balance-of-payments deficits are seen as a major factor in domestic inflation, the political pressures on government to institute still more restrictions on the multinationals become irresistible. Indeed, the international financial and corporate communities themselves become major factors pushing the government to adopt more stringent regulations. Limits are set on the access of foreign firms to local capital markets or to special credit arrangements; foreign borrowing and intracompany debt limits are more severely discouraged; and the traditionally hostile posture toward royalty payments and similar fees continues unabated.

Brazil's attitude is that foreign firms, recognizing the country's developmental potential, should register their confidence and expectations in the form of increased capital transfers from parent companies to subsidiaries. Indeed, the government that took power in the Spring of 1979 is committed to a substantial modification of existing incentive schemes and restrictions involving foreign corporations. Within the next five years the 100 percent, 360-day interest-free deposit on imports will be reduced to 50 percent. A number of incentives provided earlier by the Committee for Industrial Development will also be sharply reduced.

Brazil's leaders are betting that by the mid-1980's the country will be a major factor in the international economy and less in need of the kind of regulations that have prevailed during the last decade or more. However, this deregulation will be matched not only by capitalization requirements (such as those suggested above) but also by new and significant pressures regarding equity sharing.

Malaysia and Nigeria present somewhat different pictures. In the first place, in the medium term, they will not join Brazil as major independent actors in the world economy. Secondly, until recently both of these countries were among the few capital-rich nations in the Third World. Even today—notwithstanding sharp balance-of-payments deficits and the need to secure several massive offshore loans—Nigeria's currency, the Niara, remains remarkably firm and has been further buoyed by the rise in oil prices. In any case, the export capacity of both nations, based on extractive and plantation resources, will continue to assure that capital shortages are not the most important bottlenecks to further economic growth.

For Malaysia and Nigeria, then, not capital but organizational skills, access to foreign markets and, above all, technology are considered the most valuable contributions the foreign direct investors can provide. Where capital as such becomes a problem, the issue turns on difficulties experienced in mobilizing and directing it to the indigenous private sectors. Particularly in oil-bloated Nigeria, the generation of risk capital outside the public sector is a major governmental concern.

In both Malaysia and Nigeria, public-sector officials are more willing than others to trade off capital inflows against technology transfer. Because they value capital less, they stress such multinational inputs as management contracts, licensing arrangements, turnkey and fade-out contracts, and so on. Nigerian officials are increasingly reluctant to permit packaged loans for specific projects in either the public or private sector; they favor instead large-scale, undifferentiated direct loans to the government generated by international financial consortia.

Not surprisingly, private-sector leaders demur. Nigerian businessmen and Chinese entrepreneurs in Malaysia are not quite so confident in the judgment and managerial capacity of government officials. Nigerian businessmen in particular believe that loans to the federal or regional government encourage erratic investment behavior. They are sharply critical of foreign firms that seem to abet this pattern—indirectly if not directly—when they fail to enter the Nigerian economy with more capital of their own. The international banking community, insofar as its lack of knowledge or timidity leads it to prefer to lend to governments, contributes heavily to this distorted pattern.

One Nigerian, who makes an excellent income by bringing foreign companies together with local partners, notes that the multinational practice of coming in with minimum capital and repatriating it as quickly as possible creates a series of conflicts. First, there is conflict over who in the arrangement will put up how much. Second, there is similar conflict whenever expansion requires additional capital. Third, this practice underscores the underlying conflict of views as to what is the most desirable way for a foreign firm to enter a local market. On the corporate side, of course, there is the reverse complaint that Nigerian local partners want to obtain the required 40 or 60 percent of the action without putting up any capital at all.

There is extensive agreement among participants in the study that non-equity arrangements, except in clear and limited situations, are unsatisfactory on both sides. A Nigerian lawyer with considerable experience in these matters calls attention to the *political* side of the problem. If the foreign firm, he says, does not put enough hard cash up front, it is difficult to persuade the government, or the critics of multinationals, that the company is really serious about doing business in Nigeria. Undercapitalization from abroad signals a lack of confidence in the country, an unwillingness to show that the foreign investor has a real stake in Nigeria's future.

The Influence of Home-Country Governments

It is true, of course, that parent companies are not entirely free to accommodate this need or demand. Their investment strategies reflect *home-country* governmental policies and regulations. Countries like Britain, France, Sweden and Japan do not hesitate to regulate foreign investment when adverse balance of payments seem to require it.[2] Even the United States, which prides itself for greater permissiveness on this score, has responded similarly in the face of balance-of-payments deficits.

If the United States is more liberal on overseas investment controls, American business claims that the Federal Government is substantially more rigid than other governments with respect to reporting and taxation requirements. The overall impact of these home-country regulations is manifestly difficult to measure. But the fact that they affect investment strategies is evident in the wide variety of issues involving the multinationals that come up in bilateral negotiations between home- and host-country governments.

MNC's from Different Countries

From the perspective of host-country elites, the investment strategies followed by U.S.-based MNC's are not strikingly different than those pursued by other multinational firms. Basically, the leaders believe that foreign firms will try to come in with as little cash as possible and hope to take out as much in profits as the traffic will bear. More thoughtful respondents do not moralize about this, but simply argue that the host country should drive tougher bargains, at least up to the point where foreign direct investment itself begins to shrink.

Nevertheless, there are some stereotypes expressed in their responses. Some Nigerian elites in the study think that U.S. firms in particular make "impossible demands," or that they "are particularly concerned not to risk their own money." But such attitudes are relatively rare, and almost never articulated in Brazil or Malaysia. Insofar as practice may support the claim, the tendency is based less on American investment strategies per se and more on other factors.

For example, American firms are understandably less familiar with Africa than are their European counterparts. They are likely to be more uneasy about investments there, less confident about the *political* prospects of a country like Nigeria. Furthermore, as many host-country leaders and

[2]C. Fred Bergsten, Thomas Horst, Theodore H. Moran, *American Multinationals and American Interests*. Washington, D.C.: The Brookings Institution, 1978, pp. 32-40.

corporate managers point out, American companies looking at the U.S. market generally have a wider range of investment options than do their European competitors. Where the need for capital is high, and American confidence in the overseas investment environment is low, management will inevitably seek higher rates of return from capital before acting at all.

There is a widespread feeling overseas that American managers can be distinguished from the European and Japanese along several attitudinal dimensions that relate to investment strategy. First, the Americans are identified as having much more rigid expectations regarding return on investment (ROI). Europeans, it is said, are willing to live with lower profit levels, even with longer and more problematic pay-back forecasts. Second, Americans are held to be more likely to say: "Do it our way or we won't play." Third, American managers are said to be immensely more legalistic than the others. Particularly in the Third World this propensity creates a certain amount of bewilderment among host-country elites—and perhaps some lost opportunities for the U.S. firm. Some of these national differences among MNC's tend to be reflected in other aspects of corporate philosophy, organization and behavior as well.

Joint Ventures

If host-country pressure for equity sharing is universal, willingness of multinational firms to respond favorably to such demands is not. Few managers of any nationality prefer joint ventures as an operational strategy. Uniformly, respondents recite a litany of problems and disadvantages created by equity-sharing arrangements with private- or public-sector partners overseas. Given these difficulties, it is entirely understandable that, wherever possible, the multinational corporation will prefer that its overseas subsidiaries be wholly owned by the parent company.

But the investment environment is rapidly changing on this score. Particularly in the developing countries, political pressure to assure that indigenous groups and organizations share in the ownership of modern industrial enterprise is very strong.

Multinational corporate response to these pressures seems to vary by nationality. American companies included in this study generally fear joint ventures more than Europeans, and American managers will go to greater lengths to resist them. At the rhetorical level, U.S. managers often insist that they will actually abandon a market before taking on local partners. European managers almost never say this. Moreover, where joint ventures *are* undertaken, Americans seem less comfortable than Europeans as these arrangements unfold in corporate operations abroad.

Host-country elites pay close attention to the rhetoric. The American posture seems to reinforce local beliefs that the United States likes to throw its weight around, and that American corporations do not make an unequivocal commitment to sharing in the problems, as well as the profits, of industrial development in the Third World.

There are some ironies here. For example, perception and practice do not always coincide. In Nigeria and Brazil, American firms, in fact, do *not* lag behind European counterparts in their willingness to enter joint ventures. What is true for Brazil can be generalized to all of Latin America; by and large, the U.S. firms will be similar to the Europeans in adjusting to the changing conditions and requirements for operating abroad.

Nevertheless, the image of American rigidity about joint ventures is reinforced when some of the largest, most prominent, and powerful U.S. firms not only talk publicly about refusing joint ventures but sometimes actually abandon a given country. Events of this kind are quickly picked up by the media, and the impression is created that what may be true of only a handful of American companies is typical of all of them.

An important problem in joint ventures turns on majority and minority equity control by the parent. Here American verbal resistance to minority shares seems to coincide with practice. European firms not only express less concern about accepting minority shares, they actually seem more ready than American companies to accept a minority equity position. Typically, European managers report that the inherent difficulties of a minority position can be surmounted, and that, in any case, having a piece of the action is often better than having none at all.

Data recently compiled by the United Nations Commission on Transnational Corporations seem to confirm these impressions. The Commission examined the ownership patterns of 1,276 manufacturing affiliates of 391 U.S. and non-U.S. multinational corporations established in developing countries between 1951 and 1970-1975. In this period, the proportion of wholly owned affiliates of the 180 major U.S. multinationals remained highly stable at about 45 percent. The proportion of minority-owned ventures increased from about 10 percent to a quarter of the total. Among 135 European and U.K.-based multinationals examined, the proportion of wholly owned affiliates declined from 32 percent in 1951-1960 to 19 percent in 1966-1970, while the proportion of minority-owned affiliates rose from 28 percent to 42 percent in the same period.[3]

United Nations data no doubt understate the proportion of U.S. companies actually involved in joint ventures in developing countries. Many medium-sized and even smaller U.S. companies participate willingly in various types of equity and joint-venture arrangements in Brazil, Malaysia and Nigeria. The statements—and, more important, the actual behavior— of a few of the largest U.S. firms should not be taken as a microcosm of the entire universe of American companies that venture abroad. Furthermore, host-country officials with knowledge about corporate practices in their countries agree that U.S. firms do as well as any others in conforming to such governmental policies as the Indigenization Program in Nigeria, or the New Economic Policy in Malaysia.

---

[3]Centre on Transnational Corporations, *Transnational Corporations in World Development*. New York: United Nations, 1978, p. 229.

It is possible to sum up the differences in American and European attitudes by citing the views of senior managers. The head of a major U.S. corporation in Malaysia says simply: "We are 100 percent foreign owned, and we will always remain so." A European, who heads a British-based firm, laments equity sharing but adds that his company would never think of leaving Malaysia. Rather, he has taken the lead with the Malaysian government, specifying the proportion of equity his company is prepared to divest and is now prepared to negotiate the issue. The idea here is that the bargaining psychology will be less favorable if the firm waits for the government to make its demands. European managers seem to believe that more stringent equity requirements should not be confused with expropriation or other catastrophes, although necessity may lead to rationalization. Thus, the head of another European company says: "I cannot see our company controlling only 30 percent of its Malaysian affiliate by 1990, but I can't see 100 percent either. In fact, I wouldn't even *want* to be 100 percent, especially in a developing country."

Japanese MNC's

Although no Japanese firms were included in this research, available information reveals a fairly distinct pattern of joint-venture behavior. For example, one study of 50 Japanese corporations with 417 overseas subsidiaries finds that 342, or 82 percent, were joint ventures. Furthermore, in 304 of the joint ventures, the parent company held a minority of the equity.[4]

Data like these conform well to the conventional wisdom that the Japanese manifest the highest joint-venture propensity. However, closer inspection requires that this view be tempered. Because of the import-substitution strategy followed by the Japanese parent companies, their joint ventures overseas—even those in which the parent owns only a minority of the equity—are still tightly controlled by the parent and heavily dependent on the parent for intermediate materials or components. For the most part, these enterprises were designed to serve the local market and to perform only limited manufacturing or assembly operations. Their function vis-á-vis the parent has been primarily to maximize exports from Japan to the subsidiary, according to the author of the study quoted above.

Further, as Japanese firms have developed more globally oriented production and marketing strategies, there has been an increasing tendency to demand 100 percent ownership of their overseas affiliates. As another student of Japanese MNC's has recently observed: "Long gone are the days when Japanese firms preferred positions of minority owners, while going through trial and error practices of managing their overseas ventures.[5]

[4]M.Y. Toshion, *Japan's Multinational Enterprises*. Cambridge, Mass.: Harvard University Press, 1976, pp. 143-156.

[5]Y. Tsurumi, *The Japanese Are Coming: A Multinational Interaction of Firms and Politics*. Cambridge, Mass.: Ballinger Press, 1976, p. 211.

Whatever host-country elites may say about the greater flexibility of Japanese firms should be viewed against these conditions. In fact, officials with in-depth knowledge of the foreign investment community actually complain that, irrespective of the equity-sharing arrangement, Japanese firms tend to be excessively controlled by their headquarters. One often overlooked aspect of the much publicized, quiet paternalism that characterizes the Japanese firm is the underlying posture that "father knows best."

Investment Motivations

Essentially everyone interviewed for this study understands that companies go overseas with the expectation of making a profit on investment. Of those respondents who talked specifically about profitability, four-fifths evaluate MNC profits as "high," while the rest judge them to be "normal." Nigerians are more inclined than Brazilians to consider the average MNC's profits "high," but this may be readily explained by the relative knowledge of and experience with multinationals in each country.

High profits are not necessarily identified with *excessive* profits. By and large, respondents do not use the word "excessive" in discussing MNC profit levels. Indeed, high profits—that is, higher than typical of local firms in the same sector—are most often ascribed to the comparative advantages (e.g., scale, technology, efficiency, global distribution systems) that characterize the multinationals.

Though the profit motive—even a *high*-profit motive—is generally accepted abroad, exclusive concentration on profits is not. It is true that only a small portion of the total sample score such single-mindedness as the *most* serious defect of the multinationals. However, there is very widespread feeling that Americans display this shortcoming more than European companies. This inference is drawn not merely from the responses of host-country elites but from interviews with many overseas managers of U.S. corporations as well.

The possible systematic difference between U.S. and European firms here is far from trivial. A Swiss, who heads a very large-scale Brazilian operation for his company, predicts that average levels of ROI available in the Third World will gradually decline and that European companies will be better able than their U.S. competitors to live with this change.

American managers are prone to believe that European competitors are sometimes less profit oriented because of neomercantilism. They feel that in Japan, and in European countries as well, governments do much more to support and guarantee the overseas operations of their firms. Increasingly, the Americans are wondering whether increasing competition in the future will not require more conscious attention to this handicap.

European managers find such claims amusing, if not disingenuous. They argue that the U.S. government does not hesitate to put its considerable international weight behind U.S. business enterprise. They add that

American firms went multinational with considerable government encouragement and assistance, and that they did so in a period of exceptionally high profits. For this reason, they may turn out to be less ready or able to live in the more typical profit conditions of the real world.

Sifting the claims and evidence on all sides leads to several conclusions. There is considerable truth to the claim that American and European investment motivation and expectations operate in different time perspectives. Americans seem to take a shorter term view of many aspects of business, and their time frame comes to pervade every aspect of corporate planning, investment and operations. The shorter time frame is reflected in assignment of managers to overseas responsibilities, pay-back requirements, and increasingly to ongoing assessments of the health of overseas subsidiaries. As one disgruntled overseas U.S. manager puts it: "The company will kill itself by managing its decisions quarter by quarter, year by year. They try to do this in the context of conceptual planning, but they aren't doing it very well. The basic question they keep asking at headquarters is: 'Can we add to how well we do this quarter, as opposed to the same quarter last year'?"

Another American manager suggests that patterns of this kind are to be blamed on the basic objectives of central management. He says: "They want their objectives achieved in three years. This infects the company managers who come here for short terms. Because you are going to be somewhere else in three years, anything that produces developments for the company *after* three years is out."

A Brazilian industrialist suggests that parent companies make short-term demands on subsidiaries that "very definitely reflect the single-minded focus on return on investment, and the overpowering concern of how the corporation may look in the eyes of its own shareholders after the next quarterly report comes out." Although this respondent does not claim such practices to be exclusively associated with American firms, he echoes the views of many others that U.S. firms are far more prone to this approach than are European companies.

American managers believe that this difference places U.S. firms at a distinct disadvantage in the international business arena. If and when other structural advantages of the American firm—such as marketing techniques and systems of financial control—are reduced, they expect that the competitive balance will shift more in favor of European, Japanese and even Third World countries that are deeply involved in the multinational industrial community.

The American corporate posture regarding profits, equity sharing, and many other aspects of doing business overseas is deeply affected by the sheer size of the American domestic market. As many writers have noted, American firms were much later in going overseas *because they did not have to.*

European managers and host-country leaders are well aware of this special circumstance. In the limiting case of a Swiss firm, with close to 100 percent of sales abroad, it is simply unthinkable that its managers will threaten not to enter—or to leave—an overseas market unless everything conforms to their preferred investment and operational philosophy. The existence of the European Common Market has not yet changed the basic European managerial conviction that to be successful requires being in business overseas, on almost any basis. It is striking that this philosophy can now be readily implemented by directing capital to the United States—as the most attractive foreign investment environment in the world.

Chapter 10
Personnel Policies

CORPORATE POLICIES and strategies regarding expatriate and indigenous managers are a continuing source of tension for firms operating abroad. As with other host-country requirements, those pertaining to the replacement of expatriates by indigenes, training local personnel, and so on, constitute the external parameters for corporate strategy; individual corporate structure, needs, philosophy and style determine how the firm responds to these requirements.

Indigenous Managers

Indigenization of affiliate management abroad is a highly ranked objective in Brazil, Malaysia and Nigeria. Where countries differ as to the urgency of indigenization, differences typically reflect the progress already made in localizing management and existing levels of industrial development. At higher levels of industrialization, when countries have had longer experience with a variety of multinational enterprises, we expect to find greater use of local managers as well as greater acknowledgment among host-country leaders that international firms are paying attention to this problem. These are exactly the findings in evidence from the field. Over half of those interviewed commented on the progress by the multinational community in localizing management. Their estimates are summarized in Chart 12.

The data indicate that most of the respondents in all three countries believe indigenization levels are low. However, not all those interviewed ventured a judgment. Host-country nationals everywhere are acutely aware of the fact that MNC's are frequently more comfortable with expatriate than with indigenous managers. Although they recognize that the availability of local high-talent manpower is a major stumbling block, they often add that the multinationals hide behind this excuse and, in any case, do not do as much as they could—and should—to improve and enlarge the available local manpower pool.

Corporate managers who discuss this problem often rely on aggregate numbers designed to show that the firm overseas has made marked progress in adding locals to the work force. These figures frequently fail to treat middle- and upper-level managerial categories separately and, therefore, wind up obscuring what progress has been made in reducing the number of expatriates in these categories.

Host-country elites, on the other hand, are less interested in gross numbers than in more precise calculations. Thus, when they talk about "adequate" levels of indigenization they refer less to the *number* of local managers than to the *kind* and *level* of corporate responsibility to which the locals are assigned.

Chart 12: Progress in Placing Indigenous People in Management, as Reported by Interviewees Making a Judgment▲

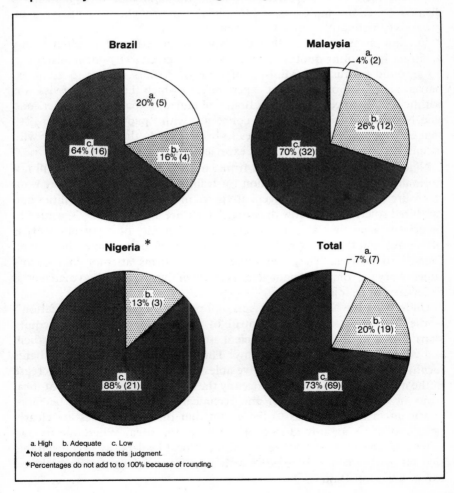

a. High   b. Adequate   c. Low
▲Not all respondents made this judgment.
*Percentages do not add to to 100% because of rounding.

National Experience

Foreign firms operating in *Nigeria* face by far the toughest restrictions on the use of expatriates. Indeed, a number of multinational managers insist that pressures to "Nigerianize" their managerial and technical staffs constitute the single most vexing problem they face in Nigeria, much more trying than requirements of equity sharing. Firms that wish to employ expatriates must obtain a permit from the ministry of Internal Affairs, a process which normally involves lengthy and frequently exasperating negotiations. Expatriate quotas may be obtained for positions not reserved for Nigerians (accounting is a reserved position, for example) if it can be proved that qualified Nigerian personnel are not available. Quotas, even then, are usually limited in duration and the government has frequently reduced the number of expatriates that foreign companies can employ. In addition, there are severe restrictions on the ability of foreign firms to dismiss Nigerian employees, and civil action brought by employees on grounds of wrongful dismissal is common.

Foreign firms complain that the Nigerian government is often highly arbitrary in granting quotas and that projects agreed to by one ministry can go aground because the Ministry of Internal Affairs refuses to grant expatriate quotas. Some recount experiences in which the necessary visa was withheld, even once a quota was finally obtained. Expatriate managers add that Nigerian officials are overly concerned with "paper qualifications"— that is, they will permit companies to bring in only those expatriates with extensive certification, while work experience itself is discounted.

Nigerians respond that foreign firms, unless severely pressured, will not normally make adequate provision for training local managers. They want to ensure that Nigerian managers are given meaningful responsibilities and not hired solely as "window dressing." They are also extremely sensitive to perceived racial slights. They believe that the quality of expatriate staff is often low, and that foreign firms do not send their best people, their "high fliers," to Nigeria. They claim that foreign firms attempt to pass off supervisory personnel as managers, even when they have had no managerial experience or training.

Underlying the Nigerian criticisms and posture about "Nigerianization" is the fundamental issue of control of enterprise. Nigerians see equity sharing as a necessary but insufficient step in the direction of giving them full control over their own economy. They argue that selling equity shares locally will not achieve this objective unless it is matched by a sharp increase in the number of indigenes who occupy the "commanding heights" of local firms in both the managerial and technical sectors. They will be more confident in foreign firms to the extent that these companies are clearly perceived to be committed to cooperation in this area. Where the foreign firms are seen to evade this responsibility, local leaders say it is inevitable that the government will respond with even more stringent restrictions on expatriate quotas and visas.

Until recently, in *Malaysia* the issue of indigenization was much less urgent. The Chinese community, with its active business interests and experience, provided cadres of disciplined and qualified local managerial staff; the Malaysian government, following its post-independence policies, did not apply too much pressure on foreign firms to make greater use of indigenes in management; and the quality of life in Malaysia ensured a substantial pool of expatriate executives content to remain in that country almost indefinitely. Companies with "pioneer status" were required to maintain a racially balanced work force, but there were no restrictions with regard to the use of expatriates in management.

The New Economic Policy introduces substantial new requirements on foreign firms to make greater use of Malays at all levels of their operations. As in Nigeria, equity sharing by the Malay community is seen as just part of the story. Beyond shared *ownership* of wealth, the NEP aims at restructuring the racial pattern of *employment,* without, of course, decreasing employment for any race. The immediate objective, and the one that impinges most severely on foreign firms, is to move Malays out of jobs in the traditional sectors of the economy into the more modern, high-productivity sectors. Within these sectors, firms are also expected to promote Malays upward to more highly skilled and responsible technical and managerial positions. All of this is presumably to be accomplished without firing or otherwise discouraging those non-Malays—mainly Chinese—who occupy most of these places at present.

The NEP may be even more burdensome when the government requires that all firms sharply increase the proportion of their business going to Malay service and distribution companies—Malay in this case defined as 100 percent Malay owned. As the head of one of the largest foreign operations in Malaysia observes: "This is really where the tensions start. Equity is an issue for the future. Employment is an issue we have to deal with on a day-to-day basis."

The multinationals are faced with a serious dilemma here. Even if they succeed in finding highly qualified Malays for technical and managerial positions (admittedly a very tall order), they are expected to carry off this transformation without destroying the job security and the morale of the non-Malays. Understandably, the Chinese in Malaysia are skeptical about this policy.

The kinds of problems of indigenizing managers found in Nigeria and Malaysia are ubiquitous in the Third World; they are also circular. It begins with a shortage of skilled manpower. The shortage, experience has shown, is only minimally alleviated by sending young people abroad to be educated: Most fail to return home, and many who return do not stay very long. Indigenous persons who do possess relevant skills can ride a heady merry-go-round, jumping rapidly from one job to another. Head-hunting becomes a way of life for the companies faced with strict indigenization requirements, and salaries are bid up out of all proportion to the nature of the jobs involved. These high salaries serve further to widen the amenities gap between rich and poor.

In a booming environment like Nigeria's, the circle is closed when many of the best trained and highly skilled locals drift out of the productive sector altogether. They either charge foreign companies rents for serving as sleeping partners, or they become facilitators or middlemen who take their cut from the top for making connections for the foreign firm. The company that takes the greatest initiative in upgrading the quality of indigenous personnel may find to its regret that it is serving as a free university or technical college for other firms, both foreign and local, and for government agencies bent on hiring away the brightest and the best.

These booming environments are characterized not only by a multiplicity of goals but also by a drumbeat of demands and criticisms that have political implications. The foreign firm is often caught in the middle, unable to fully understand where, if at all, the host-country government is able and willing to draw the line between efficiency and training. An American manager, whose company does construction work in Nigeria, underscores the contradictory impulses that drive Nigerian leaders: "They want better roads and buildings *now*. But they also want Nigerianization *now*. Foreign companies cannot do both at once: They cannot do their best in terms of product and at the same time carry a heavy responsibility for training Nigerians. If they are not allowed to use sufficient expatriates, and have to spend a lot of time training Nigerians, the final result will either be less adequate or it will take longer to produce."

Although *Brazil* differs markedly from Nigeria or Malaysia, there are some parallels there as well. For example, even though Brazil has a much larger pool of high-talent industrial manpower, the rapid development of the country during the last decade or two has resulted in severe shortages of industrial managers. Shortages, in turn, are translated into salary inflation that today makes Brazilian industrial managers among the highest paid anywhere in the world. As many parent companies have come to learn, holding on to first-rate Brazilian managers often entails compensation at levels that many parent-company personnel find enviable—and even astonishing.

If Brazilians are relatively more satisfied with the tempo of indigenization, this should not be confused with an absence of pressures to speed up the transformation. On the one hand, Brazilian pragmatism is reflected in a willingness to listen to and understand the difficulties companies face in replacing expatriates with indigenes. On the other hand, Brazilian officials prefer to see hard evidence of systematic replacement programs as opposed to verbal assurances that the firms are concerned with this problem. Moreover, Brazilians are highly sensitive to the frequent use of "figurehead" senior managers—often in the form of politically well-connected corporate presidents who lack other qualifications and have no significant power over corporate decisions and operations.

Nevertheless, on the critical issue of training locals for higher level managerial responsibilities, Brazilians are more satisfied than either Malaysians or Nigerians. Of the small number of respondents (under 40 percent) who addressed the specific question regarding the quality of training provided by the multinational firms, a markedly higher proportion of Brazilians than of the Malaysian or Nigerian groups indicate that programs are "adequate" or "exceptional." No Brazilian thought it "inadequate." By way of sharp contrast, not a single Nigerian describes corporate training programs as adequate, and three-quarters of them score the training programs as inadequate. The configuration of responses to this question is provided in Table 22.

Some foreign companies wrongly believe that if they can show a change in the proportion of locals who hold managerial positions, popular criticisms in this area will diminish. In reality, such advances will tend to be recognized and appreciated only by a small minority of local leaders and officials who are extremely well-informed about the foreign corporate community.

Within this group of well-informed local leaders, evidence that the number of expatriate managers has actually been on the *increase* in Brazil in recent years causes great consternation. Commenting on this tendency, a former Brazilian Cabinet minister expresses the view that "the multinationals are actually going backward here." He says that the reason for this retrograde step is less the scarcity of local talent than the overreaction of multinationals to nationalistic Brazilian managers. Foreign firms, he argues, must learn that Brazilian managers will retain a high sense of Brazilian identity and loyalty and that, by and large, this fact should not be disquieting for the foreign company operating there. "Local managers," he cautions, "do not develop a corporate personality. They are patriotic. They tend to see things from the point of view of their own countries. They will believe in Brazil first, and then in their company."

Companies with a deeply ingrained sense of corporate identity will have some difficulty accepting the idea that this tendency is without costs. Furthermore, the Brazilian environment seems to require greater use of expatriates. Firms operating in Brazil insist that the recent growth in the proportion of expatriates derives primarily from the rapid expansion of industry there. For example, the head of a British-based firm reports that the number of managers in the Brazilian affiliate grew from 80 to 400 in just six years. The senior manager of a large-scale Italian enterprise underscores the same problems. He adds that, at similar levels of training, experience and responsibility, it is now strikingly cheaper to send over Italian managers than to hire locals.

Expatriate Managers

Host-country pressures and requirements set external parameters and, therefore, tell only half the story about indigenization. The other half is

Table 22: Quality of Local Management Training by MNC's

Evaluation	Brazil[1]		Malaysia		Nigeria		Total	
	Number	Percent	Number	Percent	Number	Percent	Number	Percent
Exceptional........	3	21%	6	15%	—	—	9	14%
Adequate.........	10	77	16	39	3	25	29	44
Inadequate.......	—	—	19	46	9	75	28	42
Total..........	13	100%	41	100%	12	100%	66	100%

[1]Percentages do not add to 100 because of rounding.

provided by corporate practices and predispositions regarding the expatriates themselves.

Two questions are fundamental in this regard. First, what does the parent company expect from its expatriate managers overseas? Second, what kinds of personnel are generally sent abroad? Answers to these questions help to detemine what is likely to be the individual firm's response to indigenization pressures.[1]

In general, it is clear that multinationals of whatever nationality rely on expatriates to keep a tight rein on the overseas operation and to pursue the overall interests of the parent company. Many firms are, therefore, reluctant to place indigenes in the topmost positions. In American firms, the position least likely to be turned over to locals at an early stage is that of chief financial officer. Some companies will appoint locals as managing directors or chief executive officers, but there is also reluctance there. Although some companies say a local president can open doors, more believe that one never knows whether a local at this level is "our man or someone else's." Often the solution is the one the Brazilian respondents lament: A local president is appointed but turns out to be nothing more than a figurehead.

By and large, the positions abroad that are most readily turned over to locals are those in personnel, legal affairs, and public relations. The underlying assumption is that these are functional areas where knowledge of the local culture is a prime requisite for effective management. For similar reasons, locals also eventually filter into managerial responsibilities in marketing.

On the important and delicate question of who should handle an affiliate's external relations, and particularly relations with the host-country government, there is considerable difference of opinion and variation in practice. The impression from this study is that American companies are more likely than European to use local personnel in this function. One reason, included in the comments of an American manager, is a certain amount of timidity about dealing with government officials: "I'm a bit worried about getting into the government sector because the hand is usually out somewhere along the line. Things like that would be against our code of ethics. I find I do not want to get directly involved."

American firms will often rely on local consultants or law firms to handle their relationships (and problems) with the political and public administrative sector. European managers take a quite different view, holding that only the most senior expatriates should represent the company's interests in dealing with the host-country government. In the words of a European manager in Malaysia: "The Americans are more likely to use a local in relations with the government. They will always try to send in a

[1]Burton W. Teague, *Selecting and Orienting Staff for Service Overseas.* The Conference Board, Report No. 705, 1977.

Malay. We like to do it ourselves. It is really a question of how much you want to delegate. I am willing to delegate minor things but I feel it is necessary to do the major things myself. Who is to say that the Malay manager will really have our company's interests at heart?''

Another important difference between European and American firms lies in the varying extent to which an overseas assignment is seen as temporary or permanent—as a major responsibility for highly trusted and seasoned managers, or as another of many varied assignments for those on their way to important responsibility at corporate headquarters. European managers tend to stay abroad longer, with the expectation all around that extended service overseas will not be detrimental to a managerial career. American managers move in and out of managerial positions at home and abroad more frequently, and expatriates are unlikely to stay away from home any length of time if they can avoid it.

A young American manager, working in Nigeria for a major U.S. multinational, says that in his company people like himself go out of the country to gain overseas experience. They get points for taking on a tough overseas assignment, but they have to get back to headquarters to move upward in the organization. Some people do go out and stay; they get accustomed to life overseas and never come back. But they lose the opportunity to climb up the corporate ladder.

European firms generally expect their people to work their way up through the ranks and to create a job suited to their own particular skills and interests. When this involves taking an assignment abroad, it is likely to be for an extended period. One consequence is the frequency with which European managers learn local languages, marry citizens of host countries, and genuinely integrate into the local society.

One can readily argue the pros and cons of either the American or the European approach. From the vantage of host-country leaders, however, frequent turnover of expatriate managers is open to much criticism. It seems to them self-evident that whirlwind managerial tours will rarely lead the manager (or his company) to develop genuine understanding of the host country.

Frequent turnover of managers is often identified as the most serious hindrance to the advancement of U.S. corporate interests abroad. The case of an American firm in Nigeria posting three different general managers to its affiliate there in less than seven years is not unique. Indigenous leaders cannot believe that companies following such personnel policies are taking the local operation very seriously. Where the suggestion is made that frequent turnover and assignment to a wide range of responsibilities makes for better top managers, they are skeptical and unimpressed. What concerns them most is that their *country* represents a very brief way station in corporate careers.

Many respondents also feel that the American manager who remains overseas for an extended period is not likely to count for very much inside his own company. They are aware of the widespread American corporate practice of putting managers out to pasture by sending them abroad.

This discussion may suggest that the entire international management system requires rethinking at a more basic level. A European manager in Brazil insists that the multinationals must develop a new *conceptual* approach to overseas business. He says: "We need fewer technocrats, and more businessmen who can see that the world has changed. You can create a system that will give you information about the total country, but that information has to be filtered through people in the country itself who have a broad conceptual base, who have had, above all, extensive local experience. U.S. firms that have men here for just a few years do not get that kind of experience."

Transformations of this kind are not without potentially high costs. A European manager says: "Where we are required to have more local than expatriate managers, there will be great difficulty in maintaining the cohesion of our company." A British manager in Nigeria echoes this view: "The expatriate always looks on Nigeria as a place where he works, but he responds to somewhere else." Furthermore, he adds that certain positions in the company require the manager to be "*totally* loyal to the company, without outside commitments." He is at a loss to suggest what will evolve once the Nigerians succeed in enforcing Nigerianization throughout the upper levels of multinational affiliate management.

The trade-offs that go with indigenization are both subtle and complicated. If, as many claim, European affiliates abroad have greater local autonomy than their American or Japanese counterparts, will parent companies be able—or willing—to continue this pattern when highly trusted compatriots are replaced by locals? What happens to the "old boy" network so crucial to the internal coherence of these organizations when more local managers, many of whom do not belong or aspire to a place in this network, are brought into the company?

Pushed to the extreme, indigenization will compel major changes in corporate management-training formats. It will surely make a difference if, as some Brazilian officials insist, expatriate managers may not exceed 10 percent of a firm's local management pool. Who goes overseas to do and to learn what kinds of things is certain to be a major question corporate headquarters will have to face.

As the proportions of indigenous managers grow, companies will also have to review incentive and compensation schemes, as well as their policies regarding transfer, promotion, demotion and dismissal. Standard American management techniques on demotion and dismissal often appear extremely harsh to host-country nationals. "Americans have no conscience," a Nigerian says. "They hire and fire without blinking an eye."

European and Japanese companies appear to be at the other extreme, going to the greatest pains not to dismiss a manager or to cause him serious loss of face in reassignment. A number of European managers report that they are not sure whether the European approach is good for the firm; they acknowledge that these may well be an important positive dimension to the more "brutal" American approach.

Locals find American managers personally more open, friendly and informal than Europeans or Japanese. In places like Brazil, Malaysia and Nigeria (and they are typical of most countries) these agreeable qualities are misinterpreted as signs of personal loyalties and commitments. Therefore, the locals are shocked and angered when these same people fire employees who do not fit successfully into the organization. If this approach to personnel policies is considered essential for corporate success abroad, host-country leaders may reply that European and Japanese companies that consciously avoid this aspect of American management practice do not seem to be at a disadvantage.

Chapter 11
The Organizational Connection

CORPORATE ORGANIZATION is a reflection of the company's past development and its present mission. Corporate structure, in turn, sets the parameters in which investment strategies, personnel policies, and other corporate activities are defined and elaborated. Frequent alteration in organizational structures, perplexity about optimal organization, and changes from one organizational system to another frequently mirror a corporation's wider uncertainty about its mission or overall strategy.

In many American corporations, such uncertainties are increasingly manifest in efforts to give organizational meaning to changes in the relationship between traditional domestic commitments and newer involvements abroad. Whatever the factors that take a company overseas, the evolution of the "global firm" requires enormous attention to the organizational "connection" between center and periphery.

Uncertainty and the tensions it creates can be highly beneficial. Executives under pressure may be forced to transcend existing organizational modes and to innovate formats that will serve a multiplicity of old and new objectives. It will not be the first or last time that what corporations do out of necessity will be translated into a *theory* of corporate organization.

At the same time, frequent reorganization can confuse and demoralize those within the corporation. Experienced managers are well aware that reorganization may become a surrogate for hard decisions. Beyond reflecting a firm's basic philosophy and objectives, its strategic posture and operational style, organizational decisions in the future will have to reflect (much more than in the past) host-country requirements and constraints of the kinds that have been discussed. The global economy is not only an abstraction, it is a fiction. That economy is more appropriately called international—implying that it is deeply conditioned by what nation-states want and do. This requires careful attention to the views of host-country elites, including affiliate managers, regarding organizational forms.

Centralization and Autonomy

Two basic facts emerge from this research and from an examination of recent literature on multinational corporate organization. First, in definitive majorities, the host-country elites interviewed believed that multinational affiliates are excessively controlled by corporate headquarters. Second, notwithstanding these attitudes, it appears that centralized corporate control is actually increasing on a global basis.

The summary of views from Brazil, Nigeria and Malaysia illustrates the first point (see Chart 13). Less than half of the respondents—44 percent—discussed this issue, but more than nine out of ten of the Brazilians who did, believe that control from the center is excessive. The Brazilian case is interesting: In effect, the greatest concern about lack of local autonomy is expressed by respondents from the country that has had the longest and most varied experience with the multinationals of those in the study. The most sophisticated Brazilians interviewed appear to believe that management philosophies—and not some ironclad theory or logic—account significantly for differing degrees of autonomy.

In all three cases, nationalistic feelings run high. Respondents in these countries are particularly critical of any evidence that independent control over the economic affairs of their country is being infringed upon. That some of these leaders may be overreacting does not diminish the importance of these feelings.

Raymond Vernon notes that centralized control is increasingly the rule among the multinationals. According to Vernon, research findings show that: "...over the past few decades an increasing proportion of the world's largest firms have tended to favor an organizational structure that breaks down the enterprise primarily by product divisions, with each such division having the world as its domain. With the global status of the product occupying the top strategic echelon of the firm, differences based on national factors have been obliged to take a second place."[1] A recent Conference Board survey of shifting patterns of international organization of U.S. firms underscores this conclusion, at least for American corporations. Of those executives reporting a major alteration in international organizational structure, almost all describe a shift from a traditional geographic organization to one based on global product lines. These organizational changes are prompted, in the words of one executive cited in the survey, by "the increasing complexity of our business, the need for better coordination within a business, and the need for better rationalization of resources."[2]

---

[1] Raymond Vernon, *Storm Over the Multinationals,* Cambridge, Mass.: Harvard University Press, 1977, p. 31.

[2] James R. Basche, Jr., *Shifting Patterns in International Organization: U.S. Experiences in the 1970's.* The Conference Board, Information Bulletin No. 42, September, 1978, p. 10.

Chart 13: Attitude on Degree of Headquarters Control of Affiliate

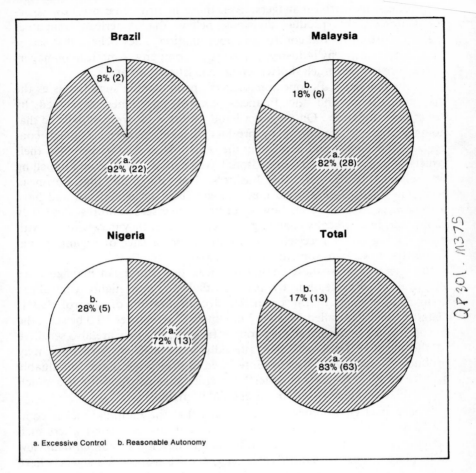

Brazil

b. 8% (2)

a. 92% (22)

Malaysia

b. 18% (6)

a. 82% (28)

Nigeria

b. 28% (5)

a. 72% (13)

Total

b. 17% (13)

a. 83% (63)

a. Excessive Control   b. Reasonable Autonomy

Comments of this kind often imply that there may be substantial and systematic differences between U.S. and European corporations on the issue of centralization versus autonomy. Although the data in this study, based on a relatively small sample of 18 European and American firms, cannot supply a definitive statement on this question, it seems most unlikely that the differences found among them can be explained *without* reference to the *nationality* of the company. Beyond industrial sector, product differentiation, market structure, age of technology, and other factors that impinge on center-periphery relationships, it seems to make considerable difference whether or not the company is American. Moreover, the idea that the American firm tends to be much more controlled from the center is widely held not only by host-country leaders, but also by American and European multinational affiliate managers in Brazil, Malaysia and Nigeria.

European industrial managers, even those in firms that are now structured along global product divisions, believe that American companies make a fetish of central control and coordination. They believe that sector by sector, industry by industry, company by company, American managers abroad are kept on much shorter tether than Europeans are.

On the one hand, European managers openly admire such things as the marketing skills and the financial control techniques developed by American companies. On the other hand, they are far from convinced that going global, or organizing by product division, requires so much concentration of power and decision at the center. They tend to deny that their American colleagues and competitors have devised a precise and impelling way of conducting worldwide business. They point out that European companies have been abroad much longer than the Americans and have learned a good deal about how to optimize overseas ventures. And they claim that, in a radically changing overseas climate, they may wind up with more staying power precisely because of the persistence of organizational forms that Americans sometimes dismiss as obsolete.

In concrete terms, these comments mean that European managers are skeptical of organization by product division with highly centralized control, as well as of the ostensible decentralization of control that is claimed for the so-called "matrix" or "mixed" structures.[3] To be sure, the Europeans are interested in corporate efficiency, but they are also sensitive to the negative trade-offs that allegedly more efficient structures may produce. In particular, they are interested in preserving the most valuable aspects of the "mother-daughter" structure that carries with it a much looser relationship between the parent and its affiliates.

Where local environments become such that the multinational is compelled to pay more attention to the demands of host countries; where such demands require, for example, that the parent develop a total *national* view of its place in a given country's economy, many European managers believe that the centralization and coordination of product division activities *located in that country* is absolutely essential. When local officials demand that the foreign company in their jurisdiction deal with them through a single individual, irrespective of the number of product divisions represented there, the Europeans believe they already have in place a form of organization that the American companies will be compelled to adopt.

Control points in U.S. corporate organization are normally remote from host countries; they are located in regional headquarters, in international divisions at the center, or at the top of global product divisions. Affiliate

---

[3]Allen R. Janger, *Matrix Organization of Complex Businesses*. The Conference Board, Report No. 763, 1979.

managers of U.S. companies that introduce regional structures are generally aware that if the regional group gives a country's operation more visibility at corporate headquarters, it also carries with it, despite what the theorists say, a *diminution* in local autonomy.

Host-country leaders are well aware of this pattern. A Brazilian businessman says: "Only in a small number of MNC's does the Brazilian executive have true authority. He can go up to a certain point, and beyond that the decisions escape his control. The subsidiaries are always tightly linked to the parent and the basic decisions are made abroad." And a Nigerian manager in a U.S. affiliate echoes him: "Too many people who know little about local conditions pull strings by remote control from outside of the country."

A number of respondents contend that because of excessive central controls, it takes American firms inordinately long to reach a decision or to commit itself to a line of action overseas. People on the spot seem to have little authority or discretion. It is suspected that the people who finally make the decisions have relatively little knowledge of local conditions.

An extreme formulation, articulated by many respondents, is that American firms are not multinational at all, either in basic attitude toward overseas investment environments or in their methods of organization and operation. One respondent says: "The United States tends to confuse know-how with the American way of doing things. We have seen this very often here and in Europe."

About his own U.S. company, a Brazilian manager in São Paulo says: "I honestly think first, and this is fair, in our behavior here we are just an American company that happens to be operating overseas. I'm comparing us with other multinationals that have *real* operations overseas. What happens here is that policies are stated outside Brazil without any consideration for our situation."

An American expatriate, working for this same company in Asia, makes the same point: "We are very much an American company that works overseas only *after* it has served its American needs. And this is a company that will withdraw at a moment's notice from an overseas operation to go back to the United States to fill a need there."

It is also possible that some American companies will misunderstand and misuse "internationalism." For the company, being international may mean piling up a lot of managerial experiences from many different parts of the world. But for any given host country, the international or multinational company is one that should go to considerable pains to understand *that country's* needs and situation. For example, Malaysian bureaucrats, who had recently completed a series of negotiations with a number of U.S. and European companies, complain of the American companies' continuing stress on their internationality. To carry out negotiations in Malaysia, they assembled their toughest possible negotiating teams from around the world. The Malaysians complain that these tactics were designed to initimidate them, and to flaunt the company's "multinationality."

An American banker in Hong Kong underlines the dangers of this approach: "You can't take the experience gained in one part of the world and overlay it on other parts. What we learn in Africa or Latin America cannot often be transferred easily to Asia. It is a very dangerous form of internationalism to think that experience in one area of the world creates an ability to understand cultures and business practices in other parts. The most effective managers overseas are those who recognize the *differences* among areas of the world, and who do not press to see only similarities."

Local Autonomy and Centralization

European multinationals may *not* be *less* centralized, according to a young American manager. A first question about centralization would be: How do units constituting a single system, organized both horizontally and vertically, relate to each other? A second, related question is what is the level of organization at which central authority over all of the units located in any given geographic area is exercised. For example, one can readily demonstrate that individual product divisions are *highly autonomous of each other* in the typical multiproduct-division American firm operating overseas.

Even where there is an entity representing the entire corporation in that country, local product managers are likely to report directly to divisional headquarters at home, and only indirectly to the country manager. What looks like autonomy among major divisions of a single corporation from the perspective of "corporate" turns out to be maximum lack of autonomy from the standpoint of host-country observers.

European firms organized along the "mother-daughter" format permit their product divisions strikingly less autonomy overseas, particularly in developing nations. At the level of the host country, the European multinationals are much *more* centralized than American companies. Local product managers are directly responsible to the country manager, the overall chief executive officer who speaks for the company in that country in fact as well as in theory. As a highly seasoned and trusted executive with typically long experience in that same country, he frequently enjoys considerable autonomy from the corporate center. This structure can function well, even if product divisions are the company's profit centers, and even if some staff services provided by corporate headquarters are highly centralized at corporate headquarters or regional divisions.

The American pattern of product-line autonomy combined with centralized control at product divisional headquarters is often the source of considerable difficulty for firms in dealing with host-country governments. Increasingly, these governments wish to deal with a local executive who has overall responsibility for all of the divisions of the parent located there.

When American managers reply that each of the product groups operates independently, such comments draw bewildered, skeptical and increasingly hostile responses.

Host-country technocrats wonder if Americans are dissembling when the ostensible country head of a multinational corporation tells them that he cannot control the activities of his company's people there. Nevertheless, this is exactly what many American managers are compelled to say. The general manager of one U.S. company in Brazil comments: "It is almost impossible for me to 'speak for' the corporation. I have no direct authority over the product lines here. I don't work for a product line and no one in my chain of command does. I have very few direct reports. Almost everything I want to do, I have to get someone to do who does not report directly to me. But that is not really his job."

Concentration of effective power in the product divisions of multinationals can complicate the overseas side of operations from the point of initial investment. Tensions regarding overseas commitment of corporate resources between product divisions and international divisions are well-known. An American manager notes that his company's international division "targeted Nigeria as an area of opportunity. But Nigeria is not at all critical to the company on the product side. And it is the product lines that make the basic investments. So our job is to convince the product people to be interested."

In general, product-line managers, particularly in the United States where they may have been strikingly successful in managing profit centers, are not greatly interested in the international side of business. They see the domestic operation as the major part of the overall business; they are comfortable about the American operation; and they want to keep the balance skewed to the domestic side.

Given the high degree of autonomy that American product divisions enjoy, it is clear that a good deal of management's time must be devoted to intracompany negotiations. This is true not only for the domestic sectors but also—and especially—for the international division. Asked how he manages to keep his own particular and successful overseas operation afloat, an American manager replies: "Through a mixture of cajoling, arguing, doing favors, and trying to educate people."

The European multinationals follow a different pattern. Overseas they are as concerned as are host-country governments that the company be able "to speak with one voice." Where there is, in fact, one person who can speak authoritatively for all branches of the parent company located in a given country, the Europeans believe that they can make a credible claim about their *localness*. They then have an easier time persuading public officials that their local operation is important to national economic development plans and can be readily blended into the plans themselves.

In order to carry off this strategy, European companies demand and get a high degree of teamwork and coordination among their product-line managers. Coordination may require, for example, that one product division located in a given country source little or nothing outside the country in order to buttress another product line there that will require high levels of imports.

It is possible that European respondents overstate the degree of genuine independence they enjoy from corporate headquarters. Nevertheless, as European companies are structured, the pressures on country managers—and, more important, on the product managers operating within their geographic jurisdiction—to work things out at the country level without having to ask for intervention from the center are very great. Even so, a number of respondents believe that the claimed differences between U.S. and European firms may actually be more apparent than real. A Malaysian suspects, for example, that the cable traffic from London to Kuala Lumpur is not much less than that emanating from New York, or that the headquarters language from London is not notably less demanding or rigid. The difference may lie in the pains taken by European companies to obscure rather than to flaunt their international character; to emphasize the affiliate's local, rather than its multinational, identity.

The Influence of Collegial Governance

The use in European organizations of collegial formats of decision making and control at the top, as well as special committee arrangements for dealing with overseas aspects of the firm's commitments and operations, is also noteworthy. Top management in very large European corporations seems enchanted with the idea of a small group at headquarters who have known each other in the firm for a long time and who genuinely share in the responsibility of providing direction for the enterprise. Their sense of how they operate contrasts sharply with what they hear about the all-powerful chief executive in American companies. They are of mixed views regarding the kind of radical change the direction of the company can take simply because one CEO has been replaced by another. To the extent that the Europeans acknowledge that there is a top man in the company, they prefer to describe him as "first among equals"—and certainly not as "the boss."

The European pattern of more collegial corporate governance is a result of two factors frequently absent in the American firm. First, top European managers stem largely from the upper-middle and upper classes of their societies. Second, European managers will have experienced much less movement from one firm to another and much longer experience in a single firm. Both of these factors combine to give these managers high confidence that they know how the others think and, therefore, how each person will react to given situations. In this setting, more formalized American modes of corporate discussion and decision are felt to be unnecessary. The chief financial officer of a British firm, who makes exactly these points, insists that neither the explicit language nor the volume of intracompany written communication typical of the American firm is necessary in his company. This manager, like other Europeans who discussed this issue, expresses astonishment at the amount of internal information required by the headquarters and regional units of American corporations. They suspect that much of it is not really necessary and, further, that relatively little of it is actually read.

The use of committee structures as a top-level method for managing overseas business is another form of collegial oversight found in many European firms. Members of "overseas committees" are typically those with extensive foreign experience. At headquarters, each of them may well combine area responsibility with oversight of one or more of the company's product lines. This system is designed to minimize the tensions that occur between top-level product managers and others who are associated with the international divisions and operations of the company. In one major European multinational operating on a worldwide basis, both members of the overseas committee and country managers of the company refer to committee members as the "godfathers" whose prime responsibility is to represent not merely the interests of the product divisions but also those of specific countries and geographic regions at corporate center.

Interpretation

The corporation is a system—a highly complex organizational "package" whose structures, missions and policies interrelate with and affect each other. From time to time, corporations change along one dimension or another, and such changes will radiate throughout the organization and require additional changes and adjustments.

But fundamental change—of investment philosophy and strategy, of personnel policies and operational style, or of basic organization itself—is likely to occur much less rapidly than frequent corporate reorganization schemes and announcements suggest. This is one of the reasons why the mother-daughter format among European companies seems to have survived the introduction of product divisionalization in these companies. This is also why, in the American case, the huge outflow of foreign direct investment since World War II seems to have had a limited effect in "internationalizing" many of the most basic decision-making and operational characteristics of these companies.

Attention has been called to certain differences between U.S.-and non-U.S.-based multinationals that seem to affect the way in which companies deal with host countries. Differences can be exaggerated, and generalizations about American or European "types" may also easily lead to the erroneous conclusion that there are no exceptions on either side. No such oversimplification or distortion is intended.

Insofar as the differences are valid, it may be important to explore why they exist. Four factors seem to impinge on the kinds of issues addressed in this and the previous two chapters. They are: a company's age and overseas experience; its technology and technological development; the nature of its home market; and the nature of the parent company's national government and corporate relationships with it.

Age

Many European companies are older—often much older—than U.S. firms, and many have had much more extensive international experience.[4] In those cases in which their govenments acquired colonial empires, national firms soon followed the flag. In some cases—in West Africa, the Malay peninsula, and the Indian subcontinent—British companies preceded their government and formed their own political organizations.

The age of a company and its overseas experience inevitably are reflected in its organization and operational style. Companies with heavy endowments of overseas experiences have learned a good deal about foreign cultures, and particularly how to work with local leaders. Equally important, local leaders have learned about them, too, and about their ways of doing business.

It is a myth that European colonial powers crudely and rigidly implanted their own institutions in the territories they took over. The Europeans quickly learned how much easier it was to avoid saying bluntly, "do it our way," and to try instead to blend European and indigenous ways of doing things. The apparent emulation of British, French or other European social, economic, governmental or cultural traits in former colonial territories should not be confused with blind, indiscriminate substitution of one system for another.

Whether information and wisdom regarding overseas environments came to European industrial managers through colonial missionaries, colonial administrators, or businessmen who ventured abroad, this knowledge itself is a considerable asset. It gives European managers the confidence that they can operate more successfully than anyone else in foreign investment environments. Furthermore, far from retaining great hostility toward the metropolitan powers, leaders of former colonies actually prefer to do business with them. As one Nigerian official laconically put it: "We prefer to deal with the devils we know."

Technology and Technological Development

This dimension of a company's history may offer even more insight into its organization and style. As several writers have emphasized, European companies first ventured overseas as exporters and traders and later in full-

---

[4]Mira Wilkins, *The Maturing of Multinational Enterprise: American Business Abroad from 1914 to 1970.* Cambridge, Mass.: Harvard University Press, 1974.

scale production, spurred by the need to secure resources and to exploit materials-saving technologies. This type of technology tended to direct European corporations toward the production of goods for which there was a stable existing demand and which might be manufactured more cheaply than before through the use of synthetics, and through the discovery of innovations that reduced dependence on imported raw materials. American firms, on the other hand, went abroad in search of labor-saving rather than raw-materials saving opportunities. American firms also tended to emphasize the comparative advantages associated with product innovation, and sought to exploit these advantages in new overseas markets.[5]

The European pattern involved firms in intimate dealings with host-country governments. Their tendency to replicate abroad manufacturing processes that were material- rather than labor-saving was strongly encouraged by host-country governments because of the new jobs that such overseas production implied, and also because the European firms could establish full-scale production abroad under an organizational format that permitted the overseas affiliate to operate with considerable independence from the parent company. The European firms learned to live comfortably in a "negotiated environment" in which frequent and informal dealings with host-country governments were accepted on all sides as the natural way of doing business.

Size of Home Market

The importance of this factor cannot be overemphasized. Not only did American firms become multinational later than most of their European opposite numbers, but there was also a basic tendency to treat overseas investments as mere extensions of a vast domestic market. Within this domestic market, economies of scale could be realized much more readily than elsewhere. Coupled with the American emphasis on product innovation, it was natural that this structural factor would lead American companies to conceive of overseas opportunities largely in terms of exploiting growing interest in the purchase of new products.[6]

For all of these reasons, including a relative lack of intimate knowledge of foreign cultures and business environments, American managers took a radically different view of foreign operations, and overseas business played a substantially different role within the corporation, in terms of the development of corporate policy and organization. For many European companies there may be no choice except to stick it out. Where this is true, the situation will naturally be reflected in investment strategies, personnel policies, and organizational forms. The contrast between U.S. and

---

[5]Lawrence G. Franko, *The European Multinationals*. London: Harper and Row, 1976.

[6]A. Chandler, *Strategy and Structure*. Cambridge, Mass.: MIT Press, 1961.

European firms on this score may become even sharper as the United States, for a variety of reasons, becomes one of the most attractive environments anywhere for additional industrial investment.

National Governments

National governments of industrialized countries influence the international activities of their own corporations in many ways. Governmental assistance to business ventures abroad is provided by several European governments—on a scale that is relatively unknown and unacceptable in the United States. The United States government is loath to develop "national champions" in the competitive world of multinational enterprise, except in those rare cases where there may be only one obvious American company involved in an international competitive bidding situation. Furthermore, the days are gone when the U.S. Government might send gunboats or land marines to protect American business interests in foreign countries.

In the years since World War II, the American national government has played an important role in encouraging U.S. firms to expand internationally. Beginning with the Marshall Plan, the Federal Government has provided all sorts of assistance and incentives designed to encourage a greater American industrial presence abroad. Information about potential markets, specific surveys, and studies of industrial development opportunities, access to low-cost loans, special insurance schemes against expropriations without adequate compensation, tax deferral provisions, the Hickenlooper Amendment conditioning foreign aid on specific provisions regarding expropriations—these are only a few of the U.S. governmental policies that have facilitated the enormous growth in American foreign direct investment that took place beginning in the 1950's.[7]

In addition, as European firms are quick to point out, much of the cost of basic research and development that created notable competitive advantages for American industry was borne, directly or indirectly, by the Federal Government. European managers are likely to consider somewhat disingenuous, therefore, American claims that they and their government are the only ones who practice neomercantilism.

Nevertheless, there are some striking contrasts to be noted. In the first place, because many European economies are much more centrally planned than that of the United States, European firms come under more overall scrutiny and control than American firms. Planning formats and targets inevitably bring national governments to ask more probing questions about the overall impact of corporate policies on the national economy, and particularly on the balance-of-payments position of the national govern-

[7]Wilkins, 1974.

ment. European governments are more sensitive to the need to provide assistance to their exporting companies.

On the other hand, in very specific areas, American firms are subject to much more rigid and stringent controls than is the case in Europe or Japan. One need merely mention antitrust and trading-with-the-enemy legislation to make this point. In addition, recent investigations of the Security and Exchange Commission and of the United States Senate on Foreign Relations' Subcommittee on Multinational Corporations suggest that the long arm of the Federal Government can and will extend to aspects of the overseas conduct of business that European governments prefer to ignore. As one American executive reflecting on the stringency of American regulations puts it, the one force that can put the typical American company out of business overseas in the shortest time is the U.S. Government.

In the second place, the effects on American firms of the profoundly adversary quality of government-business relations in the United States should not be underestimated. Distrust of big business is deeply rooted in the American national psyche. If there have been times when Americans extolled the virtues and the benefits wrought by business enterprise, there have also been points at which leaders of industry were called "robber barons" and government was called upon to reduce the power and influence of the industrial sector.

U.S. businessmen tend to be much more uncomfortable than Europeans in dealing with their own national government. European managers who are more comfortable than Americans dealing with host-country officials are simply extending abroad the relatively easy, informal network of contacts they maintain with national governmental officials at home. Evidence gathered in this study strongly documents this difference. European managers are much more likely than Americans, for example, to say that they often turn to their own governments for help and find governmental assistance extremely useful in their overseas operations. Unlike most American firms abroad, European companies do not limit their contacts with their national governments to those occasions when an initial investment is contemplated or, even worse, when a local situation has gone sour.

To sum up, European companies and managers have grown up in domestic and overseas environments where the border between the public and the private sectors is less distinct than in the United States. They expect the government to take a more active role in the economy and in the affairs of individual firms. No matter how they might evaluate overall economic planning schemes at home, or economic development plans abroad, they have come to appreciate that ignoring political and administrative factors that affect business would be done at their own peril.

Chapter 12
Labor and Industrial Relations

MULTINATIONAL CORPORATIONS are widely acknowledged to have stimulated employment in *industrialized* host countries, especially when they have opened up new plants. The impact of these firms on job creation in the *less developed* nations is open to greater controversy, both at home and abroad. Recent studies estimate that MNC's have created about two million new jobs in the Third World—a substantial figure, although small when compared with the total labor force in these countries.[1] Moreover, critics of multinationals insist that two effects of multinational investment in the Third World require much more careful inspection than they have thus far received. First, there is the claim (not strongly substantiated by data) that the principal companies that venture abroad are highly capital intensive. Second, there is is the related (and also weakly supported) claim that the net effect of foreign direct investment in the developing nation is actually job displacement. The reasoning here is that local jobs are lost when highly automated firms enter economies characterized by lower levels of technology. Host-country leaders are increasingly pressed to deal with allegations of this kind. Indeed, some companies with high levels of technology and automation have begun to experiment with overseas adaptations that introduce more labor-intensive production and distribution than would be possible or acceptable in industrialized countries.

Many firms, however, consider such adaptations very risky. Host-country legislation may ensure, for example, that it will be next to impossible ever to reduce a given labor force once it is in place. Even in industrial countries such regulations can be so severe, and the social welfare components of the cost of labor so high, that affiliates prefer to pay overtime rather than add workers they may later find it impossible to lay off. Efforts to avoid such booby traps may lead the multinational affiliate

---

[1] International Labour Organisation. *The Impact of Multinational Enterprises on Employment and Training.* Geneva: International Labour Organisation, 1976, p. 31.

to freeze existing levels of employment. This strategy may lead to scathing criticism from indigenous trade unions, political parties, and governmental officials.

In dealing with host-country governments, multinationals now face a wide array of questions about their impact on local labor markets and working conditions. On the issue of job creation, particularly in the developing world, they may be able to demonstrate that a fundamental factor operating here is the economic policies of the host-country government. Lawrence Franko, a leading student of multinational corporations, suggests, for example, that where these policies are export oriented and there is a large multinational component in the local economy, MNC affiliates seem to produce high levels of job creation. On the other hand, where national policies are primarily of the import-substitution, protectionist kind, high levels of MNC involvement in the local economy seem to be associated with much lower levels of job creation. This appears to be the situation that prevailed in many Latin American countries during the 1960's.[2]

Overall aggregate statistics on employment effects in developing nations, however produced, can be misleading. As noted earlier, foreign direct investment is increasingly concentrated in a relative handful of Third World countries that play more and more important roles in the international economy. The effect of foreign investment on their employment profile and industrial relations policies can be profound. Brazil, Malaysia and Nigeria are among the developing nations in this special category. Their attitudes toward the labor and industrial practices of the multinationals deserve careful attention.

Salaries and Conditions of Labor

In countries with highly developed, industrialized economies, multinationals are generally found to be well within the average norms as far as wages are concerned. The rule seems to be that they neither lead nor lag behind local firms. In places where local firms are lax in providing the most modern facilities and the safest work environments, the multinationals may actually be singled out as exemplars. In Italy, American firms, in particular, are lauded for everything from standards of plant safety and worker amenities to information disclosure about their local operations.

Of the 70 respondents in Brazil, Malaysia and Nigeria who addressed the issue of wages, almost three-quarters judge multinational wages to be "normal" or "high" by local standards (see Chart 14).

The bulk of Nigerians employed by foreign firms are in white-collar jobs.

---

[2]Lawrence G. Franko, *Multinational Enterprise, the International Division of Labour in Manufacture, and Developing Countries*. Geneva: International Labour Organisation, Working Papers, World Employment Programme Research, October 1975, pp. 18-20.

Chart 14: Evaluation of Wages and Salaries Paid by MNC's

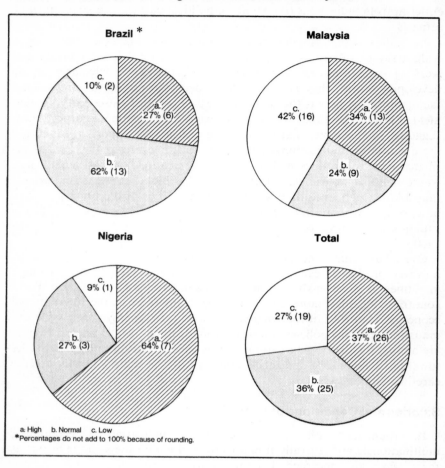

Brazil *

c. 10% (2)
a. 27% (6)
b. 62% (13)

Malaysia

c. 42% (16)
a. 34% (13)
b. 24% (9)

Nigeria

c. 9% (1)
b. 27% (3)
a. 64% (7)

Total

c. 27% (19)
a. 37% (26)
b. 36% (25)

a: High   b. Normal   c. Low
*Percentages do not add to 100% because of rounding.

These positions in general involve substantially higher wage scales than one finds in most other sectors of the economy. This may explain Nigerian perceptions that MNC's pay more than local companies.

The Malaysian response is initially more puzzling, but less so in view of the pains to which the government has gone to lure major foreign companies to its shores. Beginning in 1970, the government went in search of labor-intensive export-oriented multinationals whose establishment in Malaysia would help mop up unemployment, considered a major cause of the communal riots a year earlier. Malaysian responses indicate that the respondents believe that low wages are paid in many of these export-oriented industries, and are critical of this practice. As one local labor leader put it: "The government keeps emphasizing that cheap labor is abundant in Malaysia. The foreigners get this impression and come here. And they exploit the workers to the maximum."

When low wage rates are also associated with multinational activities felt to be unrelated to local industrial development, criticisms of local labor leaders become even more sweeping. In the words of another Malaysian trade unionist: "Employment creation is a joke! There is still 12 percent unemployment in this country. How many people does the so-called manufacturing sector actually employ? And the employment that is created is not stable. Those factories can close as quickly as they open."

The Brazilian situation also involves a special twist. Respondents believe wage levels paid by multinationals are at least normal by local standards and even, perhaps, high. Those local standards, however, have involved a continuous erosion of the real wages of industrial workers in the last several years. This pattern is in sharp contrast with the direction that managerial salaries have followed during the same period. Not only are Brazilian managers among the highest paid in the world; such salaries also make a major contribution to the extreme inequality of income that has been characteristic of Brazil.

Insofar as the multinationals contribute, actively or passively, to this inequality, they become the targets of highly volatile political attacks in Brazil. A number of managers of firms that collaborated in this study say that they lose no opportunity to stress to officials at Brasilia how short-sighted and dangerous such wage (and regressive taxation) policies are. These managers know that, if and when a political explosion occurs, the foreign firms will be among the first to suffer. Nevertheless, the companies are loath to press for wage policies that might be objectionable to the national government, to say nothing of the indigenous industrialists who prefer to pay lower wages. Even they, however, have recently begun to urge a modification of government policy.

Brazil provides a good example of how competition for high-talent manpower, often inaugurated and spurred by the multinationals, can bring about unintended distortions and other adverse consequences. The gap between the salaries of those at the bottom of the managerial cadres and those at the top of the most skilled labor categories—above 1000 percent in many cases—has its parallel within the wage-rated categories.

In the first half of 1979, Brazil began to experience levels of labor unrest unprecedented since the military took power 15 years earlier. Spurred by promises that the political system would be somewhat democratized, fueled by expectations that the deterioration in real wages would slow down, and enraged by levels of inflation approaching 60 percent, industrial workers began a series of strikes that could only be alarming to industrial managers. The managers themselves understand that equity, political validity, and continued economic growth require an attenuation of the wage problem.

The Question of International Parity

Respondents in all three countries take the view that, although wages paid by the MNC's may be better than those paid by local firms, they are still lower than what the multinational would have to pay workers doing similar jobs at home or in other developed countries. In most cases respondents are not suggesting that Nigerians or Brazilians or Malaysians should be paid precisely what their counterparts receive in the industrialized countries. Their comments reflect two concerns. The first of these arises whenever it is demonstrated (or suspected) that expatriates are paid more than indigenes who are doing the same work. If such episodes are relatively rare among Brazilian as compared with expatriate multinational managers, they occur frequently enough in most overseas environments to elicit pointed criticism.

The second concern is essentially psychological: The types of persons interviewed in this study do not like to have their countries thought of as inexhaustible pools of cheap labor. A Nigerian journalist, who specializes in labor problems, puts it this way: ''The Nigerian labor movement, with its heavy preponderance of white-collar workers, feels that they should have the same 'place' as overseas employees. The point is not so much exact parity in pay as to move away from the prevailing concept of 'cheap labor' in the developing countries.'' His surmise is that where the concept of ''cheap labor'' prevails, indigenous persons are widely and mistakenly perceived as being less competent and less able to learn. Where this is so, opportunities for advancement within the Nigerian affiliate of a given firm will not be the same as the opportunity structure operating in the parent company, or in other affiliates outside the Third World.

Attitudes about lower labor costs vary. Many respondents are aware that if labor were as costly abroad as it is in the parent company's home country, fewer companies would transfer operations abroad. Sharp increases in salaries and wages are, therefore, understood to imply an erosion of a significant comparative advantage enjoyed by the less-developed countries. Most believe that this is a situation that should remain untampered with, at least into the indefinite future, particularly at a time when major groups in countries from which foreign direct investment emanates are now attempting to slow down or even stop the outflow of capital.[3]

Working Conditions

Respondents from the three countries in this study acknowledge that conditions of work in multinational affiliates are superior to those found in local firms. A Brazilian businessman says: ''Working conditions are better in general than in the national industries. The MNC's have a very good

---

[3] James Greene and David Bauer, *Foreign Investment and Employment: An Examination of Foreign Investments to Make 58 Products Overseas.* The Conference Board, Report No. 656, 1975.

wage structure and they care a lot about social benefits. In this sense they are very different from the national entrepreneurs who only care about social issues when they are under pressure."

Contrasts are even more dramatic in Nigeria, where there is universal agreement that concern for health and safety standards, as well as for illness and disability, is much higher in most foreign-owned companies than in indigenous businesses. As a result, Nigerian labor leaders think twice about indigenization. While they strongly favor the government's indigenization program in principle, these leaders expect to find it immensely more difficult to bargain with local owners for better wages and better conditions in the work place. According to one labor leader: "The labor movement is, of course, happy that our economy is being transferred into indigenous hands. But many of us feel that this will also make labor's task more difficult in persuading indigenous owners to conform to modern standards. We strongly favor it on political grounds, but have some reservations on economic grounds. Indigenous companies make life difficult for labor. They have bad labor practices; their human relations programs are bad; and they try to disrupt trade union organization."

Similar considerations are apparent in Brazil. A great many Brazilians believe that, left entirely to their own devices, the indigenous industrialist class would do little to improve either wages or working conditions. If a few of the larger Brazilian-owned industries pride themselves on wage levels and worker safety and amenities policies that rank with the highest international standards, many more exemplify the form of exploitative capitalism prevalent in the western industrialized countries in the 18th and 19th centuries.

Training

Third World trade union leaders, as well as other elites, are acutely aware that the training programs of multinationals provide one of the important paths to economic modernization. About one-third of the respondents discussed this issue. Although three-fifths of them judge MNC training programs to be "adequate" or "exceptional," some striking country differences are depicted in Chart 15.

Once again there is a clear relationship between elite attitudes and the level of economic and industrial development. Brazil leads these three countries in level of infrastructure, industrial and technological development. Respondents from that country show the greatest satisfaction with MNC training efforts. Nigeria is at the other extreme, where over half of the respondents judge programs as inadequate, and not one of them evaluates MNC training efforts as "exceptional."

The underlying dynamic that explains these differences in attitude should be made clear. Brazil's sophisticated industry and economy, and the tempo of its development, require a highly trained and specialized labor force. Companies that want to be successful there will go to great efforts to supplement whatever the Brazilian education system provides by way of in-service training programs. In Nigeria, there is relatively little local manufacturing, and companies tend to be found in relatively isolated enclaves. For the country as a whole, demand for highly skilled labor is low, and the multinational affiliates respond to this local situation.

The Nigerian situation reflects one of the dilemmas of un-derdevelopment: In a less-developed economy, multinational corporations have less need for skilled workers and, therefore, less incentive to train them. Relatively speaking, training is not an issue in Brazil because the multinationals must train the work force that will permit them to remain viable; training is a biting issue in Nigeria because the need for training programs is not imposed by the economy itself.

Chart 15: Evaluation of Worker Training Provided by MNC's

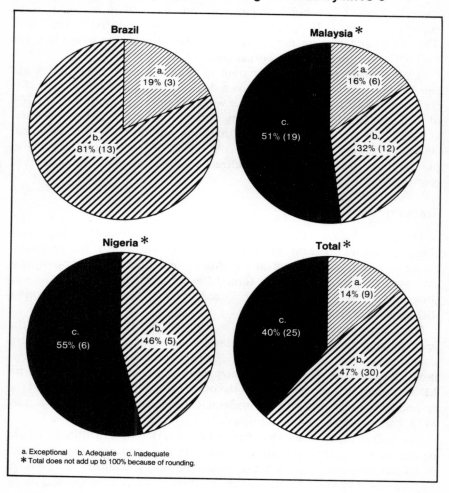

a. Exceptional   b. Adequate   c. Inadequate
* Total does not add up to 100% because of rounding.

Behind the acknowledgement that MNC's are engaged in upgrading the quality of local labor pools there lurks the suspicion that they hold back on the inculcation of certain essential skills. Such views are similar to many expressed about technology transfer: There is the residual belief that the developed countries know more than they are willing to reveal, and that the best and most useful wisdom is held back.

Reservations of this type must not obscure the overall finding: Almost universally the training efforts of the multinationals are judged to be superior to what local firms are doing. A Chinese politician in Malaysia insists that this is so even if one can show that some MNC's are less concerned than others about training. His point is that local enterprise has not evolved to a point where training is seen as integrally related to the profitability of the firm: "Most local firms have no conception of training. They expect people to learn as they go along. It is only in recent years that some of the bigger local companies have even begun to think in terms of training their workers."

A Brazilian businessman notes that the superiority of foreign firms in the training area is built into the very definition and meaning of industrial multinationality. The MNC's accumulate worldwide experience in the best—and the worst—ways to approach worker training. Beyond sheer experience, they also have the administrative know-how and the financial resources to put training schemes to the most effective use. The local firms may be similarly motivated, but they lack the resources that permit them to compete with the multinationals.

As suggested earlier, many respondents consider training programs to be a vital part of technology transfer. A Brazilian industrialist points out that some of the workers trained by the MNC's will move on to national forms and raise the level of skills in these places. In Malaysia, one striking reason for elite criticism of the government's export zone policy is that it invites to Malaysia exactly those multinationals that make the weakest contribution in imparting industrial skills. For these Malaysians the creation of employment is not enough to justify the incentives the government provides the foreign investor; technology transfer in all forms, but particularly in the form of worker training, must be given more official attention.

These elites argue that an effective training program is a ncessary condition for optimal industrial development. Precisely because they excel in this function, the MNC's are increasingly called upon to make training a central aspect of their overseas operations.

Some multinational managers complain that they are often asked to assume responsibilities overseas that appropriately belong to governments. A top political figure in Nigeria, while not excusing the MNC's from a heavy share of training responsibility, acknowledges this point. The lack of skilled workers, he says, does represent a failure of the MNC's. "But to a greater extent it represents a lack of honesty on our part. It represents a failure by Nigerians to create a powerful drive to train Nigerians. What

Nigeria needs is a major effort sponsored by government, extending perhaps over 50 years, to create an adequate cadre of trained Nigerian technicians. It is useless to complain about what foreigners have not done to train Nigerians when we have done so little ourselves."

Side by side with such objectivity will go greater insistence that the multinationals shoulder more of the training burden. A top official of Nigeria's national bank put it bluntly: "Foreign firms will be judged in the future by their willingness and their ability to train Nigerians to carry out the development of Nigeria".

The leaders of the developing nations are harried by the gap between national aspirations and national capacity. Because economic and political needs are so intimately connected, firms can expect pressures for stronger commitments to training to increase markedly in the years ahead. The assistance the multinationals can provide to close this gap will be well received for political as well as economic reasons.

Trade Unions and Industrial Relations

Trade unions operate under severe legal and political restraints in all three countries. Compared with the developed nations, very few workers are found in unions at all, although the more industrialized sectors of Brazil are closer to the Western than to the Asian or African pattern. Nevertheless, by comparison with other major Latin American countries like Argentina or Chile, the Brazilian trade union movement has historically been quite weak.

Since the Revolution of 1964, Brazilian organized labor has led a precarious existence. Freedom to organize trade unions is severely curtailed; the only trade union structures that are accepted at all are those that have received official blessing and authorization. Brazilian industrialists continue to believe that organized labor was a prime cause of the economic chaos under President Joao Goulart that brought the military to power and led to the prohibition of free political party and trade union organization.

Labor leaders in Brazil believe that the indigenous industrial community has used this history to rationalize persistent low wages and other unacceptable working conditions that characterize the economy. The degree of their growing antagonism is evidenced in recent and escalating labor unrest in the teeth of official prohibitions against strikes. Leading members of the multinational community in Brazil are not only in favor of wage improvement but are also convinced that greater permissiveness regarding trade unions is a vital aspect of the political détente that the new President and his government have promised. Indeed this view is shared by some members of the Brazilian cabinet. Differences of opinion as to how much concession should be made on wages was a prime reason for the resignation of one cabinet member in the Summer of 1979.

In Nigeria and Malaysia the labor unions are, if anything, even weaker than in Brazil. Under Nigeria's military regime, unions have not been permitted to function openly and freely, although that situation may change as the country returns to civilian rule. Malaysia, which is the most liberal of the three countries as far as labor organizations go, will experience greater unionization as industrialization proceeds. As in Nigeria and Brazil, a more articulated trade union movement in Malaysia is almost certain to be highly fragmented, reflecting the communal divisions within the country.

What about the attitudes of trade union leaders toward the multinationals? Such evidence as is available suggests the description of "schizophrenic." On the one hand, union leaders quickly recite the litany of wrongdoings practiced by the multinationals; on the other hand, they also acknowledge that the multinationals have satisfactory labor and industrial relations practices and, indeed, have better relationships with local union organizations than do most national companies.

The head of a white-collar union in Nigeria believes that the multinationals are much more advanced than Nigerian-owned companies about recognizing the legitimacy of labor organizations. A Nigerian specialist on labor matters cites the greater willingness of foreign firms to recognize the need for cooperation with the labor movement. While multinational affiliates may go so far as actually to encourage union organization, indigenous employers take a personal and paternalistic view of their factories or businesses. They say: "This is my company and things will be done the way I say." There is much more tension and many more strikes in the indigenous business community." Local labor leaders, political representatives, and members of national bureaucracies voice the same complaints about indigenous business leaders—especially their paternalism and their sense of outrage that labor organizations might want to interfere with the prerogatives of ownership. Although similar attitudes can be found within the multinational sector, they are generally conceded to be more rare.

Nevertheless, the multinationals certainly do not escape unscathed from the scrutiny of indigenous labor organizations. In Malaysia, for example, one encounters extremely hostile feelings toward allegedly wide-ranging multinational exploitative practices, and equally hostile feelings toward governmental policies that encourage or permit these practices. One labor leader comments: "The government helps the multinationals to be socially irresponsible. It enacts laws that prevent the workers from taking industrial action for better pay. So why should the MNC's pay high wages? The multinationals are like princes and we give them royal treatment even though they exploit us."

A Malaysian-Indian politician denies this, insisting that the union leaders overstate the case. He insists that these leaders, most of whom are Indians, fail to negotiate with firms on a consistent basis. Because of frequent change in union leadership, negotiations proceed in fits and starts. More important, in his view, is the undeniable fact that the multinationals treat their employees much better than local firms. This contrast makes it extremely difficult for the union leaders to direct their criticisms primarily against the multinationals.

In general, local union leaders come to expect more hostility from indigenes than they do from foreign managers. This is true within the multinational corporation itself. Union leaders expect to receive less understanding and greater opposition from multinational affiliate managers who are indigenes, than from expatriates. Part of the time the explanation for this difference is said to be that local managers are often drawn from the country's higher classes and even from the aristocracy. One does not expect a Brazilian multinational affiliate manager from a leading Brazilian family to show the same degree of tolerance toward organized labor that one would expect from a typical American expatriate manager.

But the contrast may persist even when local managers are recruited from a broader social and economic base. Thus, the head of a major industrial union in Malaysia says about Malaysian managers of MNC affiliates: "Local managers tend to have a miserly attitude. Especially when they come from lowly or rural backgrounds, they will minimize the workers' needs. Expatriate managers, on the other hand, have a more generous conception of what workers need to live decently."

Chapter 13
Codes of Conduct and Social Responsibility

FEW RESPONDENTS in this study perceive multinationals as birds of prey; few recite the roll call of depredations that the multinationals are often alleged to commit in the Third World. Most respondents are pragmatic about what it takes to keep the multinationals behaving well: If there are clear, strong and coherent policies that are well administered, the multinationals will behave accordingly. As one Brazilian administrator puts it: "Some multinationals have impeccable conduct; others do not. By and large, what they want is to have the rules of the government defined for them. Once they know the rules, they accommodate."

Codes of Conduct

Partly as a response to several spectacular examples of corporate misbehavior, partly as an effort to stem the flow of government regulation, partly to demonstrate that the best regulators of corporate behavior are the corporations themselves, a large number of firms—almost exclusively American thus far—have drafted "codes of conduct"—sets of norms designed to guide corporate behavior.[1]

Critics of the multinational corporation are far from enthusiastic about the codes. They reject the idea that multinational corporations will regulate themselves to minimize those negative aspects of overseas corporate behavior that these critics allege to be endemic. According to the critics, nothing short of binding *international* codes of conduct, enacted by organizations like the United Nations, UNCTAD, or the International Labor Organization (ILO) will suffice to bring corporations into line.

How do respondents interviewed for this study react to these company codes or international proposals?

[1] Robert Black, Stephen Blank and Elizabeth Hanson, *Multinationals in Contention: Responses at Governmental and International Levels*. The Conference Board, Report No. 749, 1978, Chapters 6, 9 and 10.

In the first place, knowledge about existing or proposed codes is very low. Half or more of the respondents were unable to articulate any views at all about them (Tables 23 and 24). Where they did, more had comments on international codes than on company codes (50 and 32 percent, respectively). One reason for this disparity is that the United Nations' discussion of codes has received extensive publicity, particularly in countries of the Third World. Another reason is that host-country leaders simply do not look to corporations as organizations likely to be very diligent in self-regulation. Indeed, among respondents who are aware of company codes, the general reaction to them is likely to be highly skeptical. Those who consider company codes "useless" or "impractical" outnumber those who see some utility in them by three to two. But over half of the knowledgeable respondents suggest that international codes may be at least "marginally useful." About one respondent in ten believes that either kind of code is useful or essential.

Country differences are illuminating. Brazilians seem more cynical about the entire code exercise—more likely than others to deride codes, international or corporate, as useless. More Malaysians claim to be informed about codes than either Brazilians or Nigerians, and tend to be more optimistic about their usefulness. Two factors may account for this: First, as noted earlier, Malaysians are concerned about the failure of international firms to establish more than distributing and assembly operations there, and about the tendency of many multinationals to see Malaysia primarily as a source of cheap labor. Codes might help limit and correct this tendency.

Second, Malaysians worry about the expansive propensities of their own government, and the possibility that public-sector power will be used to favor one ethnic group at the expense of another. Conceivably, an international code of conduct might include rules that constrain such impulses.

Nigerians are least familiar with codes. Of the three countries, Nigeria has had least experience with multinationals (other than the oil companies), and little experience, in particular, with U.S. firms.

The Utility of an International Code

What useful functions might be performed by an international code of conduct? No one suggests that a code should—or could—take the place of national law. Few respondents even suggest that an international code should be mandatory if, by that, it is meant that the code should supersede *national* law. Almost unanimously they would agree with these words of a Nigerian elder stateman: "A code of conduct for multinationals in foreign countries, in the final analysis, must be this: that foreign companies should study the rules of the host country and follow them carefully. They must either obey the rules of the host country or not go into that country at all."

Some feel, however, that an international code can serve as a valuable

Table 23: Attitudes Toward International Codes of Conduct

Attitude	Country							
	Brazil		Malaysia		Nigeria		Total	
	Number	Percent	Number	Percent	Number	Percent	Number	Percent
Essential	1	2%	—	—	3	7%	4	2%
Useful	1	2	11	13	2	5	14	8
Marginally useful	3	6	20	24	5	15	29	17
Useless	9	18	7	9	2	5	18	10
Impractical	3	6	16	20	3	7	22	12
No opinion	33	66	28	34	25	61	85	50
Total	50	100%	82	100%	41	100%	173	100%

Table 24: Attitudes Toward Company Codes of Conduct

Attitude	Country							
	Brazil		Malaysia		Nigeria		Total	
	Number	Percent	Number	Percent	Number	Percent	Number	Percent
Essential	1	2%	6	7%	—	—	7	4%
Useful	1	2	8	10	4	10	13	7
Marginally useful	—	—	1	1	1	—	1	1
Useless	14	28	13	16	1	2	28	16
Impractical	1	2	6	7	—	—	7	4
No opinion	33	66	48	59	36	88	117	68
Total	50	100%	82	100%	41	100%	173	100%

supplement to national legislation and regulation. Particularly for developing nations, where operating rules for foreign companies are still uncertain or incomplete, an international code might establish a general framework or a baseline for corporate behavior. Such codes might also alert host countries to issues requiring national legislation and serve also as a model for local rules and regulations.

Debates about an international code and the code-drafting exercise itself has great value, some respondents argue. One, a Brazilian technocrat who has had international experience in this area, believes that the shaping of international opinion is the critical contribution codes of conduct can make. "When my colleagues at UNCTAD want a surveillance body or a judicial tribunal, I say 'No.' The important thing is not to create tribunals but to have the international community say 'This is what should be done. Let's do it.' "

A Malaysian civil servant believes that an international code of conduct might also be highly useful for business. It might serve as a guideline that would help business leaders improve their appreciation of local problems and interests. It might lead to greater standardization of national regulations affecting foreign companies and thus to greater predictability and certainty for multinational corporations. A code might also serve as a yardstick for evaluating both business performance and national regulation as its affects enterprise.

Would an international code be practicable? A quarter of all respondents with an opinion doubt that a code could be implemented. They point to the lack of common norms among the nations of the world. The difficulty in gaining agreement on the terms of a United Nations code, for example, mirrors the sharply divergent values and interests of the UN membership. Even if the basic terms of a code could be worked out, a Brazilian planner warns, the mechanisms for international coordination are lacking. Taxation is a case in point. Even in the unlikely event that the premises of an international policy on taxation could be agreed upon, the means for implementing such a policy do not exist. Enforcement would require an unheard of degree of coordination of national fiscal policies, disclosure requirements, payment procedures, and so on—to ensure at a minimum that particular nations would not be advantaged or disadvantaged by the operation of the code.

As noted earlier, few respondents desire mandatory international codes. This attitude sharply contrasts with the public statements of many Third World leaders, who typically demand an enforceable international code of conduct for business. National leaders interviewed for this study, however, are *not* willing to countenance international rules and regulations that supersede the laws of their own nations.

Only a handful of respondents were at all concerned about the lack of international enforcement capacity. A Malaysian says that a UN code would not be effective because of its lack of power. "A UN code is more moral than binding—and of course the world is not governed by morals." In his view, therefore, a code formulated at the regional level has a better chance to succeed: "An ASEAN code that is discussed and agreed upon by ASEAN nations can be implemented in the region." But the competition among ASEAN members for technology and capital make an effective code, even at the regional level, rather unlikely—exactly the critical stumbling block that hampered the regional agreement of the Andean Group.

A few respondents say that they feel the multinationals are too powerful to be bound by an international code. A Chinese-Malaysian politician states: "The MNC's are not concerned about codes. They only respect strength. Malaysians must demonstrate resilience. We must be confident of our own capacities." He, too, opts for a regional approach, although not a regional code: "One way we can increase our strength is to promote regional cooperation. If ASEAN can negotiate as a bloc, this will demonstrate our mutual strength." Other respondents feel that behind the facade of corporate self-regulation or corporate good citizenship, MNC's possess an arsenal of legal talent and other sophisticated means of circumventing laws and regulations. In the words of a Brazilian technocrat: "MNC's do not evade taxes because, ultimately, they don't need to evade taxes. There are other mechanisms for concealing profits, like inflated remittances, intracompany interest payments, and so on. They can play at a more sophisticated level." Thus, they say an international code would be no more successful at ultimately controlling the multinationals than local legislation.

Several respondents argue that the most powerful of the multinationals should champion international codes, and seek to persuade individual firms to develop company codes. Norms associated with these codes would serve to make market behavior more orderly. More important, they may inhibit the type of corporate behavior which, even if rare, damages the image and the reputation of the multinational community.

According to this argument, it is up to the firms themselves—especially the largest and most prominent among them—to set the tone for honest and responsible business throughout. Failing this, it is predictable that the less honest types will determine the rules of the game, until governments are finally provoked to intervene with massive regulatory systems.

In an earlier study conducted in Canada and Italy, host-country elites expressed concern that corporate codes of conduct might in themselves be unwelcome evidence of too much control of local affiliates by their parent companies.[2] No one interviewed in Brazil, Malaysia or Nigeria condemned corporate codes as representing, in the words of an Italian businessman, "the arrogance of the center."

[2] Joseph LaPalombara and Stephen Blank, *Multinational Corporations and National Elites: A Study in Tensions.* The Conference Board, Report No. 702, 1976.

On the other hand, respondents in the developing countries agree with the Italian and Canadian view that corporate codes are, in almost all cases, likely to be an American phenomenon. European companies have pursued and refined the "corporate social audit," but the focus thus far (with some notable exceptions) has been limited to domestic concerns. On the whole, European businessmen have been unenthusiastic about company codes. Indeed, European managers are not only dubious about the utility of corporate codes, but believe that these codes may turn out to be a net disadvantage to the firm.

Expatriate Managers and Corporate Codes

If corporate headquarters drafts a code of conduct, the managers in the field have to live with it. The reactions of expatriate managers to codes of conduct vary greatly and, most notably, in typical responses of European and American executives.

A U.S. expatriate in Brazil says: "Corporate codes are a contribution that the American mentality is bringing to world commerce." He says that he comes down on both sides. "I'm a line guy who has to live with it. The only way to live by it is to be hard and strict." In the long run, he feels that corporate codes of conduct will help the United States and the host country, but he acknowledges that in the shorter term the companies that develop codes of conduct will labor under certain disadvantages overseas. "Most businessmen overseas are used to payoffs. They believe that you will go under if you don't make them. But this is really nonsense. They can live without payoffs. They can live with these codes."

A typical European expatriate view of corporate codes is that, as a Swiss general manager in Nigeria observes: "They are pure fiction. If you have good conduct, you don't have to stress it. If you don't, a code of conduct isn't going to change it. Too much fuss is made about all of this. As long as I am here, I will see to it that we behave as well as possible, but there's no need to talk about it every day." Another European executive, sitting at corporate headquarters, agrees that corporate codes are useful, perhaps even necessary, but very difficult to formulate. "A corporate code comes out a bit like being against sin and for motherhood," he says. His company "communicates" a code to its overseas affiliates, that are urged to "express" the code in terms appropriate to local customs. But he opposes making the company code public: "It would be foolish to publish a company code. It would be too easy to ridicule. Besides, to publish a code can itself be taken as evidence of past bad behavior, or at least of a bad conscience." This conforms precisely with the view, reported in the earlier study, of an Italian manager of a U.S. company operating in Italy: "The very least that people who read our libretto will think is that if we have published it, there must be something we are trying to hide."

Social Responsibility

In a world of extreme skepticism about the corporation, many firms are increasingly attentive to the requirements of "good citizenship" or "socially responsible" corporate behavior. These interchangeable terms are said to signal a new corporate awareness of the impact of the firms on the overall environment.

Corporate social responsibility is inevitably seen through the eyes of the beholders. What is promised in Kansas City or Los Angeles may not be equally appraised in São Paulo, Lagos or Kuala Lumpur. It is essential, therefore, to gain some perspective as to the evaluations that host-country elites make of the overall operations of the foreign firms in their midst. It is equally important to learn how these persons define socially responsible corporate behavior.

As Chart 16 shows, only a negligible number—four in all— of respondents believe that the multinationals' conception of social responsibility is well-formulated in *their* respective countries. A quarter of them state that multinationals lack any sense of social responsibility at all. Just over a third suggest that the multinationals display a preliminary and diffuse sense of what social responsibility in their countries might require.

It is apparent that Brazilians are the most skeptical, with almost two-fifths of the respondents claiming that the MNC's have no sense of socially responsible behavior. Malaysians are not so skeptical; almost half suggest that the multinationals are at least making a beginning in this area. Nigerians perhaps do not yet have sufficient experience with the MNC's to make strong assessments one way or the other.

The basic complaint overseas is that the multinational seems to equate good citizenship and social responsibility with corporate good deeds, or with scrupulous adherence to local laws. For many respondents, good deeds are irrelevant and obedience to local law is no more than corporations owe their host countries. When asked how they would describe socially responsible corporate behavior, three-fourths of the respondents emphasize that corporate business plans and operations should conform to national development programs. Another 17 percent discuss the general economic impact of the multinationals on the local economy.

One searches in vain for clear-cut definitions of what good corporate citizenship would require. On the other hand, host-country leaders complain that the multinationals themselves do not have well-reasoned ideas, philosophies or programs on the basis of which good citizenship and social responsibility might be gauged.

Elites in these countries suspect that the multinationals are significantly *less* responsible overseas than they are at home. It is no answer to this charge simply to show that the multinational firms behave better than indigenous enterprises. Many knowledgeable host-country leaders insist the multinationals should behave in their environment exactly as they would in their home countries. An Indian civil servant in Malaysia, for example, scores the MNC's for not paying as much attention to welfare and the environment as they do in the developed countries. "When they leave their home bases," he says, "they run wild and do whatever they want, regardless of the consequences to their hosts."

Not everyone agrees with this harsh assessment. Others note that vast and varied corporate experience makes the multinationals more open than local firms to trade unions and modern industrial relations; more sensitive to environmental protection, health and safety requirements and employee training; more responsive to the demands and regulations of government; and more willing to support community affairs.

Although corporate philanthropy abroad should not be confused or equated with social responsibility, its importance can easily be underestimated. When foreign companies establish libraries, build specialized schools, or endow university chairs, host-country elites take notice.

Chart 16: Assessment of MNC Sense of Social Responsibility

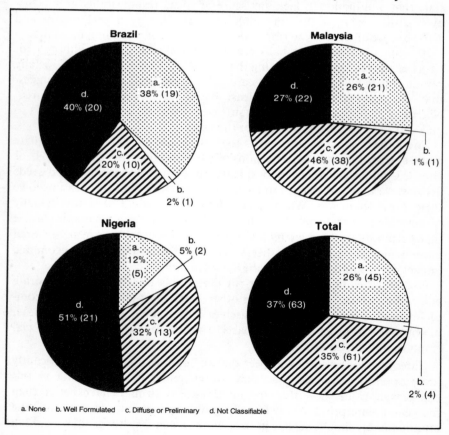

a. None   b. Well Formulated   c. Diffuse or Preliminary   d. Not Classifiable

196

A few respondents relate a company's willingness to take part in this kind of activity to its national background. An official in a state-owned enterprise in Brazil notes that some MNC's are very "welfare-oriented." "One, for example, set up the best hospital for tropical diseases in the world. Some enterprises have excellent social programs, and others are more conservative. That depends on the country of origin—the mentality transplanted from their home country. Americans and Scandinavians, for example, tend to be more oriented toward social issues."

Host-country elites expect the multinationals to bring to their shores the very best in technology, managerial talent, training programs, research and development, and environmental protection. If the multinationals are applauded for doing more of all of these things than local firms, they are often condemned for doing so only under duress. In the words of a Nigerian banker: "They have been good citizens, reluctantly, grudgingly, and have sought to find loopholes in government regulations wherever possible. If foreign firms are not trusted in Nigeria, they do not deserve to be trusted." A Brazilian technocrat sums it up: "When the multinationals act responsibly—for example, to avoid polluting the atmosphere—they do so under pressure. And there cannot be public responsibility under pressure."

In many cases the MNC's are caught in a cleft stick and can be condemned no matter which way they go. Pushing the economy ahead may lead to greater environmental destruction; transferring certain kinds of highly desired technology (e.g., nuclear power) may have unfortunate social consequences; costs of production may inadvertently undermine regional development plans.

Brazilian respondents who perceive these dilemmas relate them less to corporate social responsibility than to the failure of the state to establish a system of national priorities and to require that corporate operations conform to this. Discussing pollution control, a Brazilian engineer says that this is not a function of corporate citizenship. "I insist this is a function of legislation. If the law does not require companies to control pollution, they won't. As long as the prevailing atmosphere here is one of the Wild West, companies will act according to these rules. Nobody creates social responsibility if it is not imposed." It is not a problem of legislation another Brazilian argues, as much as one of *priorities*. Multinationals (and local firms) may cause pollution, but they provide jobs, generate income, foster economic development. What does the country want? Establishing priorities is not a task that individual companies can undertake. They will adjust, guided by profitability, to whatever system exists.

Although most Brazilians stress the role of the state in imposing responsible standards of conduct, a few point to the absence of well-developed community and consumer attitudes in Brazil as a major problem. A young technocrat observes: "The Brazilian market is still too quantitatively oriented. There is no consumer mentality in the style of Ralph

Nader. This is what creates public responsibility, these kinds of pressures and mechansims."

Malaysians are more apt to discuss the voluntary side of corporate behavior. Several suggest that the government's role should extend beyond setting standards and regulations. Officials should exhort and persuade firms to do *more* than the law requires. The multinationals, in turn, should recognize that this behavior has a real payoff. One respondent says: "Many parent companies expect their subsidiaries to show greater social responsibility. To do so is not only good for profits, but the goodwill and image that are created are important considerations, too. Our local firms can get away with murder, but the multinational corporations can't afford this." Efforts to go beyond local requirements may give the strongest impression of socially responsible behavior. Corporations may, in fact, sometimes be able to act where the local government cannot.

A Malaysian bureaucrat in the Cabinet Office explains that Malaysia has several "governments"—state governments, the federal government, even the state bureaucracy—all of which have different views on such subjects as environmental protection. It is not sufficient to say "follow the law," when the laws are so inchoate. And there are situations in which the private firm might be in a better position to act than the government. The federal government, for example, might be unable to impose pollution regulation requirements on a recalcitrant state government determined to heighten its growth rate. A foreign firm can choose the easier state standards, or it can act more responsibly by adhering to federal or even to its home standards. "It is the easiest way out for the foreign firm to say that it has done everything the government is doing and should not be asked to do more. But in the end, if they do not do more, they will get it in the neck."

Although individual respondents list a wide array of specific acts or requirements that constitute good corporate citizenship, it is relatively easy to summarize and classify them. There are, first of all, responsibilities to workers—ranging from wages to conditions of work and worker training. Second, there are responsibilities to the economy and environment that encompass technology, local sourcing, production for export, and a wide variety of other specifics. Third, there is the responsibility to the host country as such, to its developmental needs, potential, aspirations and policies.

A Nigerian businessman and economist produces a simple and pointed list of requirements:

• The multinational should be seen to respect the sensibilities of its local partners and not attempt to circumvent the authority of senior Nigerian managers or the Nigerian members of the board of directors.

• Foreign companies must realize that even if they own a majority share of the local subsidiary, the interests of the subsidiary are not 100 percent those of the parent.

- The foreign company must develop local managerial skill.
- Finally, foreign firms must realize that the strength of the multinational corporation lies ultimately in its ability to adapt to host countries and not to insist that host countries adapt to them.

In the less-developed nations, especially those that have not reached the level of Brazil, social responsibility may be overwhelmingly associated with the willingness of the foreign company to develop local human resources—that is, to transfer technology, both technical and managerial; to train workers at every level; and to share operating authority in its subsidiaries with local people. In the least developed nations these requirements may involve corporations in a much broader range of responsibilities than they have previously encountered.

A Nigerian with wide experience in government insists: "Firms should help their staff to overcome the basic practical difficulties of life here—for example, by helping to provide public transportation, housing, medical care, and indeed, in helping to arrange such matters as education and health care for their families."

Experiences at home do not prepare companies for demands of this kind. Yet they will face persistent pressures to adapt to local conditions in exactly this way. Such adaptation goes side by side with the growing need to align the company's mission and operations overseas with the national plans and aspirations of host countries.

This form of adaptation is immensely more valued than corporate good deeds or acts of philanthropy. However much they may be appreciated, such acts rarely head the list of host-country definitions of social responsibility. Indeed, such acts may actually be resented by locals who are wary of corporate paternalism, and by governments that may feel the programs serve to underscore their own weaknesses or negligence. Furthermore, major social conflicts (for example, ethnic or racial conflicts) may run dangerously close to the surface in apparently nonpolitical arenas. Involvement in university development in many new nations, for example, might have long-term and unpleasant political ramifications.

The message of this chapter is clear: Neither corporate codes of conduct nor occasional good deeds can substitute for what the multinational corporation does in its day-to-day operations to satisfy the deeper and more demanding expectations of those in host countries who are potentially the most important supporters—or detractors—of multinational enterprise.

Part Four

Chapter 14
The "Brazilian Model": Summary and Conclusions

WHAT are the wider implications of the analysis of foreign investment policies in Brazil, Malaysia and Nigeria—and of their leaders' perceptions and attitudes that determine how these policies emerge and affect the foreign investor? Perhaps the most interesting, although tentative, speculation is that countries of this type, the more advanced of the developing nations, may be moving in a similar direction insofar as their attitudes and policies regarding the foreign investor are concerned, and that a pattern or model may be seen emerging across a range of countries.

The Brazilian Model

The analysis suggests that, within limits, one can think of Brazil as constituting a model of the kinds of demands, bargaining posture, and regulations multinational corporations will encounter in other developing nations. Brazil, of course, is in a class by itself. It is not Chad or Peru: The latter cannot weigh as heavily as Brazil in their relationships with the multinationals.

Despite such obvious caveats, the concept of the Brazilian model is appealing. In its basic posture toward foreign investment, Brazil seems to fit what many observers would expect from nations as they develop economically and politically. The Brazilian case makes it perfectly clear that a developing nation can introduce a wide range of stringent policies and regulations without turning off the flow of foreign direct investment. Brazil seems also to represent a novel middle ground between laissez-faire capitalist and socialist assumptions about the need and value of foreign investment—and what form such investment should take.

The Brazilian model is usefully considered along the following major dimensions:

Ideology. Preconceptions are less rigid about capitalism and socialism, or about the relative superiority of private or public ownership of the instruments of production. However, most leaders agree that the state constitutes a major factor in the economy—as a source of investment capital, as entrepreneur and producer, as planner and regulator of industrial and agricultural enterprise.

Some degree of centralized planning is accepted. The need for coordinating the Brazilian public and private sectors, as well as the private foreign investment sector, is widely acknowledged. Also the need to bring into harmony developmental plans and policies of governmental units throughout the federal system is conceded.

Attitudes Toward FDI. Attitudes are favorable but not uncritical. The basic commitment is to encourage a continuous flow of foreign capital, to treat the foreign investor fairly, and to accept modes of resolving conflict typical of the industrial world. A growing commitment is that the kind and levels of FDI should be more consciously attuned to the developmental needs and priorities of the nation.

The multinationals are seen as major factors regarding a range of problems of great concern to Brazilian interest groups, political leaders, and policymakers. These include the balance of payments, servicing foreign debt, import substitution, exports, the rationalization of national industry, and so on. Because of this, regulation and control of the multinational is considered a prime requisite of effective internal economic management.

Significant Actors. In the normal negotiation and day-to-day operations carried on by the multinational in places like Brazil, the most significant host-country actors are found in the upper reaches of the military and civilian bureaucracies. Key figures in these sectors seem to be permanent; they generally manage to survive many changes of presidents, cabinets and governments. They also probably account for most of the policies directed toward the multinationals and their administration. Among the strategic elite categories of host countries, this one is the most important.

These actors in Brazil are *tecnicos*—well-trained professionals who, by and large, know what they are doing. Their internal economic and political managerial capability is high. They approach multinationals with self-confidence. Their praise and criticism of the foreign direct investor, their demands and concessions are, more often than not, likely to be based on direct experience.

Significant actors are not limited to the military or civilian bureaucracies. As the political system is liberalized, they will appear increasingly at the head of labor unions, the mass media, and political parties. Within the universities and other intellectual circles, there are always those whose views about the foreign direct investor are more than marginally important. It must be taken for granted that actors from these categories will often make the multinationals the objects of much of their criticism of society. On the whole—and for a variety of reasons—such criticisms are likely to remain circumscribed within bounds that will not seriously threaten the foreign investor.

Indigenous industrialists and entrepreneurs are also significant actors. They are neither merely potential "sleeping partners" for foreign companies nor necessarily natural allies of the multinational corporation. They are also potential competitors, often highly influential, who may try to keep some foreign investors out; and they are potential partners in joint ventures who will want to share management control. By and large, the impact of these groups is favorable both to the preservation of the private sector and to the encouragement of a continuing (but regulated) flow of FDI.

Bargaining Style. Because the stakes are high, Brazilians seek to drive hard bargains. As the world's tenth largest economy, Brazil will no doubt escalate the demands it makes not only on foreign investors, but also on international banks whose offshore lending practices are considered demeaning or offensive.

Brazilians are also pragmatic negotiators. This means that, despite what may appear as formal legislation or regulation, they prefer to deal with issues on a day-to-day, case-by-case basis. They prefer not to stand too rigidly on legalistic formulations. Their bargaining style is indirect, opaque, nuanced and polite. Learning to read the gestures, intonations and other hallmarks of nuance is a major requirement for those who wish to operate successfully in Brazil.

Bargaining Strategies. The basic strategy is to keep the other side off balance, but to do so within a context that clearly implies a rational and pragmatic approach to negotiations. Beyond pragmatism, Brazilians are empiricists; they want to gather and analyze the relevant facts. They are likely to be as capable of arranging data to suit their own arguments and purposes as those they deal with.

They emphasize that their policies and their implementation will be coherent, predictable and efficient. In exchange for this, Brazilians will demand much greater efforts by foreign investors to integrate their business plans into Brazil's developmental schemes.

Managerial Capability. As the foregoing suggests, managerial capacity is high, and no doubt much higher than in many Third World countries. There is also extensive interaction and collaboration among elites in government and in the private economy. Brazil has undoubtedly been a leader in this development—what some have called the "new corporatism." For this reason, the kind of authoritarian political system that exists there today must not be confused with the more historically typical form of military or authoritarian political systems. Brazil, many feel, is in this basic sense very much the wave of the future.

Political Stability. High-level managerial skills may reduce the probability of explosive political developments but they will not entirely remove it. This is especially so where economic development brings about extreme levels of inequality, as it has in Brazil. Indeed, the history of nations since World War II suggests that the more open the political system, the greater the probability of economic turmoil, political fragmentation, and political repression (military or otherwise).

Levels of current inequality in Brazil, measured by class, geography and race, are acknowledged to be excessive. If the real wages of industrial workers in the cities have been steadily decreasing for some years, their income, on average, is still four times that of the agricultural peasant. If inflation has battered purchasing power in Brazil's industrialized Southwest, rising prices of food and other necessities have been devastating in the countryside. If Brazil can boast the largest black population outside Africa and many truly remarkable achievements in racial integration, it cannot escape the fact that groups at or below the poverty line are overwhelmingly black or Indian.

Brazil's political leaders acknowledge that better wage, price and taxation policies would reduce existing extremes of inequality. Some effort to develop such policies is under way. On the other hand, the leadership wants to resist populism or falling into the easy trap of thinking that the level of inflation can be reduced without austerity.

Brazil's leaders believe the way to resolve current economic problems is through continued economic growth. They say that if they are to succeed in this mission, they will require a high degree of understanding and cooperation from the international banking community and from the multinational firms operating there.

Brazilians, in short, understand the implications of integration into the world market and the interdependence this implies. They wonder whether those who provide capital and direct investment for the developed nations also understand these implications. The dialogue they want to pursue, as well as the policies they put in place, will certainly attract imitators throughout the developing world.

Summary and Conclusions

Even if Brazil, Malaysia and Nigeria are atypical, knowledge about these three countries as investment environments has implications for many other developing countries, such as Mexico, Argentina, Egypt, South Korea, India, Indonesia and Taiwan. Such countries are not just strong magnets attracting risk capital, nor just promising domestic markets. This is also where indigenous multinational firms exist or will emerge; these are the countries evolving a special kind of interdependence with the industrialized world; and, like the OPEC group, they will be significant factors in the world economy.

These three countries are also exemplars because of the influence they exert in their respective regions. What happens to foreign investment in Brazil and Nigeria, particularly, will have major consequences throughout the continents in which they are located.

Host-Country Elites

In most places abroad, the fate of foreign-owned multinational enterprise is guided or influenced by the attitudes and behavior of the host-country's strategic elites. With variation from country to country, these elites are the leaders of political parties and trade unions, influential industrialists and educators, opinion makers in the mass media, highly placed officials in the executive and legislative branches of government and, above all, the civilian and military managers who occupy the commanding heights of public bureaucracies. Not riots or revolutions but the attitudes, policies and behavior of these elites toward the multinationals is what affects most of these companies in most countries most of the time.

Brazilian, Malaysian and Nigerian leaders tend to be ambivalent toward multinational corporations. This is true even of those who wish to encourage foreign direct investment, and who acknowledge that its continuing flow is a necessary condition for economic growth. Essentially all national leaders would prefer that a nation be able to move forward under its own power. When dependence on the outside world is forced on them by the nature of the international economy, it is unrealistic to expect that they will be unqualifiedly grateful.

Beyond the generalizations discussed earlier, it is useful to reflect on the following patterns and tendencies among host-country elites.

(1) The most generalized suspicions of the MNC's are likely to exist in countries at the lower levels of economic development, especially those that have only recently become independent. Here foreign capital has been traditionally associated with extractive industries and has dominated the cash economy. Their leaders will typically have had limited experience with the multinational firms, and it is predictable that the foreign investor will be viewed as essentially exploitative.

(2) Almost by definition, the least developed countries are also in greatest need of outside inputs of capital and managerial, organizational and technological know-how. Thus, suspicion is matched by felt need. The frustration this engenders will sometimes lead to aggressive policies and behavior toward the foreign investment community.

(3) Where developing countries possess significant capital resources of their own, it is natural to expect more demanding and stringent regulation of the foreign investor. Nigeria is a good example and Mexico, visibly flexing its new-found economic muscles, is another.

(4) It would be premature to suggest, however, that as Third World countries discover new resources, or reach higher levels of economic development, their attitudes toward the multinationals will become more hostile. An equally plausible hypothesis is that the development of the economy will lead to more integration of these nations into the world economy, to more

economic and financial interdependence, and, therefore, to a mature and sophisticated approach to the foreign investor.

(5) Brazil provides strong evidence that the latter is the more probable tendency. The Brazilian case suggests that more sophisticated approaches to the multinationals should not be equated with a more liberal or permissive climate of regulation. Brazilians have a precise understanding of how the multinational firm works, and what place it should have in the economy. One result is that foreign investors in Brazil are spared not only sweeping negative judgments, but also the kinds of general laws that raise anxiety levels among those investors. Another result is that the more knowledgeable and experienced Brazilian elites have produced a wide array of specific regulations designed to cope with the multinational-related problems they have pinpointed for attention.

(6) Far from causing high anxiety or panic among investors, policies and regulations of this kind might be welcomed. They suggest not only that governmental elites know what they are doing, but also that, within limits, they perceive foreign investment problems as predictable and manageable. Moreover, insofar as regulations result in unanticipated consequences for either side, they are open to further discussion and negotiation—although administrative elites in all of the countries studied claim to be more rational and pragmatic than they believe they are judged to be by multinational corporate managers.

(7) Although host-country knowledge of industrial enterprise varies by sector and country, it is apparent that the knowledge gap is narrowing everywhere. Nigeria and Malaysia may be less well-endowed than Brazil on this score, but all three countries are in better shape than most developing nations. Horror stories about bureaucratic corruption or inefficiencies should not be too readily generalized for all of the Third World, or reported as if they do not find counterparts in the West. It is generally a mistake to assume that one's business is so complex that no one in the host country can understand it.

(8) Elites in Brazil, Malaysia and Nigeria are not of one mind regarding the role of the public sector in the ownership and management of enterprise. Many are committed to maintaining a dual economy in which the market and the private sector remain fundamental. Even in those cases where leaders advocate direct public ownership in certain sectors, there is usually recognition that private property, free markets, and profitability are necessary to attract foreign direct investment. Nevertheless, these same leaders do not anticipate that state-ownership trends will be reversed; and they believe that central planning of economic development is not only desirable but essential.

Officials in the three countries pay lip service to the desirability of a vibrant private sector. But public administrators in Nigeria may greatly muddle this matter by acquiring pecuniary interests in business and thereby "privatizing" the public sector. Malaysians claim a commitment to free enterprise, but the state has picked up the tempo of acquiring equity under the NEP. The Brazilian government is committed to returning state-owned industry to the private sector. But state assets in manufacturing enterprise there have almost doubled in ten years reaching 30 percent—and are unlikely to be markedly reduced. In all three countries the state will remain a major investor in the economy for some time.

(9) Bureaucratic elites in particular defend the entrepreneurial role of the public sector. Those who manage state-owned enterprises will not passively accept efforts to return these firms to the private sector. In tomorrow's world, they will find allies at many points in the political and interest-group spectrum. The multinational firm must, therefore, be prepared to deal with the public managers not only in their traditional regulatory roles, but also as potential competitors, joint-venture partners, and so on.

(10) Nationalism should not be confused with xenophobia. It means nothing more than greater self-consciousness on the part of elites of host countries that they can—and should—secure the greatest benefits for their countries that bargaining circumstances will allow.

Many implications follow. For example, it is doubtful that many indigenous managers will put loyalty to company before loyalty to country. Companies that have been slow to indigenize overseas managers are often aware of this. As the mix of expatriate and indigenous managers changes, it will be necessary to redefine overseas managerial roles—and corporate expectations regarding overseas managers.

It is equally doubtful that, in dealing with governmental officials abroad, multinational firms will be able to overpower them with the underlying logic—the so-called imperatives—of industrial enterprise conducted on a global scale. These and other local leaders will resist accepting truncated subsidiaries; they will insist on full-scale production, on production for export, on a wide range of conditions that restrict the freedom of the corporate center to optimize its worldwide operations.

(11) When elites think about the benefits multinationals bring, the transfer of technology tops almost everyone's list. There is no way around this issue with host-country leaders who are increasingly able to tell whether the "black box" has anything of value in it. The problem of discussing technological value added becomes exceedingly complicated where host-country pressures are high and where, as in Brazil, local joint-venture partners intend to share in the management and control of the firm. More than ever in the past, negotiations will center on this issue and, therefore, may well require modified corporate negotiating strategies and skills.

Organizational Considerations

The basic issue here is how much autonomy does the multinational subsidiary really have. Closely related is whether the parent company speaks with one voice in the host country, or in as many voices as it may have subsidiaries operating there. Autonomy is the issue at the center of the clash between the logic of national development as opposed to the logic of the international firm. The number of corporate voices relates to the perceived capacity of the multinational to attune its overseas operations to the developmental policies of individual host companies.

It may be that the perceptions of foreign elites are mistaken. There may, in fact, be less central control from headquarters than they fear or imagine. Organization of the firm by product divisions with centralized global responsibility in each division may not impede country-level coordination among subsidiaries overseas. Host-country elites who favor the traditional European model of corporate organization may fail to appreciate how much central control of the full spectrum of a company's overseas operation this format permits.

The beliefs of these persons are important, irrespective of what the facts may be. They claim to have enough direct experience with both of the above matters to be able to show that their beliefs are based on solid evidence. In the American case, it is often the company's own claims about its global reach and the advantages it derives from centralized planning and control that reinforce precisely what local leaders suspect. In any case, indigenous economists, businessmen and public managers—often trained at leading American universities—recite in detail the theory and practice of the international firm.

Matrix or other organizational devices aimed at blending product division, functional and geographic aspects of the global firm are less reassuring abroad than they may be at the corporate center. Neither subsidiary managers nor host-country leaders who want more autonomy fail to note that what looks organizationally like *more* decentralization may actually be *less*. From the standpoint of São Paulo or Lagos, it is not clearly a gain that effective control of local subsidiaries may shift from New York to Coral Gables, or from London to Houston.

The challenge to the international firm is whether it can take on the coloration and nationality of the host country and still be multinational as well. Can a subsidiary be reasonably or acceptably Brazilian or Nigerian and also be integrated into a global corporate entity whose central system is located elsewhere? Where is the point at which, from the standpoint of the host country, the subsidiary loses the nationality of the parent company or, from the standpoint of the parent, the subsidiary surrenders its identity with the company?

Whatever may be the longer term mode of organizational adjustment, the short- and medium-term objectives are to improve corporate capacity to read those aspects of overseas environments that come increasingly to affect the success or failure of enterprise abroad. Attention will have to be paid to the public policy process and to the major groups and organizations that influence it. Forecasts will have to be derived to assess what kinds of policies affecting the foreign investor are being advocated, which policies are actually in the pipeline, and which have the best chance of being adopted as law. Beyond the policies themselves, it will be essential to produce sophisticated readings of the public administrative bodies and processes that are responsible for policy implementation. Just as the success of enterprise is based in part on the accumulation and careful assessment of economic data, the future will require that a stronger basis for making relevant political and administrative assessments be put in place.

Appendix

Appendix
Profile of Respondents

THE GENERAL APPROACH and methodology of this study are described in detail in the Appendix to *Multinational Corporations and National Elites: A Study in Tensions* by Joseph LaPalombara and Stephen Blank (Conference Board Report No. 702, 1976). As in the earlier study the authors take the view that the perceptions, attitudes, expectations and demands of key *strategic elites* in the three host countries, as these refer to foreign investment and multinational corporations, constitute the principal variable that affects and limits the activities of foreign corporations in these countries. The research strategy hinged on the identification in each country of those occupations and individuals in the public and private sectors who influence—either directly or indirectly—the making and implementation of national policies that affect the foreign investor. Once this enumeration had been completed, a listing of 75 to 100 individuals was selected from this group for in-depth interviews. Interviews were carried out in three countries by the project team, utilizing a systematic open-ended interview guide.

Interviews were completed with 173 local elites: 50 in Brazil, 82 in Malaysia, and 41 in Nigeria. Table A-1 shows the distribution of these elites by occupational or professional category. Almost a third are members of the national bureaucracy, while about one-fifth are local businessmen or bankers. Academics constitute about 8 percent of the group and members of the mass media (in fact, all newspaper reporters) almost 6 percent. Political and other constraints abroad sometimes inhibit the researcher's ability to interview persons in certain categories. Thus the set of respondents contains fewer trade unionists than would have been preferred. The same might be said for leaders of the political opposition.

It should be added, however, that the number and range of political leaders included in the sample is quite large. This becomes apparent when one considers not just the primary but also the secondary occupational classification of the respondents (Table A-2). Almost 10 percent of the group either are involved in party politics at the present time, in addition to another occupation, or have served in key political posts in the past.

Table A-1: Distribution of Elites by Elite Category (Primary Classification)

Category	Brazil Amount	Brazil Percent	Malaysia Amount	Malaysia Percent	Nigeria[1] Amount	Nigeria[1] Percent	Total[1] Amount	Total[1] Percent
Cabinet	—	—%	7	9%	—	—%	7	4%
National bureaucracy	16	32	23	28	15	37	54	31
Regional bureaucracy	3	6	3	4	—	—	6	4
State enterprise	6	12	5	6	—	—	11	6
National legislature	—	—	2	2	—	—	2	1
Regional legislature	1	2	2	2	—	—	3	2
Trade union	—	—	4	5	1	2	5	3
Mass media	4	8	3	4	3	7	10	6
Local business	6	12	11	13	5	12	22	13
Manager of MNC (non-coop.)	—	—	2	2	3	7	5	3
Intellectual/Economist	—	—	—	—	1	2	1	1
Intellectual/Other	2	4	—	—	—	—	2	1
Academic	3	6	8	10	3	7	14	8
Liberal profession	1	2	3	4	5	12	9	5
Banker	6	12	3	4	1	2	10	6
Interest group	1	2	6	7	2	5	9	5
Other	1	2	—	—	2	5	3	2
Total	50	100%	82	100%	41	100%	173	100%

[1]Figures do not add to 100% because of rounding.

Table A-2: Distribution of Elites by Elite Category (Secondary Classification)

Category	Number	Percent
Former cabinet members	7	4%
Former national or regional bureaucracy	12	7
Politicians, either party leaders or members of national legislature	10	6
Local business	9	5
Liberal professions	16	9
Economists—in training	23	13
Intellectuals—Other	13	8
No secondary classification	83	48
Total	173	100%

Respondents were asked to indicate their orientation toward the present government of their country. On the basis of their answers, they were placed in one of four categories: those who support the government and its policies regarding foreign investment; those who oppose the present government; those who support the government but are critical of its foreign investment policies; and those who seem to be neutral on both counts. A few responses could not be classified. A bare majority of the total group fall into the first category. Broken down by country, however, this group includes only 32 percent of the Brazilian respondents, but 57 percent of the Malaysians and 76 percent of the Nigerians. More than a third of the whole group are critical of their government's policies toward foreign investment and foreign investors. Again, country differences are illuminating. This group includes a majority of the Brazilian respondents, more than a third of the Malaysians, but only about a sixth of the Nigerians. Critics, of course, do not always lean in the same direction. While most of the Brazilians who criticize their government's foreign investment policies demand more stringent regulation of the MNC's, a large number of Malaysian critics (who are likely to be Chinese-Malaysian businessmen) want less government involvement and regulation in the economy.

A tiny minority of those interviewed can be considered opponents of their governments. This figure may reflect more the problems faced by investigators working in these countries than the actual degee of political opposition there. Still, it provides some evidence to suggest that the view that political upheaval and revolution is a likely event in the near future in any of these countries is probably in error.

Table A-3: Respondents' Orientation to Own Government

	Brazil		Malaysia		Nigeria		Total	
	Amount	*Percent*	*Amount*	*Percent*	*Amount*	*Percent*	*Amount*	*Percent*
Pro..................	16	32%	47	57%	31	76%	94	54%
Neutral.............	5	10	3	4	—	—	8	5
Critical of government policy.............	26	52	28	34	7	17	61	35
Anti-government......	—	—	1	1	1	2	2	1
Not classifiable......	3	6	3	4	2	5	8	5
Total...............	50	100%	82	100%	41	100%	173	100%